Rethinking
DisAbility

Re-Thinking

New Structures, New Relationships

Dis-
Ability

René R. Gadacz

The University of Alberta Press

First published by
The University of Alberta Press
Athabasca Hall
Edmonton, Alberta
Canada T6G 2E8

Copyright © The University of Alberta Press 1994

ISBN 0-88864-260-1

Canadian Cataloguing in Publication Data

Gadacz, René R.
  Rethinking disability

  Includes bibliographical references and index.
  ISBN 0-88864-260-1

  1. Physically handicapped—Social aspects. 2. Physically handicapped—Services for. I. Title
HV3011.G32 1994   362.4'048   C94-910675-5

All rights reserved.

No part of this publication may be produced, stored in a retrieval system, or transmitted in any forms or by any means, electronic, mechanical, photocopying, recording, or otherwise, without the prior permission of the copyright owner.

Printed on acid-free paper. ∞

Printed and bound in Canada by
Quality Color Press, Inc., Edmonton, Alberta, Canada

COMMITTED TO THE DEVELOPMENT OF CULTURE AND THE ARTS

For Nataliya,
　　and her generation

Contents

Preface xi
Acknowledgements xv
Introduction xvii
    The Research Process xxi
    Putting the Disabled Consumer Movement
       into Context xxv

I DISABILITY—SOCIETY'S HANDICAP

1 The Politics of Physical and Mental Differences: Struggles for Identity and Autonomy 3

Social Movement: The Recovery of Identity 9
Theoretical Inspirations 13
The Concept of Community 19
Breaking the Mold 24

2 Fact into Fancy: From Disability to Handicap 27

The Social Meaning of Disability Statistics 34
Image into Stigma: The Body as Vehicle
   of Meaning 36

Stigma into Deviance: Perceptions into Actions   42
The Situation of the Disabled: Decontextualization
   and the Transformation of Subjective Reality   47
Rethinking Disability   52

II SOCIAL CHANGE IN THEORY AND PRACTICE

3 Consumerism and Independent Living: Focusing the Concerns of Disabled People   59

The Emergence of an Alternative Perspective   62
The Rise of the Disabled Consumer Ethic   71
The Means and Outcome of Empowerment:
   Towards Independent Living   76
Independent Living   83
The Path to Self-Determination   91

4 Beyond Minority Protest: Social Movement and the Meaning of Empowerment   93

Social Movement as a Product of Society:
   Old Approaches   95
The Duality of Social Movement   98
Society as a Product of Social Movement:
   New Perspectives   100
The Role of Empowerment in Social Movement   104
Defining Features of the New Social Movements   109
Social Movement as Learning and Becoming   116

III IMPLEMENTING CHANGE

5 Organizing for Empowerment: The Disabled Consumer Organization   121

From Objects to Subjects: Empowerment
   and Agency   123
"A Voice of Our Own": The Disabled Consumer
   Organization   128

Alberta Committee of Citizens With
    Disabilities   135
Coalition of Provincial Organizations of
    the Handicapped   149
New Relationships, New Structures   156

**6 New Solutions and Innovations for Empowerment
and Community Building   163**

"Taking Charge": Experiments and Innovations
    in Independence   166
Independent Living Centres   169
The Formation, Organization, and Structure of
    IL Centres   174
Independent Living Centres as a Social
    Innovation   179
The Idea of Supported Independence   182
The Joshua Committee: A New Initiative in Personal
    Support Networks   184
Service and Agency Brokerage: Individual Empowerment
    and Personal Accountability   189
The Basis for Brokerage: The Role and
    the Process   192
The Community as "Expert"   198

IV TOWARDS EQUAL CITIZENSHIP

**7 Emancipatory Politics: Equality Rights and Reasonable
Accommodation   205**

Federal Government Initiatives   207
The Struggle for Charter Protection   213
Equality and the Disabled Consumer Movement   219
Discrimination and the Law: A Basis for the Concept
    of Reasonable Accommodation   224
Intentional and Unintentional Discrimination   227
Defences to Allegations of Discrimination   231
Reasonable Accommodation: Definitions and
    Legal Issues   234

Implementing Reasonable Accommodation   238
Reasonable Accommodation: The Political
  Response   242
Accommodating Our Citizens: Community
  Obligations   246

**8 Personhood and Consumerism as Part of the
Community-Building Process   255**

Personhood: A Prerequisite for Community
  Building   257
Barriers to Community: The Production and
  Maintenance of Disability   263
The Promise of the Disabled Consumer Movement:
  Self-Determination as a Universal Right   272

Bibliography   279
Index   309

Preface

Rethinking Disability: New Structures, New Relationships is an issues or "perspectives" book that provides a human and a social dimension to "disability," which has all too often been treated only as a medical and technical phenomenon. During the 1980s and 1990s the general public's awareness and consciousness has been raised by the efforts of disabled people and by authors, playwrights and artists. Disability—a social category whose membership is always open—has come to be portrayed with realism, compassion and understanding. Motion pictures such as "Rain Man," "Born on the Fourth of July" and "My Left Foot" are examples of efforts to see disability as part of the human condition. These efforts have had the effect of encouraging a much-needed openness about the subject. *Rethinking Disability* is a continuation of this consciousness raising, albeit from a more scholarly and analytic approach. This is not a technical or scientific book about disability or about specific kinds of disabilities. Nor is it about particular groups in society who are chronically ill or who are disabled.

This book seeks to complement works already published on disability by offering an analytical framework. In Evelyn Kallen's *Label Me Human: Minority Rights of Stigmatized Canadians* (1989, University of

Toronto Press) and Diane Driedger's *The Last Civil Rights Movement: Disabled Peoples' International* (1989, St. Martin's Press) disabled people and their organizations are discussed in significant detail, but the motivational and structural dimensions of the independent living movement are not examined. In my study, the concept of empowerment and the process of social movement are used as analytical tools to present a multidimensional treatment of this important social phenomenon.

In the sociology and health literature there are many descriptive books of what it is like to be disabled or to be ill. Good examples of the "illness narrative" are Robert Murphy's *The Body Silent* (1987, Henry Holt), Irving Zola's *Missing Pieces* (1982, Temple University Press) and Arthur W. Frank's *At the Will of the Body* (1991, Houghton Mifflin). Murphy and Zola are disabled social scientists; Frank, a sociologist, survived two serious illnesses: a heart attack, and cancer diagnosed one year later. Murphy, an anthropologist, suffered a gradual deterioration of his spinal cord due to a benign tumour that resulted in quadriplegia. All describe illness and disability from personal experience, and bring social theorizing to bear on their accounts. The "insider's" narrative is invaluable in shedding light on the truisms that all bodies sooner or later fall apart and that society overvalues body surfaces and so judges individuals—stigmatizing them and spoiling their identities in the process (Kleinman 1988). My approach in *Rethinking Disability* is to complement these existing narratives by studying collectivist orientation movements whose goals are to develop strategies that do something about how disability is perceived and how disabled people are treated in society.

There has been a marked increase in our society of disabled or chronically ill people—over four million Canadians according to the 1991 Census of Population. There is also the general aging of the population to be considered and the disabilities in one form or another that often come with age. Environmental degradation, exposure to toxins and the hazards of the workplace are responsible for disease and trauma suffered by individuals. Some conditions may be temporary, but all too often they are permanent. Through education the number of AIDS and AIDS-related cases may not be increasing at the rate once feared, but estimates of the number of persons infected with

HIV, in Canada and elsewhere, makes this health issue one of the most important of this, and possibly the next, century.

Illness narratives or simple sociological categorization somehow seem inadequate to the task of showing how some individuals are working to reform their society to accommodate disability and change attitudes. Change is in order if we are to sustain ourselves and support each other in a community of fellow citizens. *Rethinking Disability: New Structures, New Relationships* shows how some disabled citizens in Canada envision and have initiated this process of social transformation.

Acknowledgements

This book would have been impossible to write without the unselfish and generous assistance of the staff, board and friends of the Alberta Committee of Citizens With Disabilities (Edmonton) and the Coalition of Provincial Organizations of the Handicapped (Winnipeg). Nancie Krushelnicki, Muriel Keeling, Leroy Thompson, Edna Coffin, Brian Laird, Irene Feika, Michael Huck, Jim Derksen and April D'Aubin—some of whom are still with these organizations and some of whom are not—had on numerous occasions gone completely out of their way to accommodate my research and source material needs. Their dedicated pursuit of a "culture of ability" was clearly reflected in the ways they helped me. Interpretations of data, policy statements and organizational documents, as well as errors of ommission or commission, naturally remain my own responsibility. I also do not purport to "speak" for the disabled consumer movement in this book, for the simple reason that, for me, there still remains one significant barrier between having a sympathetic and an intersubjective understanding of disability and illness. I know that disabled citizens will not begrudge me that.

I would like to express my gratitude to Dick Sobsey (Severe Disabilities Program, University of Alberta), David Bai (Department of

Anthropology, University of Alberta), Gordon Fearn (Athabasca University) and Evelyn Kallen (Social Sciences, York University) for their expertise and generosity of spirit during the most intense writing phases of this book. Funding for the research was provided in part by the Social Sciences and Humanities Research Council of Canada. Tables 2.1 and 2.2, and Figures 2.2 and 2.3 are provided through the cooperation of Statistics Canada [readers wishing further information may obtain copies of related publications by mail from Publications Sales, Statistics Canada, Ottawa, Ontario K1A 0T6, by phone at 1–613–951–7277, national toll-free 1–800–267–6677; readers may also facsimile orders by dialing 1–613–951–1584].

My capacity as an evaluation researcher in 1991 with the Victorian Order of Nurses (Edmonton) on their frail elderly day care program permitted me to gain some valuable insights into disability, but from the other end of the human lifespan. After periods of participant observation and interviewing I would always take the time to reread one of my favorite phrases from Erik Erikson's *Insight and Responsibility*: "Any span of the [life] cycle lived without vigorous meaning at the beginning, in the middle, or at the end, endangers the sense of life, and the meaning of death in all whose life stages are intertwined." I am grateful to Vicki Strang (Faculty of Nursing, University of Alberta) and Jean Greschuk (Executive Director, VON Edmonton) for the opportunity to participate in their work and for their continuing friendship.

I want to thank Norma Gutteridge, Director, University of Alberta Press, for believing in the potential of this book and Mary Mahoney-Robson, Editor, for guiding me, with her excellent humor, through all the editorial and business details that are a necessary part of the publishing process. Others deserving my thanks include Penny Oman, whose artwork graces the cover and the text, the Press's designer and production manager Kerry Watt, Karen Chow, editorial assistant, and Hendrika Beaulieu who helped me prepare the index.

The University of Alberta Press acknowledges the financial support of the Alberta Foundation for the Arts, a beneficiary of the Lottery Fund of the Government of Alberta, in the publication of this book.

Introduction

Rethinking Disability: New Structures, New Relationships is a description and analysis of the Independent Living movement of disabled people in Canada. It is also a study of the process of individual and collective empowerment. The independent living philosophy that both motivates and is an outcome of this movement is an integral part of what is called the disabled consumer ethic. This ethic, or worldview, emerged among disabled citizens in Canada, the United States, Europe and in other parts of the world over twenty years ago.

Through the independent living/disabled consumer movement, this historically excluded and abused collectivity emerged from a context of powerlessness to pursue its vision of integrated community living and a meaningful social life. This social reform movement, also referred to as the Disabled Consumer movement, has as its primary objectives the empowerment of disabled people in relationship both to identity formation and the reformation of community relations. The movement and its associated discourse on empowerment are understood as aspects of struggle by the disabled to gain control over the form and content of their own identity formation, and to achieve autonomy and independence in daily living through integration into redefined community (social, economic and political) relations. The struggle for empowerment consists largely, though not exclusively, of the struggle *against* professionally dominated forms of medical/psychological diagnosis, prescribed treatment and service delivery, and *for* the mobilization and securing of resources required to achieve personal choice in service consumption, and the capacity for independent, integrated community-based living.

From the perspective of the independent living philosophy as articulated by action-oriented disabled people, the disabled citizen is no longer the passive "case," "client" or "patient" receiving donations, rehabilitation therapy or services under what are called the charity and medical/professional ethics. Under the new consumer ethic he or she is becoming empowered to participate actively in the decision-making that is part of the treatment and service provider/consumer relationship within the general disability services market. The disabled citizen is becoming empowered to participate in the social, economic and political life of mainstream society, despite formidable attitudinal and physical barriers. Participation in these ways is considered essential by the disabled consumer movement in achieving reintegration into community life. The various grassroots structures and organizations disabled people are creating represent not only empowering efforts to consciously structure the contexts of their own existence, but they represent efforts to build a community in which they, and others, can participate more meaningfully.

The independent living/disabled consumer movement is an example of what is occurring on a larger and wider scale. Conscious action to renew social structure, build community and achieve meaning in social life involves trying to overcome by various social, legal and political means a large number of *imposed* language, cultural, gender, homophobic, age and other "handicaps"—not only physical or mental ones. Thus, the disintegration and decontextualization of disabled people from community and social life is not fundamentally different from what is experienced by certain language, religious, ethno-cultural, gender, age and many other stigmatized minorities. What disabled people are trying to accomplish can be clearly understood as part of a much larger context of social reform movements and community-building in which other minorities are involved.

The activities of action-oriented disabled people in the work of two high-profile disability-focused organizations—the Coalition of Provincial Organizations of the Handicapped (Winnipeg) and the Alberta Committee of Citizens With Disabilities (Edmonton) are focused on in this book. Founded in 1976, COPOH represents a national cross-disability coalition of over 85 provincial consumer organizations claiming a total membership of approximately 30,000 disabled Canadians. COPOH was one of a small group of organizations that successfully challenged the federal government in 1980 and 1981 to include the rights of the physically disabled and mentally handicapped in the Canadian Charter of Rights and Freedoms. The Alberta Committee was founded in 1972 under the name Alberta Committee of Action Groups of the Disabled, and provincially now represents a coalition of smaller, local, single-issue groups of disabled persons. These organizations are recognized by many, including government, as powerful voices of disabled citizens on disability issues.

Disabled consumer activists are engaged in changing the ways in which they interact not only with able-bodied people, but with each other as well. Disabled people historically have been, and still are to a great extent, labelled and stigmatized as deviant, sick, dependent and as somehow abnormal. In turn, policies and legislation have reflected and perpetuated these largely negative stereotypes and myths. Disability, in fact, has been created, maintained and perpetuated by the decisions of law and policy makers in such areas as rehabilitation, health care, employment and education. My interpretation of the meaning of disability and my discussion of the disabled consumer movement, its independent living model and the idea of community-building is presented in Chapters 1, 2 and 3.

By being excluded from mainstream community life because of the effects of misguided public policies, bad laws and legislation and the paternalistic attitudes of medical and health care professionals, disabled individuals have had little or no opportunity to develop their potential. Neither have they had the chance to even demonstrate their capabilities. Disabled people are seeking to end their oppressed and disadvantaged position in society. By literally creating the conditions of their own liberation, they are shifting the focus from "disability" to "ability." In the process, not only are persistent stereotypes and myths about disability debunked, but more fruitful and beneficial means of socially interacting with other members of society are achieved. Chapter 4 looks at how this is accomplished by examining social movements, the processes of domination in post-industrial society and the role of empowerment.

In Chapters 5 and 6, the disabled consumer movement's independent living model is linked to a discussion of the movement's broader organizational strategies and to its more specific empowerment solutions and innovations. In these chapters, the workings of consumer organizations (the Alberta Committee of Citizens With Disabilities), coalition structures (the Coalition of Provincial Organizations of the Handicapped), independent living centres, peer support groups and several kinds of brokerage systems are detailed. These self-created structures provide the contexts in which disabled persons learn and put into practice, often for the first time, new motivational, interactional and participatory skills. This self-creation and organization is the essence of empowerment and the basis for social movement. The various grassroots self-help organizations disabled people are creating serve to challenge dominant beliefs of what disabled people are capable of and what their abilities are.

How these structures can also serve as organizational bases for public education and lobbying efforts whose aim is to influence social policy and legislation directed towards disabled people is discussed in Part IV, Towards Equal Citizenship. In the final chapters of *Rethinking Disability* an analysis of the movement's approach to equality and human rights in its attempt to secure and protect some of its achievements, and to ensure a future voice for disabled citizens in the ongoing process of community-building is presented. In order for substantive equality to be realized, it is essential that "reasonable accommodation" and affirmative action programs in employment and education for disabled Canadians be put in place throughout the country. Some of the key supporting human rights and public policy concerns and interests of disabled consumers from the point of view of community-building are outlined in Chapter 7. Chapter 8 concludes the book with a discussion of the implications of the movement with respect to the process of community-building and the political economy of consumerism.

The Research Process

Personal interviews with members of the Alberta Committee and COPOH, follow-up unstructured interviews and impromptu talks in 1985 and 1986 eventually led me to the focus and theoretical orientation of this book. References to brokerage systems, Joshua Committees, Independent Living Centres, the development of an independent living philosophy and model, and the consumer ethic personally intrigued me. Here was evidence of social action and organized social movement such as I had not heard of or seen before. My earlier reading of the work of Alain Touraine (1977a, 1981) on social movements and that of Anthony Giddens (1984) on structuration theory convinced me that I could attempt an interpretive analysis of what the Alberta Committee, the Coalition of Provincial Organizations and other organizations that are part of the disabled consumer movement had accomplished and what they are still working to accomplish.

I made trips to Winnipeg and Calgary, especially to the Walter Dinsdale Centre/Calgary Association for Independent Living (now called the Walter Dinsdale Centre for the Empowerment of Canadians with Disabilities). During those years I was introduced to some key players of the movement, including, Jim Derksen (COPOH, Winnipeg), Henry Enns (COPOH, Winnipeg), Leroy Thompson (ACCD, Calgary and Edmonton) and Michael Huck (Edmonton). Significantly, it was at the Alberta Committee's annual general meeting in Calgary in September of 1986 that I heard Henry Enns from COPOH cite the work of Paulo Freire and talk about the process of empowerment. This soon became the key concept that subsequently helped me formulate links between structuration, social movement and community-building. With reference to the independent living/disabled consumer movement in Canada, a study by Kallen (1989) also linked social movement activity to empowerment. Kallen suggests that the movement is a reform movement organized around instrumental/empowerment types of goals (p. 45), and that it is predicated on the goals of empowerment (p. 157). I elaborate on this concept and suggest that the empowerment process, synonymous with social movement, is central to discussions of social and cultural change in general, and community-building in particular.

Through interviews, discussions and reading Alberta Committee and COPOH materials, a number of key issues and themes emerged. They were the notion of independent living, social and community integration, consumerism, the independent living/disabled consumer movement (which was linked to 1960s civil rights movement in the United States), the demedicalization of disability and the deinstitutionalization of disabled persons. The growth and development of various means or strategies of independent living, for example, independent living centres, brokerage, peer support groups, networks, consumer groups and coalitions were consistently referred to.

Such principles of independent living as accountability, the idea of dignity of risk and the notion of personhood were also expounded in interviews and discussions. Later, legal concerns were explored and discussed in reference to problems in such areas as transportation, housing, education, employment, equality rights, the rights of the disabled as individuals and as an identifiable collectivity, and employment equity/affirmative action. The concept of reasonable accommodation as a means of social and community integration also was mentioned.

Related theoretical issues that emerged were the obvious ones: the political economy of consumerism (production-consumption relationships under capitalism); self-determination as a political/rights issue; social movements (contrasting older with newer approaches); and the idea of community-building and social reform in the context of social/cultural change in general. I also became interested in situating collective action in the context of action theory, especially in the relations between the actions of organized disabled citizens, the organizational structures they were creating, and the vision of reintegration into mainstream social and community life that they were pursuing (Lamoureux et al. 1989).

I decided to expand upon the major themes of the disabled consumer movement and to adopt a macro-approach. This meant looking at larger socio-cultural patterns and institutional processes in specific relation to the issues, in order to see how they are tied together in a larger framework that gives them meaning, for example, action, structure, social movement, social and cultural change and the idea of community. The data/theory relationship was two-way. Beginning with what is referred to as the grounded theory approach in sociology and anthropology, my involvement and immersion into the life of participants in the consumer organizations led to the discovery of the main themes of the movement. Once I became aware of what the themes and issues were, and how pervasive they were in the consciousness of disabled consumers, I searched the social science literature for revelant theory that was useful in shedding light on their meaning.

Social science literature exists for the study of social movement, for empowerment, the theory of structuration, action theory, self-actualization/self-determination, consumerism, stigmatization and labelling theory, and deviance theory. All this was helpful and I saw my task to be the synthesis of key points in order to interpret and make sense of the actions and activities of disabled citizens. Once the relevant theoretical material was identified, I kept returning to the Alberta Committee and to COPOH to search out more data related to the themes and to keep abreast of developments in these groups and on the national scene.

The Alberta Committee's and COPOH's sizeable archives and libraries contained large numbers of research reports, studies, briefs and other material produced over the years by the groups as well as by other disability-focused organizations. These documents consisted of organizational histories, formal briefs and submissions, reports and summaries of annual general meetings past and current, newsletters, pamphlets, quarterly as well as annual reports, press releases and dozens of research papers produced by the two organization's various sub-committees (covering such areas as human rights, the Native disabled, building standards and accessibility, transportation and public relations). Of particular use were the position papers, research reports and the formal briefs and submissions to agencies, government departments and government ministers produced by the staff, board members and researchers (only a select number of titles could be included in the bibliography to this book). Supplemented by interview data, these valuable documentary source materials came to constitute my primary data.

As social products, such "native texts" are significant for the interpretive and interactional work that went into their production (Smith 1974; A. Scott 1990). In the documents that I gathered and worked with I saw a reflection of a particular social and political reality, and a social structure that has necessitated, indeed, demanded their production (Smith 1984). Being socially and culturally constituted, and having been produced by a specific segment of the disabled community, their contents naturally are biased. But the importance of this bias is in what it means, namely that it represents social/political resistance and challenge, and efforts at image-building. The biases are themselves data; they are a window into a people's social and political reality largely formed or constituted by others. These self-produced materials emerge from what may be called micro situations, yet at the same time they are the undeniable product of macrosystems (Marcus 1986: 169; Marcus and Fischer 1986: 77–110).

The understanding of the activities and documents produced by disabled people that I wanted to obtain was one that shed light on what these produced materials mean in the context of self-conscious social and cultural change. The self-produced accounts of disabled consumer movement organizations are valuable records of self-analyses of social, economic and political relations over time that are perceived to impact on disabled people in general. Historically, the spatial and temporal isolation of disabled people prevented them from gaining social and politically useful knowledge; it was this isolation that kept them from learning and developing any participatory competence. Participatory competence is related to knowledge, and the uneven distribution of knowledge among individuals and groups across society has in the past and to some extent still does placed considerable constraints on the range of practices and interactions disabled individuals have been competent to perform.

The significance of these self-produced research reports, position papers, briefs and submissions lies precisely with the fact that their production is an intentional, self-conscious and self-reflexive activity. According to the Alberta Committee of Citizens With Disabilities (1982: 4),

> Consumer monitoring and research efforts are beneficial to the community as a whole and serve an important social feedback system to appropriate authorities. Evolution of the consumer movement into a dynamic, informed source creates a valuable resource available for use by officials and service providers.... Government has the opportunity to use this pool of knowledge.... as a basis for *information*, as a means of *input* for the development of legislation, policies and programs affecting disabled consumers, as an indepen-

dent method of *monitoring* programs to ensure needs are met. [original emphasis]

Disabled consumers attach a great significance to the production of information and the monitoring process. The production of this information and knowledge represents the "learning" process in action, something that is at the core of social movement, or empowerment. Empowerment means obtaining knowledge and learning how "the system" works, in order to resist it, work upon it, and operate within it—"to make a difference," in the words of Anthony Giddens. It is the collection and processing of information in particular that is integral to the reflexive monitoring of action in Giddens's sense, and indeed, that is understood as a key element of the empowerment process. The disabled movement's development of peer support groups, networks, coalitions and other "action structures"—especially consumer organizations—serves to generate and distribute relevant knowledge and information that is initially structurally circumscribed.

Putting the Disabled Consumer Movement into Context

The independent living/disabled consumer movement is part of a tradition of radical voluntarism that originated in the United States during the mid-1960s and soon spread world-wide. It became associated with other so-called social reform movements including the civil rights, feminist, anti-poverty and gay liberation movements. The independent living movement is founded on three basic principles: consumer sovereignty, self-reliance, and political and economic rights. These three principles also form the basis of a utilitarian model that adheres to the notion that social and economic well-being can be achieved by the rational and competitive pursuit of interests in a free and open marketplace. In essence, this model entails an acceptance of the capitalist system with its free market pluralist ideology, a free market in which people compete in a context of equal rights.

From the perspective of disabled consumers, the issue is one of translating utilitarian/autonomous individualism (freedom from dependence on the will of others) into collective terms, and protecting and guaranteeing this freedom through legislation and public policy.

This serves to rationalize the movement's goal of trying to exert self-control over disability services, and to break the real or perceived professional dominance, paternalism and state-controlled monopolies of the medical, human and social services as they pertain to disabled people. The free market is considered to provide the appropriate mechanism and context for the expression of preferences and for the equitable distribution of social goods, and it is this belief that is reasserted in the form of consumer choice *against* the bureaucratic monopoly of medical and disability services. Disabled consumers wish to redefine the relations of the marketplace.

Consumer and empowerment politics are products of the times. The desire for empowerment and the "bottom-up" participatory approach with its emphasis on self-actualization and self-reliance are the outcome of both the expansion of the economy in the 1960s as well as its decline by the 1970s and the early 1980s. The desire to increase control over one's life, that is, empowerment, can be understood in the context of several changes. First, the underlying feeling and consumer skills associated with making choices in the marketplace form an important base that serve to stimulate further demands for excellence, variety and accountability in products and services. Second, in our service-oriented society most services are very near the consumer. Health, medicine and education are prime examples. They are consumer-focussed—the consumer practically contributes to the production of the services and the rationale is that he or she has a greater say in what is being produced. Third, the expansion of education, including through the media, has had some influence on people's awareness. Finally, major political and other events have contributed to the decline in respect for authority, experts, professionals and big business, and sparked an increase in respect for experiential and personal and local knowledge

The drive for equal rights by women, for example, displayed a general anti-authority and anti-professional stance. For women in particular there was a specific effect in medicine. The feminist movement had as one of its goals the establishment of a woman's right to make decisions about her own body, including the right to reproductive freedom and freedom from doctors. It is in this very same historical context that disabled people decided they had a right to make decisions about their own bodies, and to determine what services they needed. In simple terms, consumerism in medicine, from the point of view of disabled people, has meant challenging the medical and rehabilitation professional's right to make unilateral decisions.

A challenge to authority and to professional expertise as that represented by disabled consumer action has to be qualified by an alternative expertise and competence. Empowerment lies at the base of consumerism because through this process appropriate alternatives are sought, worked out and new knowledge gained. For this to happen, the right socio-cultural, structural and legal conditions have to be created that enable people to develop workable alternatives. The independent living/disabled consumer movement is developing alternative ways of doing things, while at the same time it is trying to create the conditions that make this possible. This presupposes a "negative" role for government and the state, one that ensures the removal and elimination of barriers and disincentives to fair competition and participation in the free market. This recognition makes the legislation, constitutional enshrinement and enforcement of equality, social and economic rights important for the movement. Legislation and enforcement of rights are particularly crucial in tough economic times.

The rise of the independent living/disabled consumer movement coincides with the ascendancy of an ideology of conservative individualism. Events of the 1960s, 1970s and 1980s culminated in a wave of neo-conservatism that had an immense effect on what it means to be a citizen and a member of a powerless minority. In Canada, federal, provincial and even local governments have come to pursue policies set by Britain's former prime minister Margaret Thatcher and other neo-conservatives. In the context of shrinking national budgets and in response to fiscal crisis brought on by economic restructuring, the trimming of bureaucracy, decentralization of government, cutting public programs (for example, unemployment insurance, medicare and health insurance, family allowances, old age security) and the privatization of human and social service systems have appeared on the agendas of most governments (Russell 1991).

The emphasis on individual initiative, autonomy, free consumer choice and identity is at odds with what some people are experiencing. A major problem is that the private sector, due to a welfarist history and orientation, has had a poor record with respect to program and service initiatives and solutions. Self-help and other groups—including those of the disabled consumer movement—are mushrooming to meet new needs and in some cases to endeavor to provide direct services to needy individuals. But, the burden of providing services and the bureaucratic requirements relating to funding may limit their freedom to carry out action aimed at institutional change. The very existence of self-help groups and voluntary organizations is in constant jeopardy because of their dependence on public funding—even though they are extolled in policy papers as "partners" in the human and social services fields. Interest group politics, now more than ever, involves competing for access to scarcer and scarcer government resources.

Critics argue that the state's opting out of social programs means that it is co-opting voluntary initiatives to take over what has in the past been regarded as *its* responsibilities. There is the danger that people are going to be confused into believing that public or profit-making services are "community," while decision-making remains highly centralized. The danger is that the word "community" will be given a bureaucratic/technocratic sense by having its meaning narrowed to target populations, priorities and programs that are imposed on public institutions and on the private sector by the state. With regard to the disabled consumer movement, the principles of consumer sovereignty, self-reliance and political and economic rights are indeed worthy, but outside a context of a comprehensive political strategy could become an excuse for benevolent minimal government and public neglect.

On the positive side, I see these developments as part of a process that may be referred to as "emancipatory politics" (Giddens 1991: 210–14). This is a process by which the meaning of citizenship, personhood and a different conception of the role of government and of the state in the lives of citizens is being redefined and worked out. This is not to be blind to the human costs that are incurred , yet I see the disabled brand of consumerism, the ideas of community-building and empowerment, and the philosophy of independent living as both an outcome of economic and political restructuring, and a means of rethinking who we are as individuals and how we will interact with one another in a community of citizens. Disabled people, individually and collectively, are working to redefine and reintegrate themselves in a renewed community of citizens.

I
Disability— Society's Handicap

1
The Politics of Physical and Mental Differences
Struggles for Identity and Autonomy

Perhaps it is unthinkable to conclude that modern society has no need for people with physical disabilities and mental impairments. But, this conclusion is often reached by disabled people themselves. According to David Lepofsky, a Toronto lawyer,

> Disabled people in our society are a substantially numerous and sub-stantially disadvantaged minority. Their experience is typified by unemployment rates that are radically higher than those that would be acceptable to anyone in the mainstream of society. We are concerned when unemployment goes from 7 percent to 10 percent for the mainstream. For disabled people, there is data that shows unemployment to be from 50 to 80 percent. The data also indicates that they are disproportionately impoverished and welfare dependent (Parliamentary Forum on the Status of Disabled Persons 1988: 7).

Those individuals who try to lead conventional lives tend to repress their pariah status and the patronizing attitudes of the able-bodied, and to internalize the values of the so-called normal world. Autobiographical accounts repeatedly emphasize this (Kleinfield 1979: Vash

1981: Zola 1982: Parliamentary Forum on the Status of Disabled Persons 1988: Secretary of State of Canada 1989). Writes Doreen Demas, a disabled student living in Winnipeg,

> All of a sudden I realized that in some ways I felt really different, that I wasn't like everybody else. I think I went all through school with that attitude—that feeling of inferiority. So I think for a while I put all my efforts into being normal. Until one day I realized, normality was accepting myself for what I was. Once I broke out of that I found things so much easier. I've learned how to feel comfortable around people (Coalition of Provincial Organizations of the Handicapped 1987d: 60–61).

Personal accounts such as Doreen's are at the same time embarrassing and encouraging. They are reminders of what little progress has been made towards the reintegration and "normalization" of disabled people; but they are also testimony to the patience and persistence of people attempting to extricate themselves from the tangled web of the politics of disability. Increasingly, disabled people are facing a choice between accepting the marginal existence in which they find themselves, and actively confronting and changing the social and economic life imposed on them.

Disabled people and those with whom they interact—rehabilitation and medical professionals, service agency personnel, employers and others—are caught in power relationships that provide little opportunity for self-determination or many chances for wielding direct power (Stubbins 1988: 22). Disability can mean many things. Disability is a socially created category rather than an attribute of individuals. At the same time, disability is a formal administrative category that not only determines the rights and privileges of many people, but one that is tied to concepts of control and responsibility (Stone 1984). Disability is "big business" notes Stubbins (1988: 22–23). It provides health care practitioners, researchers, the prosthetics and pharmaceutical industries, insurance companies and academics with respectable livelihoods. Those people with political or economic interests in disabled people define the problems, the agenda and the social reality of disabled persons in ways that almost always serve their own interests more closely than those of their clients or cases. Indeed, definitions of disability both reflect and are an outcome of political and economic interests.

Medical and rehabilitation technology has progressed in solving the problems of many physical impairments by creating compensating or alternative ways of getting around, communicating and of self-care so that only the most severely disabled might still require the intensive or long-term care of institutional settings. Significantly, much less progress has taken place in enabling disabled persons to become reinvolved in mainstream social and economic activities. Advances in technology have transformed the central meaning of disability from a strict concern with physical aspects to an intense search for meaning in contexts of social isolation, underemployment or unemployment and a bewildering number of imprisoning environmental barriers. The essence of disability is the social and economic consequences of being different from the "majority" (Ainlay et al. 1986). Being disabled, like being female rather than male, black rather than white, old instead of young, is synonymous with oppression and disadvantage. Disadvantages inhere primarily in social relationships and structures. Indeed,

> Are the deaf, deaf; are blind persons really sightless? Or is it the social setting we place them in? In their social relations they communicate, they "see". . . . We place them in specific social relations that make them deaf, an unwarranted and unjustified expectation on our part. We evaluate their abilities for them (Alberta Committee of Citizens With Disabilities 1981b: 14).

Disability can be viewed as a relationship between a person with a physical or mental impairment and the social and physical environment around him or her. This relationship can be characterized as a dominant-subordinate one, with able-bodied persons generally having power over those with impairments. This power relationship is manifested by the able-bodied with respect to imposed definitions, control of the environment, and in the determination of the types of treatment, services, amenities and programs deemed appropriate to the needs of disabled people. These characteristics of the relations between the disabled and able-bodied have persisted across time and space, specific individuals and individual differences (Eisenberg et al. 1982). In fact, they are *learned* role relationships built into the structure of our institutions and our society. If power involves a relationship in which some people can constrain, coerce and determine the behavior of others, then clearly the power of medical and rehabilitation practitioners and specialists resides in their credentials, ideology, authority, their roles as "experts" on disability and in their control over access to program and welfare benefits and other similar scarce resources.

Power need not be conceived of only as brute force. In the modern state, an important source of power is the knowledge and techniques generated by science—medical or clinical. This power is not easily identified as emanating from economic and monopolistic sources, since it appears as neutral technical and scientific information (Foucault 1973; 1980). Medical, clinical and rehabilitation practitioners may not be consciously aware of how their choices of techniques and treatments are tied to power considerations (Stubbins 1988: 26; Conrad 1992: 215–18). Foucault's contribution has been to show the nature of that link in terms of the influences exerted on these practitioners by dominant political and ideological interests, and by the influence they exert on their "clients" in carrying out their assigned duties. Information is one power resource used in exerting these influences. Disabled people may know far less about those with whom they interact than vice-versa. Until very recently, most disabled people knew practically nothing about the personnel, agencies and organizations under whose care they found themselves (Frankel 1988). By contrast, practitioners and specialists know a great deal about the personal lives of disabled individuals, including very intimate details.

Not until the 1970s and 1980s were disabled persons a self-conscious constituency in the sense that medical practitioners or other "experts" are. They depended on the latter for information, and to some extent still do. Indeed, because the technical and practical knowledge needs of professionals and disabled people are different, most disabled people still find themselves poorly situated to understand how their own interests might be compromised. Power and power relations between those who are disabled and those who are not has to do with a "set of practices" (what Foucault calls the discursive formation) that gives coherence and rationality to what clinical and rehabilitation practitioners do. This set of practices, embodied in the medical/rehabilitation model, tends to reduce disability problems to dimensions and procedures that lie within relatively narrow technical disciplines and specializations. In fact, the moral problems arising from the status of disabled persons in society increasingly have been transformed into technical issues, to be resolved by clinicians, scientists and technocrats (Stubbins 1988: 29; Conrad and Schneider 1980; Conrad 1992).

Questions arise as to who mediates among competing claims to expertise in the field of disability, whether hegemonic control by one or another profession is justified in terms of the needs of disabled people, who determines those needs, and who should define the scope of the expertise required to deal with those needs. Bourdieu's (1977) notion of "field" as the locus of competitive struggles for the monopoly of symbolic capital is probably applicable to the issue of professional leadership and supremacy in the field of disability. These questions get to the heart of what the status of being disabled means to the people who live it: impairment or social disadvantage, poverty resulting from personal deficit or from the socio-economic structure, isolation caused by stigma or other socially sanctioned meaning, powerlessness or lack of social competence. Whether one is personally blamed for one's impairment, labelled deviant and deemed socially incompetent, or whether one's powerlessness, poverty, and social and physical isolation is attributed to social structures depends on which profession or which group in society does the defining (Illich 1976; 1977; Mishler 1984; Waitzkin 1983).

Medical, rehabilitation and other experts have power over disabled individuals. These experts focus on certain features concerning the problematics of disability; they conceal or ignore others (Mishler 1984). Indeed,

> As medical professionals assume responsibility for managing problems beyond the illnesses of individuals, attention shifts away from the underlying structural conditions that often are sources of individual distress. By defining social problems [such as disability and handicap] as medical, medicine becomes an institution of social control. Through medicalization, the structural roots of personal distress become mystified and depoliticized (Waitzkin 1983: 41).

A similar process is at work in areas as law, economics, politics, or wherever special interests are at stake and where professionals are involved. Whatever the origins of the current state of affairs regarding the status of disabled people, it is probable that few medical and rehabilitation practitioners, social policy planners or legislators have had much voice in actually creating it. Nevertheless, as health care and social policy "experts" intervening in the lives of real people they have considerable influence in maintaining and extending it (Stone 1984; Gritzer and Arluke 1985; Stevenson and Williams 1988).

A wide gap exists between the ideology and culture of professionals and experts, and of disabled persons. Not surprisingly, there is disagreement over what the "problem" of disability is or with whom it lies. More specifically, there is disagreement over whether physical or mental/psychological differences among individuals are more crucial than the shared social, political and economic disadvantaged status of disabled people. Pierre Majeau, a human relations psychologist, makes the point succinctly:

> A prerequisite for the social integration of a disabled individual is social and economic independence, which supposes access to gainful employment. . . . A basic requirement for real integration of disabled persons into the economic life of Canada is access to quality education as part of a regular education system rather than special schools or a parallel system. In my opinion this is the real key to integration (Parliamentary Forum on the Status of Disabled Persons 1988: 8).

Disabled people likely recognize, as perhaps do medical professionals and others, that both groups live in a socially constructed world that impacts on them differently, providing them with diverse values. There is recognition that knowledge is socially conditioned and contains or expresses social and political interests (Berger and Luckmann 1967; Stubbins 1988: 32). It is reasonable to expect that the interests, beliefs about the sources of social and economic disadvantages experienced by disabled people, and solutions to these urgent social policy issues should differ so markedly between disabled people and others in society who think they "know better."

Social Movement: The Recovery of Identity

The independent living/disabled consumer movement is a contemporary social reform movement that is concerned with revealing the processes by which the bodies and identities of disabled individuals have become the objects on which various systems of domination have converged (Giddens 1991: 217–18). Essentially contentionist in approach, its social policy reform and human rights goals have been described as integrationist in outlook (Kallen 1989: 45, 157). The movement has recognized efforts to medicalize and psychologize the social and private realm of individuals for what they really are: efforts to displace conflict, to neutralize and drain disabled individuals of all potential for protest, and to "rehabilitate" bodies and minds to internalize a specific rationality upon which modern social and cultural reproduction is supposedly based (Derksen 1980: 1–2). The overall goals of the movement are to challenge and end these efforts of domination, to reclaim "expropriated" bodies and to reappropriate the "spoiled" identities that are a result of well-intentioned but generally ineffective medical and rehabilitation practices, misguided public policies and programs, bad laws and legislation and paternalistic attitudes. In effect,

> The heart-and-soul of the self-help consumer group is the individual citizen determined to take charge of his or her own lifestyle and decision-making. He/she is prepared to recognize his/her own physical limitations and at the same time wishes to share in the responsibility of solving common community problems faced by all disabled persons (Simpson 1980: 7).

What are disabled people doing to accomplish these goals? One of the strategies of the independent living/consumer movement has been to try to reinterpret the meaning of disability by constructing counter-images of "the disabled," and by rejecting the very assumptions upon which normative definitions of disability are built. For activists in the disability field, it is not disability or the disabled individual that should be the focus of attention, but rather the social environment and social structures in which disability occurs, and which continue to produce and maintain the disability category. The movement has been relatively successful in raising awareness of the effects of the quality of working life, the politics of health and welfare administration, and the state of the physical environment on the overall physical and mental health of people in general. From this ecological perspective, then, to demedicalize and deconstruct disability is also to work towards social and cultural change.

The movement is called the disabled consumer movement for the reason that consumerism, for disabled persons, means participation in the decision-making processes within the service provider/client relationship. The disabled person is the poor deserving cripple under the charity ethic; he or she is the patient and the client under the medical and professional ethics. The consumer ethic that has emerged over the past decade or so "is the first of the ethics to be defined by disabled individuals themselves" (Derksen 1980: 11). A person who defines himself or herself as a "consumer" is not the passive recipient of treatment, services and programs, but identifies himself or herself as central in his or her own production. As disabled people claim, because of their experience of living with a mental or physical impairment, they not only know better than anyone else what their needs are, but they are in a better position to determine just how those needs are best met. The goal of independent living means

> ... the ability to examine alternatives and make informed decisions and direct one's own life. The ability requires the availability of information, financial resources, and peer group support systems. Independent living is a dynamic process, it can never be static. A person's physical, emotional and social environment and subsequent needs are continually changing and evolving (COPOH 1987d: 19).

Accordingly, the Coalition of Provincial Organizations of the Handicapped made it clear that,

> WHEREAS there is a fundamental need to ensure that disabled consumers are directly involved in the planning, evaluating and monitoring of community services related to their needs;
> BE IT RESOLVED that COPOH call upon the appropriate fed-

eral/provincial authorities to enact legislation that requires meaningful direct involvement of consumers in planning, evaluating and monitoring roles in community delivery systems... (COPOH 1985c: 22).

To consume services and goods is not only to reproduce oneself, but also the exchange relations within which those services and goods are produced. The independent living/disabled consumer movement rejects what it considers is a false opposition between production and consumption. As disabled consumer activists point out, people should be directly engaged and implicated in the production of their own health, learning and growth. In advocating the reassertion and regaining of control over the context and circumstances of this reproduction, the movement's consumer ethic represents a critique, not a rejection, of capitalist market and production relations that are an integral part of medical and rehabilitation practice, program administration and service provision. Disabled consumers reject outright the notion that people have no worth apart from their ability to sell their labor.

In efforts to reintegrate themselves into society and community life and to place themselves squarely within the production and exchange process, a specific strategy adopted by disabled people has been to develop organizational structures that are designed to provide workable alternatives to existing ones. Alternative and innovative structures include personal support networks called Joshua Committees, self-help groups, service brokerage systems, Independent Living centres, consumer organizations or committees, and coalitions of consumer organizations. According to disabled consumer activists, current structures and institutions do not enable disabled people to live independently, to prove their participatory competence or autonomy, or to demonstrate their capacity for self-determination. Instead, the existing normative and shared relevance structures of society are said to encourage and promote the marginalization, isolation, dependency and powerlessness of disabled people.

It may seem paradoxical that the process of social reintegration and community-building involves the creation of parallel or alternate*

---

* Kallen (1989: 39, 46), drawing from the work of others, distinguishes between "alternate" and "parallel" types of minority organization. The for-

structures, yet the paradox is resolved in the understanding of the importance of these structures on many levels. Disabled people do not envision themselves a parallel, alternative or separate society; change and reform are sought within the existing social order. On one level, these new mediating structures are viewed as "permanently temporary," or as a kind of "half-way house" (Kallen 1989: 38). Their purpose is to bridge or to connect existing services, programs and opportunities to the specific needs of disabled individuals by relaying pertinent information and knowledge about "how the system works." In many cases they may fill a gap where presently nothing exists at all. The Coalition of Provincial Organizations of the Handicapped (COPOH) is explicit in stating that

> Those who espouse the independent living philosophy do not wish to segregate services for disabled citizens.... The emphasis is upon having citizens with disabilities access services from mainstream service delivery systems. Independent living centres operate as transitional centres which serve to facilitate the integration of disabled persons into the community.... Once perfected these can be integrated into mainstream community service delivery systems.... To do otherwise would retard, not further, disabled citizens' objective to full participation in Canadian life (COPOH 1987d: 35).

As means to certain ends, new structures such as self-help groups and independent living centres reduce ignorance, isolation and dependency by expanding awareness and understanding on the part of individuals, bring people into contact with one another and serve to demystify the disabled person's social and political environment. They are temporary in the sense that once individuals have learned to access "the system" and to find their way around in it, they are assumed to

---

mer are typically associated with revitalization movements, while the latter are associated with contentionist/social reform movements (such as the disabled consumer movement). These are not mutually exclusive however. Because there is sometimes literally nothing in the greater society that answers to the needs of some disabled people, true "alternate" structures can, and do, emerge. This does not mean, however, that disabled people are organizing themselves along the lines of a separate society or sub-culture. In this study I will use the terms interchangeably.

be reintegrated. At the same time, these new structures and those involved in them may stimulate the further development of generic community services and programs by making explicit what is lacking, and in so doing these mediating structures could either become obsolete or develop into something more formal.

At another level, personal support networks, self-help groups and consumer organizations represent contexts, or sites, for learning and support. These parallel or mediating structures facilitate the development of social learning and participatory skills because they bring together the skills and knowledge of fellow disabled persons, specialists in clinical rehabilitation and community development, qualified attendants, volunteers and others. Not only can disabled individuals learn what is available and how to access community services and programs in these contexts, but by associating with peers, sympathetic professionals, and volunteers they can learn the motivations and interaction skills that are necessary in gathering and assessing information, determining their own needs and making their own decisions. Skills and knowledge are acquired in the context of living life, not only by being told what to do by so-called experts.

At a deeper level, then, these networks and structures are significant not only for what they are, but for what they mean. Support networks, self-help groups, independent living centres and consumer coalitions represent new ways of interacting for disabled individuals. These parallel or mediating structures bring disabled people together, often for the first time. They serve to unify rather than to isolate or alienate and are the foundation, or the structural elements, of the community-building process. While providing valuable services and contexts for learning certain skills and an organizational base for empowerment as well as the politicization of disability, they are organized on the assumptions that disabled people are not only fully capable of being directed by their own conceptions of their own identities, but that they also have a *right* to determine their own actions.

Theoretical Inspirations

The insight that society is made and imagined, that it is a human artifact rather than the expression or reflection of some underlying natural order, is one of the most significant developments in the history of the social sciences (Touraine 1981: 31; Unger 1987: 1). This insight also came to inspire the great social philosophies of liberalism, socialism and communism. These philosophies held out the vision of a society in which people could become empowered to free their practical, everyday and even intimate relationships from oppressive and imposed roles and hierarchies. If it is indeed possible to reinvent or rebuild society and community, as social scientists and those who are involved in contemporary social movements are convinced it is, it should be done without bringing back old dependencies and dominations. Ideally, it should even be possible to construct a social world where individuals do not have to give up their society-making powers, or to have them (once again) appropriated by others (Unger 1987: 1–2).

Important is the process by which institutions, structures, and preconceived beliefs and models of society come to be consciously and actively redefined. Less entrenched and more revisable sets of arrangements and beliefs should empower disabled people, individually and collectively. What is at the center of this process of empowerment or social movement is the view that the various contexts of social life can come apart and consciously be remade (Unger 1987: 80 ff; Berger and Luckmann 1967: 61). Social movement is the process by which freedom from dependence and dehumanization is sought by attempting to diminish the sometimes negatively experienced effect of rigid hierarchies and categories based on such things as age, gender, color, physical and mental ability that can severely constrain people in their social interactions.

Human and equal rights movements are recognized as expressions of general efforts to break from constraining categories of gender, age and ability but also to attain more complete control over the structural and relational contexts of social life from which categories, designations and labels emerge and in which they are maintained (Unger 1987: 6–17, 144–50). Human rights movements are a good illustration of the tendency to swing between being structure-preserving and structure-transforming activities, with the end result that structures are neither fully preserved nor totally transformed. What movements such as the disabled consumer movement face is the "failure" of structures, in Unger's words, to entirely prevent or assist in their own revision. This is both a problem and an opportunity for individual and collective empowerment, and represents the challenge facing the disabled community.

Empowerment is the developmental and learning process that some disabled people are involved in when they build and actively participate in the community structures of their own creation. This process is the essence of what is referred to as social movement. Empowerment is a construct used by social scientists and others who deal with the issue of powerlessness of so-called minority group members, for example, the poor, women, the disabled, blacks and others (Powell 1987; Boyte and Riessman 1986; Rose and Black 1985; Freire 1984; Rappaport et al. 1984; Lieberman et al. 1979; Solomon 1976). The concept has been used freely with such terms as coping skills, mutual support, community and grassroots organizing, citizen participation. It is hard to define. It can be a mechanism or process that describes the interactive and highly subjective relationship of individuals and their social environments. It can also be understood as an internalized attitude and/or as an observable behavior; it may mean either a sense of control, or actual control over events and circumstances (or both) for individuals.

In becoming empowered consumers, disabled persons learn to overcome deeply internalized expectations of powerlessness, alienation and self-blame, to deal with the frustrations of inequities in the distribution of resources, and to counter social and political intimidation. As a learning process, empowerment means learning general action skills that are useful in playing a more conscious and assertive role in the ongoing social construction of one's social and political environment, that is, structures. Empowerment is the learned ability to form, develop and maintain community structures that harness the energies of people in order to achieve desired results (Figure 1.1). What is the relation between agency (or action) and structure? The process of empowerment entails gaining an understanding of how social and political institutions work. This includes grasping the fact that structures consist of ongoing sets of learned interactions. Power structures, structures of domination, social categories and social designations are correctly understood as the outcome of interactions that are mediated by material and nonmaterial resources and are contingent on following socially accepted rules of conduct. Acquiring and

Figure 1.1 The Community-Building Process

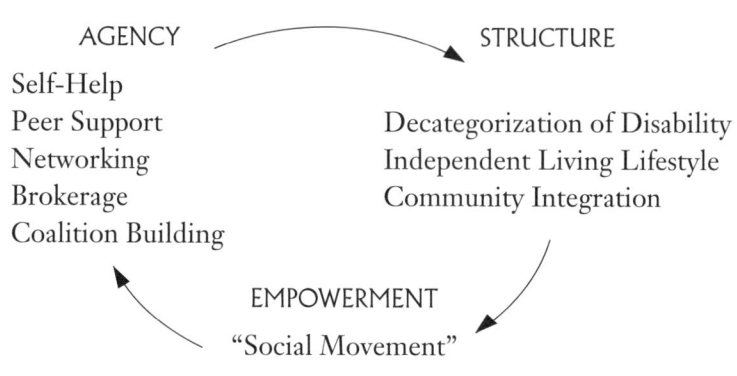

manipulating resources, trying to change the rules and so intervening in the flow of action almost ensures that some change in interaction and structure will follow.

This is a formidable task for disabled people because it requires a critical and analytical understanding of what rules and resources are crucial in reproducing the asymmetrical community and institutional power relations that are the outcome of negative stereotypes, labels, and designations. The next step is to put this understanding to use: To produce new patterned and reciprocal interactions in an attempt to reconfigure or redesign community and institutional power structures which have been, historically, the source of oppression of disabled people.

My theoretical orientation to the problem of "breaking" from imposed categories, "rebuilding" community, and "redesigning" power structures from the perspective of the disabled consumer movement is inspired by the work of Anthony Giddens and in part by the work of Roberto Unger (1987) and Alain Touraine (1977a; 1981). Using an expression possibly borrowed from Piaget, Giddens (1984) calls his approach the theory of structuration. The theory is presented in *The Constitution of Society* (1984). In earlier works Giddens (1976; 1977; 1979) prepared the way for a more comprehensive theory of action.

In one of his earliest works, Giddens (1976) discussed new theoretical currents emerging from a critique of the orthodox consensus model formulated decades earlier by Talcott Parsons (1937; 1951). The consensus model had been called into question not only by Marxists and conflict theorists, but also by symbolic interactionists, ethnomethodologists and other "micro" sociologists, as well as by anthropologists (Sahlins 1976; Bourdieu 1977). While Giddens agreed to an emphasis on the subjectivity of actors, he still considered interpretive social science too close to the orthodox consensus model in its approaches to the problems of normative meaning to be useful for the analysis of power phenomena, on both micro and macro levels (1976: 51–53). He criticized some post-structuralists (Foucault, Derrida) for almost totally eliminating the individual, and favored instead "a recovery of the subject without lapsing into subjectivism" (Giddens 1979: 39–40, 44; 1987a: 205–7).

According to Giddens, a more balanced approach is a conceptualization of social structure that does not ignore the capacity of individuals for reflection and action, but that also does not conceive of structures as totally independent from them. This led him to place the temporality and spatiality of human action at the heart of his approach (1979: 53 ff; 1984: passim). This means that the extension and reproduction of social actions and systems is specified in terms of time-space distanciation, that is, the extent to which action is face-to-face and involves physical presence/absence.

His rethinking of the idea of social action also includes a new approach to the concept of power (1979: 91–94; 1984: 14–16). Giddens attributes power to the transformative potential of all action, thus not restricting power to the actual wielding of force. He proposes that power is the capability to use resources in the sense of transformative capacity at the level of interaction and in the sense of domination at the structural level of existing institutions and systems. A clearer relationship between action and intentionality is developed in Giddens's action theory. Intentionality is seen as the capacity for self-reflective control and evaluation of one's own behavior. Action is no longer merely the execution of pre-formed intentions or of the automatic realization of internalized values and motives. Now, action is conceived as having a multiplicity of motivations, making it also possible to attribute more than one motive to every action (Giddens 1979: 58–59; 1984: 6–7).

In Giddens's framework, intentionality and reflexivity are linked together processually. This link introduces the possibility of *conscious* innovation and change in social conduct. The key notion is the overall contingency of social and cultural reproduction, and an emphasis on the individual's ability to monitor his or her own motivations and actions, and to "make" society.

Giddens does not ignore the limiting power of existing structures. Despite the creative actions by what seem to be "transcendental" actors, the approach recognizes that social structures are not produced out of thin air, but in any given instant are both reproduced and transformed. What his approach tries to overcome is the often one-sided conception of action as restricted by existing structures, precisely the kind of one-sidedness that continually gives rise to such typical oppositions as structure and agency, micro and macro approaches, or even voluntarism and determinism which Giddens rejects (1984: 139–44). Giddens's solution is the idea of the *duality of structure*, the key notion in structuration theory (1979, 1982, 1984; see also B.S. Turner 1992). This is the notion that structures have a two-fold nature that both makes action possible and restricts it, that structures are both the means as well as the result of human endeavors. Essentially, structures "exist" in manifest form only when they are instantiated in actual social practice. Structure is understood as being constituted and contingent on how people interact with one another.

Structuration theory bridges or links action and structure together in several useful and important ways. For instance, it connects an interpretive and active notion of agency to the study of the ways in which knowledgeable individuals go about producing patterned and recurrent interactions. It also links face-to-face systems of interaction with impersonal, institutionalized and "extended" kinds of interaction on the basis of temporality and physical presence or absence. Time-space is useful to distinguish between the kinds of interactions that can occur among individuals (the micro level) and between groups or more complex organizations (the macro level). Finally, structuration theory emphasizes action as "a stream of actual or contemplated causal interventions" and "the practical realization of interests." "To make a difference" or "to have acted otherwise" (phrases Giddens uses to refer to the transformative capacity of power) is to transform some aspect of a continuous flow of events, and suggests that the interventions undertaken by individuals are wholly within their control.

In what way is Giddens's approach to social action useful in understanding the activities of action-oriented disabled people and others? First, Giddens rejects any theory which ignores time and space by separating statics from dynamics. In his approach to action, an interdependence of structure and action must be predicated upon grasping the temporal and spatial aspects inherent in the constitution of all social interaction. Second, Giddens rejects both the deterministic attempts to get behind the "backs of actors," as in functionalism and structural Marxism, and the excessive voluntarism that ends up neglecting the structural context, as in contemporary action theories. Third, and most importantly, Giddens tries to mediate the dichotomy between subject and object by assigning a prime role to the knowledgeability of actors in producing and reproducing their society, while at the same time not denying that they must use societal properties in the process.

Perhaps the most useful aspect of Giddens's approach is his image of society as a continuous flow of conduct, rather than as a series of separate or discrete acts. Structuration is ever a process, never a product. Directly pertinent to the central thesis of this book is Giddens's idea of the *dialectic of control*, which means that individuals can get "in on" this process to influence, even alter, the flow of social conduct in order to "make a difference" in social life (Giddens 1979: 145–50; 1984: 14–16). The implications of a practical and political kind for the empowerment process, social movement and community-building are that it is not a given that a dominant individual or group has total or absolute control over the direction and flow of conduct, though they try to. Individuals and groups have a share in building the social world and the communities in which they live and can rebuild them differently if they so choose, and go about it in the knowledge that they can.

The Concept of Community

The task disabled citizens have set for themselves, namely their goal of integrated and independent community living through empowerment, involves the construction of mediating or alternative structures. Clearly, present social and community structural arrangements are anathema to the realization of the overall goals of action-oriented disabled people. With specific reference to Giddens's concept of the duality of structure and the dialectic of control, the struggle to "reconfigure" the categories of society (part of the social structure and part of community life) is to learn how those categories are constructed in the first place and how they are maintained. The community-building process entails learning how to build up and at the same time tear down existing structures. To achieve the goal of independent living also means "teaching" society to rethink some of its fundamental organizing principles.

The concept of community is acknowledged as important in social science theory, but is elusive and difficult to define clearly. As a descriptive and as an evaluative term, such phrases as community politics, community action, community development and community building are used. Perhaps the meaning intended to be communicated by these stock phrases relate to a sought-after rootedness, cohesion, belonging and attachment—the opposite of alienation, isolation and the loss of attachment that is apparently part of the crisis of modern mass society. Community has been linked to locality, to identity of functional interests, to a sense of belonging, to shared cultural ideas and values, and as an alternative to a highly organized and bureaucratized way of life characteristic of modern mass society that simultaneously fragments and segments people's lives.

The idea that community is "founded upon man conceived in his wholeness," that is, "in which men were to be met by other men in the totality of their social roles" as somehow distinct from the "segmentation of the person in modern urban society" is rooted in the social and political theory of the late eighteenth and nineteenth centuries (e.g., Rousseau, Hegel, and Marx; see Plant 1974: 16–17; and Nisbet 1970). This theme was central in the works of such contemporaries as Ferdinand Tönnies (his Gemeinschaft/Gesellschaft distinction), Emile Durkheim (mechanical/organic solidarity), and Max Weber (substantive/formal rationality). Continuing in the typological tradition were the works of Louis Wirth (on urbanism), Robert Redfield (the folk society and folk-urban continuum), Howard Becker (the sacred/secular distinction) and others (Lyon 1987: 18–26).

The move from communal to associational forms of organization, from Gemeinschaft to Gesellschaft, mechanical to organic solidarity, represented a loss of community, a way of life and an ethos. In turn, this loss became "a necessary condition of the emancipation of the self-conscious, self-directing individual" (Plant 1974: 31) that laid the foundation for a utilitarian individualism as a prerequisite for industrial capitalism. According to Marx, the problem of the fragmentation of society and of the personality was seen as part and parcel of industrial capitalism that replaced the communal virtues of cooperation and fraternity with those of conflict, competition and the cash nexus. Interestingly, division of labor, social class and interest groups were early recognized as both the outcome of the disintegration of community as well as a means of reorganizing or reorienting community along different, but no less satisfactory, lines. The appeal to the values of community was a critique of industrial capitalism at the same time as it provided the impetus and a positive basis for new kinds of interaction and organization.

Whether community in the nostalgic sense ever existed at all is doubtful. Whether a return to the rigid status groups of feudal society or a rural lifestyle was ever desired is also doubtful. The attempt to regain community can be seen as the attempt to recapture some sense of the wholeness of human nature that purportedly was lost in urbanization, growth of a market society, industrialization, the growth of bureaucracies and specialization. The notion of community as it was invoked in the social theory of the nineteenth and twentieth centuries can be understood as a means of trying to make sense of a rapidly changing world and to come to terms with it. One of the central problems of social theory was the "reconciliation" of the tension between the communitarian tradition that stresses identity of interests, cooperation and a sense of identity communally mediated, and the individualistic tradition that stresses personal freedom, autonomy, self-direction, contract and private property (Plant 1974: 34, and passim).

Community is an ideal form or type of organization, just as Gemeinschaft/Gesellschaft-type relations and mechanical/organic solidarity are hypothetical constructs existing for the purpose of comparison with the real world (Lyon 1987: 7). According to Lyon (1987: 16), "the community is obviously no longer a self-contained, self-sufficient, homogeneous village, but neither has it become an impotent group of unrelated, alienated, anonymous residents with little or no local ties." The community is a problematic and lies somewhere in between. It is the term's seeming looseness and imprecision that makes it so useful.

"Community" is used here in a relational and psychological sense, not a geographical, spatial or geo-political sense. As a kind of counterpoint to centralized authority in political, economic and social life, "community" is also used as an interactional field within which various forms of interaction take place that emphasizes the social-psychological elements of community. Community is a setting, a node of the macro-system, in which individuals link themselves to each other and to the larger society. From this perspective, Sarason (1974: 153) notes that,

> The psychological sense of community can have many referents, ranging from a family or a gang to a professional organization with members across the nation. I shall use the concept of referents to mean those groupings (families, fellow workers, friends, neighbours, religious and fraternal bodies) which give structure and meaning to our daily lives and whose quality and force are in some ways a function of the legal-political-administrative entity: the city, town, or village. It is that entity in which these groupings are embedded....

To Sarason's functional legal-political-administrative entity might be added the state, for it is in relation or juxtaposition to the state that communities of interests, values and ideas, purpose and goals often form. Depending on one's point of view, the state is an arbiter, mediator or coordinator of interests—or is an obstacle to their expression and realization. In a relational and psychological sense, the importance of the idea of community lies primarily with its organizing value, and in its enabling (empowerment) sense, as a process for learning and contributing to the knowledge of its members. The notion has to do with particular qualities and dimensions of social experience. Sarason states that community is "one of the major bases for self-definition and the judging of external events" (1974: 157).

The issue of community action, community-building and community development is one of citizen participation, self-realization and the fulfillment of needs both in an ontological and instrumental sense. Indeed, the liberal view of community and community-building places a great deal of emphasis on participation—

> The individual citizen has ceased to have any sense of his being personally involved: he no longer feels that he is able to identify him-

self with any organized body.... The main question then is how to promote greater flexibility in large scale institutions and to increase their systematic contact with the population or, to put it differently, how to transform formal democracy so that it becomes a living democracy. *Conscious participation of the population in the development of their own community* and readiness to share responsibility are essential if that transformation is to take place (United Nations statement on community development, *op. cited* in Plant 1974: 59, emphasis added).

From an action perspective, the community-building process involves the amelioration or transformation of structural conditions that limit, restrict, or destroy both the relational and psychological sense of community. From the perspective of disabled people, nothing is as morally hideous and destructive to the psychological sense of community as segregation—either in the form of involuntary institutionalization, specialized services and programs, rehabilitation therapies, labelling or architectural/physical barriers. Different in form but similar in impact, attitudinal and physical barriers prevent full participation in community life. As disabled citizens write,

> We expect the same treatment in respect to the dignity and integrity of all other human beings who happen to dwell on this planet called earth.... We are persons. We have specific needs, which, once met, can only lead to the public good. But to meet these needs without consultation, cooperation and ongoing participation by the disabled is to not recognize our person-hood.... And to say this, is to say that persons who happen to have a physical disability do not meet the criteria of using existing community services, but rather, need special segregated services. To not be able to gain services and the like through existing community services wherever possible, is equivalent to admitting that we are not persons (Alberta Committee of Citizens With Disabilities 1981b: 39–40).

The "quest for community" with its call for participation and personhood is a conscious learning and structuring process, one that seeks to reaffirm and ensure a democratic "culture of participation" not only in name, but in reality.

Breaking the Mold

The challenges for individuals with disabilities are complex and far-reaching. The individual is part of a unique community labelled the disabled community. But the individual is also part of a much larger community comprised of its own socially and culturally accepted practices and structures. For many individuals, the community they are part of may also be defined in cultural, ethnic, racial, religious and gender terms. In addition to the community a person may belong to, there also exists different sectors in which he or she participates or is involved with. These include the public, private, commercial, institutional, political, professional and so on. These different aspects of community present challenges to disabled people with respect to role identity, isolation, segregation, access to services and meaningful citizenship.

Historically, disabled individuals have been viewed from a "we-they" perspective. This we-they dichotomy has enabled the creation of systems, programs and attitudes which have permitted inequitable treatment because disabled people were considered different. Countless policies have been written that have underlined and emphasized individual differences, and that have helped create and reinforce certain categories and labels. Service delivery and professional care systems have been created that focus and depend on the existence of disabilities. This has led to segregated "different" services and programs. Public response to people with disabilities has all too often been reflected and supported by policies and legislation. Even language—terms such as "crippled," "suffering from," "victim of"—has served to make labels and categories more real than they really are, and have prevented the individual from being seen as a whole person with his or her own needs, strengths, weaknesses and desires.

While nondisabled people have held the we-they perspective, so too have many disabled people. The constant focus *on* disability has made it difficult to break out of that particular social category. The consequence has been that the disabled person, the service provider, policy maker and legislator, and even other citizens have often worked at cross-purposes to each other. They have not been systematically linked together in planning and creating healthy, integrated and supportive communities. Excluded from mainstream community life, the end result has been an insidious segregation and marginalization that is the direct consequence of unthinking barrier-creating attitudes of indifference, over-protection or as is sometimes the case, outright discrimination.

Citizens with distinctive physical and mental limitations have been mobilizing their talents and political will under the banner of the independent living/disabled consumer movement. The philosophy of consumerism and the independent living model have both evolved from years of personal experience with living with disabilities, and reflect the belief in the rights of individuals to take control of their own lives. Common social concerns, the disabled individual's determined sense of responsibility, and his and her right to be directly involved in the community/legislative decision-making and planning processes have resulted in the emergence of hundreds of local, regional and national cross-disability groups and organizations.

What have also emerged are a significant number of parallel, alternative or mediating structures which create the integrative environments in which organizational and structural innovation and experimentation can occur. Following Giddens's idea of the duality of structure, peer support groups, brokerage systems and independent living centres are both the means and the outcome of new interaction patterns among disabled and nondisabled people. What makes these new structures significant is that they represent empowering or learning efforts by action-oriented disabled people to restructure in a conscious way the contexts of their own lives. No less significant for an analysis of the empowering efforts of the disabled community are the self-produced materials that quite literally document this conscious and reflexive community-building activity.

2
Fact into Fancy
From Disability to Handicap

The way people interact with one another generate the social categories and structures they come to share and in which they further participate. Social categories and structures are simultaneously the means and the outcome of the actions and activities of people. The efforts of action-oriented disabled people structure the contexts of their own existence and ensure their participation in the larger community. This structuring process, moreover, is a conscious one and implies that if structures are made, they can be unmade or remade.

Part of the process of achieving the goal of independent living and community integration involves re-examining what disability is, and redefining it. Disability is socially constructed—both a product of social, economic and political relationships, and the means by which these relationships are sustained. This chapter examines the meaning of disability and attitudes towards disabled persons, what the consequences have been for being labelled disabled, and ways in which disability can be a basis for social action.

Disability, as defined by the World Health Organization (1980), is the temporary, prolonged, or permanent reduction or absence of the ability to perform or engage in certain roles and daily living activities. An impairment that causes the disability is an actual psychological,

Table 2.1 Persons with Disabilities Residing in Households and Health-Related Institutions, By Sex and Age Group, Canada, 1991.

	Population with Disabilities		Persons with Disabilities Residing in	
	Number	Disability Rate	Households (%)	Institutions (%)
Both Sexes	4,184,685	15.5	93.7	6.3
0–14	389,355	7.0	100.0	*
15–64	2,346,455	12.9	97.9	2.1
65 and Over	1,448,875	46.3	85.3	14.7
Females	2,217,640	16.2	92.2	7.8
0–14	156,365	5.7	100.0	*
15–64	1,182,145	12.9	98.2	1.8
65 and Over	879,130	48.8	82.7	17.3
Males	1,967,045	14.8	95.5	4.5
0–14	232,990	8.1	100.0	*
15–64	1,164,310	12.8	97.6	2.4
65 and Over	596,745	43.4	89.3	10.7

* Children in institutions were not included in the 1991 survey. In 1986, there were an estimated 2,499 children with disabilities in institutions.
Statistics Canada, *The Daily*, October 13, 1992: 4. Catalogue 11–001E. Reproduced with permission of the Minister of Industry, Science and Technology, 1993.

physiological, or anatomical defect in the physical and mental functioning of the body, caused perhaps by trauma or disease. These definitions are very broad, and include physical and mental conditions which might be temporary or permanent; they also include those of limited significance as well as those of immense consequence to the lives of people affected or involved.

Who is considered disabled in Canada? Based on the 1991 Census of Population, 15.5%, or 4,184,685 Canadians reported some level of mental and physical disability. Statistics Canada identified 7.0% of Canadian children under the age of 15 as having some disabling condition. Among the adult population aged 15 to 34, 8.0% reported some level of activity limitation, rising to 14.0% for those persons aged 35 to 54, and to 27.1% for those aged 55 to 64 years. Persons aged 65 years and older reported a disability rate of 46.3% (Statistics Canada, *The Daily*, October 13, 1992: 3; for comparative purposes, see

Table 2.2 Persons with Disabilities Residing in Households and Health-Related Institutions by Level of Severity and Age Group, Canada, 1991.

	Total		Persons with Disabilities Residing in			
	Number	(%)	Households	(%)	Institutions	(%)
0–14	389,355	100.0	389,355	100.0	*	*
Mild	348,300	89.5	348,300	89.5	*	*
Moderate	29,555	7.6	29,555	7.6	*	*
Severe	11,500	2.9	11,500	2.9	*	*
15–64	2,346,455	100.0	2,297,135	100.0	49,320	100.0
Mild	1,261,825	53.8	1,248,500	54.3	13,325	27.0
Moderate	737,345	31.4	725,430	31.6	11,915	24.2
Severe	347,285	14.8	323,205	14.1	24,080	48.8
65 and Over	1,448,875	100.0	1,235,955	100.0	212,920	100.0
Mild	508,095	35.1	487,420	39.4	20,675	9.7
Moderate	470,745	32.5	435,155	35.2	35,590	16.7
Severe	470,035	32.4	313,380	25.4	156,655	73.6

* Children in institutions were not included in the 1991 survey. In 1986, there were an estimated 2,499 children with disabilities in institutions.
Statistics Canada, *The Daily*, October 13, 1992: 5. Catalogue 11–001E. Reproduced with permission of the Minister of Industry, Science and Technology, 1993.

Furrie 1990 for data based on the 1986 Census of Population, and Statistics Canada 1986/87, 1990a).

The rate reported for 1991 is higher than the 13.2% disability rate reported in the 1986 Census of Population. The increase is attributed to a change in survey methodology which measured greater numbers of individuals reporting disabilities relating to a mental health condition, including learning disabilities. As well, Statistics Canada suggests that an increased awareness of disability in society may have made people more willing to report their limitations in daily activities and the barriers which they encounter in everyday life (*The Daily*, October 13, 1992: 2).

Precise breakdowns are difficult to make because there are disabilities that are related to the aging process, and because some illnesses or impairments progressively worsen. The general aging of the Canadian population (McDaniel 1986), increased air, water and chemical pollution (Bolaria 1991, Harding 1988), poor exercise, dietary practices and poverty (Bolaria and Wotherspoon 1988), are constantly creating new and complex situations out of which multiple impairments, and therefore multiple categories of impairment, may arise. Disabilities arising from work hazards and accidents are major factors as well (Dickinson and Stobbe 1988).

Any given definition of disability is further complicated by the reality of multiple impairments and physical and numerous social/environmental causes, and is at best only a partial definition. According to the 1991 Health and Activity Limitation Survey (HALS—the foundation of Statistics Canada Disability Database Program), over two-thirds of the disabled population aged 15 and older had more than one type of disability. The prevalence of poorer health, multiple disabilities as well as the severity of disability increases with age, though being old and sick or disabled is not synonymous (Furrie 1990: 35–39).

Categorization by cause and by type of disability (or by type of impairment) is largely by convenience, not necessarily by convention. The medical and scientific literature often distinguishes between four basic kinds of impairments:

1. *Muscular-skeletal* and *motor* impairments may be caused by encephalopathies, or diseases or trauma of the brain, brought on by sudden cerebrovascular disturbances. Myelopathies, or disease or trauma of the spinal cord may result in paralysis, paraplegia or quadriplegia. There are arthropathies, or diseases of the joints resulting from arthritis or rheumatism. Diseases of the muscles, or myopathies, can be acquired (for example, poliomyelitis) or congenital (for example, muscular dystrophy). Debilitating diseases such as multiple sclerosis, cerebral palsy, and Parkinson's, whose origins are still a matter of intense research, can affect all or any aspects of the physiology.

2. *Sensory* impairments may be visual, auditory or communicative. Visual difficulties may range from slight to severe, from the necessity of using corrective lenses to legal blindness. These conditions could result from birth, accident, or age. Auditory impairments range in similar fashion, and could be either congenital or acquired. Speech and language difficulties also vary in nature and

intensity, and like visual and auditory impairments, can occur as a result of brain trauma or other cerebrovascular disturbances.

3. *Organic* impairments may or may not result in significant disability, but are no less the "cause" of stigmatization than the impairments just mentioned. These include, among others, such chronic invalidating diseases as cancer, diabetes, epilepsy, cystic fibrosis and heart conditions. Obesity, for example, may also be organic in origin, and is socially and culturally tolerated to varying degrees.

4. *Mental* and *psychological* impairments vary significantly, ranging from severe mental retardation (as in mongolism or Down Syndrome) to mental illnesses such as schizophrenia, mild psychoses (for example, depression), anorexia nervosa and learning disabilities. Chromosome disorders, metabolic disturbances and neurological disorders may be among the congenital (organic) causes, while foetal infection, toxic poisoning, and accidents are among possible leading socio-environmental causes, some of which pose increasing threats to future generations of the unborn. Disfigurement due to accident (occupational, recreational, etc.) resulting in physical impairment could likewise cause depression, anxiety and so forth.

What should be acknowledged about these impairments is the considerable extent to which they overlap, are interrelated, or are points along a continuum. A particular cause or a number of causes may give rise to one or several impairments, or disabling conditions, which can vary in nature and intensity. This is not remarkable since it is recognized that the body is an interrelated whole. A stressful lifestyle in combination with a host of other things may cause a stroke or an aneurysm, which could result (not uncommonly) in partial paralysis, spasms, incontinence, speech difficulties and mental depression. A person may suffer a number of impairments, each of which varies in nature, intensity and level of severity, and each of which will be experienced differently.

Given the complex nature of impairments as causes of, or providing the conditions for, disability, it is useful to describe the kind of disability with respect to the level of ability or inability of a person to perform certain functions that are common and customary to most people. Each function might call for the individual to use a different part

Figure 2.1 Adults (Aged 15–64) with Disabilities Residing in Households, by Level of Severity and Age Group, Canada, 1991.

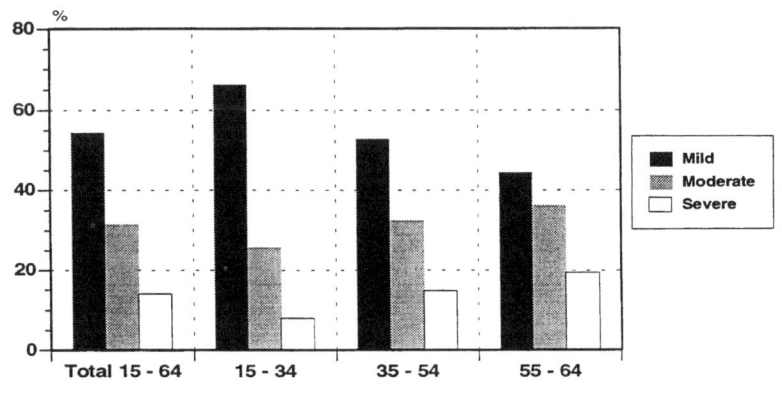

Statistics Canada, *The Daily*, October 13, 1992: 8. Catalogue 11–001E. Reproduced with permission of the Minister of Industry, Science and Technology, 1993.

or parts of his or her body. The Health and Activity Limitation Survey uses what is called the "functional limitation approach" through the use of "activities of daily living" (ADL) questions, and so focuses on six physical/mental disabilities:

Mobility—walking 400 metres without resting, moving from room to room, walking up and down a flight of stairs, carrying a 5 kg. object for 10 metres, standing for long periods (20 minutes);

Agility—dressing or undressing oneself, cutting toenails, grasping or handling objects, cutting food;

Seeing—reading ordinary newsprint, seeing someone from 4 metres with or without glasses;

Hearing—ability to hear what is being said in conversation with other people, with or without a hearing device;

Speaking—ability to speak and be understood.

Figure 2.2 Adults (Aged 15–64) with Disabilities Residing in Households, by Nature of Disability and Age Group, Canada, 1991.

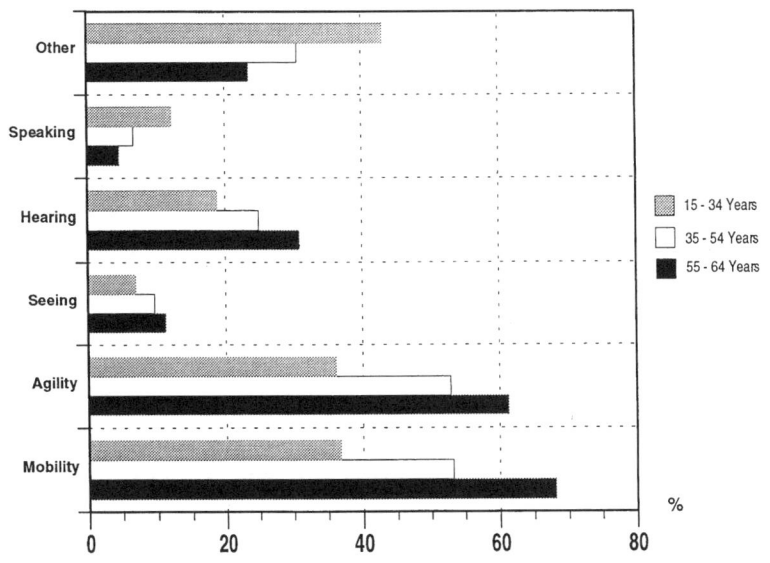

Statistics Canada, *The Daily* October 13 1992: 9. Catalogue No. 11–001E. Reproduced with permission of the Minister of Industry, Science and Technology, 1993.

The category "Other" in Figure 2.2 includes learning disabilities, an emotional or mental health condition, developmental delay, or labelling by others.

For the 1991 HALS, Statistics Canada introduced a "severity scale" that measures partial (one point) to total loss (two points) of ADL functions (Statistics Canada, *The Daily*, October 13, 1992: 13). Scores are categorized as mild (total of less than 5 points), moderate (5 to 10 points) and severe (11 or more points). Points are counted differently for adults than they are for children under the age of 15 years, and a separate measurement scale of severe disability was developed for seniors living in health-related institutions (*The Daily*, October 13, 1992: 11, 13). Data from the 1986 Census of Population/HALS were reported with respect to whether a person had multiple disabilities; data from the 1991 HALS were reported with respect to the severity scale. The advantage of the severity scale is that it measures the severity of disability in terms of multiple disabilities (for example, if two points are counted for each total loss of function, a total of four points (mild disability) might represent the total loss of two functions, the total loss of one function plus the partial loss of an additional two functions, or the partial loss of four functions).

The Social Meaning of Disability Statistics

Broad definitions of impairment and disability such as those suggested by the World Health Organization have at least two advantages. First, they draw attention to a whole range of even relatively minor or temporary conditions, rather than just the severe or chronic ones. Secondly, by inviting an awareness of physical disability at this level, the possibility is created for disabled individuals to define their conditions, difficulties, and abilities themselves. In addition, adopting these broader and more general definitions with respect to both breadth and orientation than what purely medical definitions offer, allows for the possibility of *social analysis*. The medical model of physical disability, which helps generate descriptive statistics like those in the previous tables and figures, would proceed sequentially as follows:

$$\text{Etiology} \longrightarrow \text{Pathology} \longrightarrow \text{Manifestation}$$

While perhaps adequate from a bio-medical point of view, this model includes neither the reaction of individuals to their condition(s), nor the reaction of other people to the condition of the individuals. The model does not address the consequences of the interaction between these two variables upon affected individuals, upon other people, or, ultimately, upon society. As the World Health Organization has recognized, these considerations are vital since they concern the *social consequences* of illness, disease and accident. These social consequences impact on an individual's functional abilities or inabilities to perform tasks required by the social roles an individual either has, desires to have or is prevented from attempting.

The statistics selected for presentation purport to describe a group of people or to categorize individuals in certain ways. They do not address issues relating to the social construction of disability and its consequences. This suggests that a somewhat different view of disability should be adopted:

$$\left.\begin{array}{l}\text{Disease}\\ \text{Illness}\\ \text{Accident}\end{array}\right\} \text{Impairment} \longrightarrow \text{Disability} \longrightarrow \text{Handicap}$$

These distinctions make it possible to look for and recognize the differences between conditions that may impair an individual, those that disable, and those that handicap. Impairments become physical disabilities when adequate corrective action is either unavailable, inaccessible, or not pursued for other reasons. While impairments represent disturbances at the organ or system level, disability might be thought of representing disturbances at the level of the person. A near-sighted individual, to give a simple example, becomes disabled only when adequate corrective lenses are not worn. The notion of disability thus arises with a measure of "failure in accomplishment" or "gradation in performance"; this makes it possible to distinguish relative degrees of the severity of disability.

Under some social conditions, even adequate corrective measures may not be enough to prevent existing physical disabilities from becoming real handicaps. The near-sighted individual in the example above, even with corrective lenses, may still not qualify for a pilot's license. Specific social parameters or rules have been established around the person's physical impairment and/or disability over which he or she has no control, and about which he or she has no say.

Handicaps are to be considered primarily the socio-cultural and environmental consequences of an individual's impairment. They are based on a person's assumed inability to fulfill social roles, and are "set up," consciously or unconsciously, to prevent his or her access to the various structures and institutions of society that are generally available or accessible to others. Handicaps also curtail or prevent participation in the life of the community on an equal level with others. It is not the actual physical or mental condition that is the key to understanding the position of the disabled in society and the dynamics of their interactions with the rest of society, but rather society's perception of that condition and its reaction to it. "Fact" is turned into "fancy." An individual will be as handicapped as society makes him or her out to be, even with minimum impairment.

Handicaps should be understood as *imposed* structural constraints. There are really no agreed-upon objective categories of impairment and disability (not even "purely" medical or statistical ones), despite clever attempts to make them seem that way. Any category or definition will reflect the social and political philosophy dominant at the time it is created. Also, disabled individuals distinguish between, and experience, relative degrees of intensity and severity of their impairments.

The severity and degree of impairment and disability an individual experiences depends on how certain, primarily dominant, *social* and *institutional* expectations are met. From the perspective of the individual, single all-purpose definitions of specific disabilities are the least useful. More useful are a range of definitions that relate to the incidence or prevalence of certain physical and mental conditions to specific needs that arise from them. Differing conditions and needs of individuals require a range of programs, services, and planning efforts. Definitions ultimately are important because it is when they are used as entry points to programs or as a basis for claims to social aid and income benefits that their wording and interpretation become crucial—both from the point of view of the disabled individual *and* from that of the administrator (Brown 1977: 8–20, and especially Stone 1984).

Clearly, any definitions and categories that are created would be meaningless without input from disabled individuals. This has hardly ever been the case. It is precisely over the construction of definitions and the imposition of structural constraints that conflict has emerged. It is difficult to escape the conclusion that the disability category is not only socially created, but, as something that can be manipulated, also serves as an administrative and political tool.

Image into Stigma: The Body as Vehicle of Meaning

Attitudes towards and actions against the diseased, the injured and the disabled have varied greatly. Often based on perceptions of illness or disability, resulting attitudes and treatments have ranged from complete rejection and ostracism, to semi-deification and the awarding of special privileges and honors.

In the militaristic society of ancient Sparta, as in the China of only several decades ago, physically malformed infants were killed at birth. Homer, the Greek epic poet, was blind and was venerated, and in fact in classical Greece pensions were awarded to blind persons as a matter of right. Yet the deaf in ancient Greek society were considered disabled and "incomplete." In ancient China, the visually impaired could be meaningfully engaged as musicians, poets, story-tellers, soothsayers, teachers and as scholars; there was obviously a place for them in society. Begging was still a possibility, but high political office was not out of the question for the aspiring. In Egypt, the priests of the temples taught simple rehabilitative skills to physically incapacitated veterans and civilians. In India, the degree of tolerance of certain kinds of disability was related to caste position.

Caesar's military success in what is now western Europe was not hampered because of his epilepsy (the "sacred disease"), now referred to as a hidden disability. In other societies, the presence of such symptoms as hallucinations or epileptic episodes was often considered "proof" of the ability to communicate with supernatural powers, and qualified some for the prestigious social role as shaman or medium. In medieval Europe, however, epileptics were deemed potential witches and qualified instead for the stake. On balance, Western society might be described as having a truly schizophrenic attitude towards the sick and disabled. Sometimes disabilities are "seen," and at other times overlooked and apparently irrelevant:

> Nor do we remember that Lord Byron had a club foot and Alexander Pope had curvature of the spine. Elizabeth Barrett Browning was a paraplegic. Milton was blind when he wrote *Paradise Lost*, Beethoven was deaf when he wrote the Ninth Symphony, Nietzsche was a syphilitic, and Dostoevsky was an epileptic. Edison was deaf, and Freud spent the last sixteen years of his life wearing a prothesis on his jaw. To speak of these men and women as handicapped seems a contradiction in terms (Gliedman and Roth 1980: 29).

Historically, a fundamental change in perception and attitude in the Western world toward the disabled occurred when very large numbers of injured persons returning from the Crusades resulted in institutional intervention for the first time. The Church helped create asylums for them, the earliest example (thirteenth century) and probably the most famous of which was the "House of the Three Hundred" in Paris, a hospital (an institution, incidentally, that has a long history outside Europe). That short-term solution eventually became the long-term answer in Western society for the question of where to put and what to do with disabled people. Prevailing notions about the etiology of disease or disability significantly influence the degree as well as the nature of social prejudice directed towards the afflicted.

Outside of injury in holy war, it became a firmly held Judeo-Christian ethic that physical defect is a just compensation for sin, where the visible defect provided insight into a person's inner moral and spiritual defects. Visibly ill, malformed or crippled individuals were said to be cursed or possessed by the Devil, and so were feared, persecuted and, in the extreme, tortured. As the sick individual became personally held responsible for his or her illness from the Middle Ages onward, social awareness of the individual tended to become more marked, attitudes more ambivalent and actions more drastic.

The physical segregation, institutionalization and social isolation of the disabled, the mentally-afflicted and others was well under way by the Middle Ages. The lazar houses (leprosariums) of fourteenth and fifteenth century Europe are well known; the *Narrenschiff* (ship of fools) of about the same period was the solution of some European riverine communities to deal with "vagabond madmen" (Foucault 1965: 7–8). Under James I in England, vagabonds or rogues were actually branded with the letter R, and sometimes V (Bauman 1987: 44). Often reduced to begging and so *because* of their poverty, the "immoral," "lazy" and "unworthy" were increasingly confined to hospitals, workhouses and, more often than not, to prisons. This trend became prevalent in the seventeenth century and a good part of the eighteenth century in most European countries. These places of confinement served as punitive and reformative institutions for the criminal, the poor, the sick and the insane alike (Stone 1984: 29–41; 51–55).

Through "discipline," or forced labor and corporal punishment, these unfortunates were "taught" to again become worthy, moral and work-loving. Yet even in the eighteenth century it was recognized that these institutions were not a solution, for "the hospital is an anachronistic solution that does not respond to the real needs of the poor and that stigmatizes the sick in a state of penury" (Foucault 1973: 44). The hospital was considered the "prime model involved in the early phases of the mushrooming of carceral organizations," which are associated with the rise of Western absolutist and nation-states (Giddens 1985: 182–97).

What marked these developments as a crucial turning-point in attitudes and actions towards "the sick" as constituting a biological/social category was not just physical segregation, but that for the first time *the body* itself seems to have become a *social* object upon which increasingly concerted integrative and manipulative efforts of particular systems of domination were focused (Foucault 1980: 55–62). The body, whether of positive or negative connotation, was seen as something to be controlled, neutralized, and preferably deprived of its potential to menace, in whatever way feared, the system; hence the Great Confinement, that is, the rise of the workshop, prison, hospital (Foucault 1965: 38–64, 1977: 135 ff, 1980: 166–82) and later, the factory.

Sequestration (Foucault's term) as a means of physically neutralizing and disciplining the body also occurred at about the same time such socially constructed categories and distinctions as "the deviant," the "normal" and the "pathological" began to appear. The processes of depersonalization and marginalization as a function of stigma and "deviance," with which most disabled individuals are probably familiar, clearly had their origins in the events of the sixteenth, seventeenth and eighteenth centuries.

For the last two hundred years, the meaning of illness and physical and mental disability has been specifically related *back* to the social and political structure with increasing intensity, and with the focus on the biological/physiological etiology of any particular affliction shifted elsewhere. Contemporary images of and attitudes towards disabled, mentally handicapped, and sick individuals are traceable to the melting away of the pre-eighteenth century medical dualism of health/sickness, and in its place, the gradual emergence in the nineteenth century of the dualism of normal/pathological, one that has since become established at the very center of all medical reflexion (Foucault 1973: 34–36; Giddens 1991: 144–49, 161–62). Society's initial reaction to the AIDS (Acquired Immune Deficiency Syndrome) epidemic, including carriers of the HIV (human immunodeficiency virus), illustrates Foucault's point perfectly (Schilts 1987, Social Research 1988).

The process of the typification of human differences (in the Schutzian sense, Schutz 1967) and the translation of the subsequent culturally- and socially-specific typologies into structures of interaction probably comes closest to providing an understanding of the dynamics involved in the historical shifts in perception. The creation and recognition of meaningful differences in both the physical and social worlds are basic to the human cognitive and learning processes. It is a way of organizing our experiences into some interpretive scheme, but as is the case in organizing perceptions, not only will some differences be highlighted from the perceptual horizon while others are suppressed, but not all individuals will treat the foreground differences equally either (Merleau-Ponty 1963: 68 ff).

The process by which supposedly neutral impairments are transformed by observers and ultimately by the person himself or herself into a particular disability and then into a handicap, involves (a) selectively shifting the focus away from the cause or causes, (b) selectively differentiating among the impairments (e.g., most visible to least visible, most to least severe), (c) lumping together all impairments by not differentiating among them at all, and (d) ignoring social setting and social interaction. An image of the individual is literally created by cognitive processing, one that may conform to previously constructed meaningful types and categories. The crucial point is that the image of the disabled person is thus *abstracted* from the confusing background differences (those seen but unnoticed) by the selection of salient differences (those seen and noticed), which are evaluated (positively, negatively or neutrally) by way of normative construction.

Once abstracted, the image is conferred on the person, and may become further socially approved and socially distributed (i.e., learned). The individual, so abstracted, has ceased to be female, a mother, Native, a Liberal back-bencher or a hockey team fan. Much like racism, ageism and sexism, the person's attributes are globalized to their whole being, rather than perceived as only a facet of their physical being (Russell 1989). The individual has been depersonalized, an effective way as any to sequester or marginalize them within their own community and society.

The differences between human beings that are either noticed or suppressed will depend on both what is relevant in a particular time and place, and on the kind of interaction taking place between individuals. As Douglas (1970: 37) pointed out, human interaction can only be adequately explained in reference to the situational context in which it takes place. Relevance structures of human differences that focus attention on some differences and directs it away from others are socially, culturally, and historically distributed and maintained. Although individual relevance structures do not exist completely apart from categories that are socially derived and approved, the relevance structures that determine how individuals react and respond to differences in the interactional context of the immediate moment are personal in nature.

Foreground differences, or those which are relevant or salient for particular types of social interaction, are also positively or negatively evaluated, and cognitively stratified or hierarchically arranged. Since the interpretive schemes which organize perceptions of these foreground differences include cognitive as well as normative constructs, the relevance structures that help maintain an assumed shared sense of reality thus imbue perceived differences with a kind of moral value and significance (Berger and Luckmann 1967: 104–16). Interpretive schemes clearly are normative constructions. While it is the *human body* that constitutes the perceptual horizon from which foreground differences are selected, any positive or negative valuations or moral judgements that are conferred or imposed upon the bodies of individuals also have *social* consequences for them (B.S. Turner 1984, O'Neill 1985).

Though the cognitive and perceptual processing of human body differences is universal, it is when particular human differences are evaluated negatively and imbued with negative moral meaning that the basis for *stigma* is created; stigma as a distinctly social phenomenon is a special case in the typification of difference. Goffman's classic study of this phenomenon remains unsurpassed, and he offers this definition: Stigmatized persons possess an attribute that is deeply discrediting and are viewed as less human because of it (Goffman 1963: 3–4). Human differences singled out for negative emphasis include what Goffman would call abominations of the body, blemishes of individual character and tribal stigma.

As Goffman suggests, stigmatization tends to lead to the "master status," the attribute that dominates the perception of the entire person, which has the social effect of neutralizing positive qualities and "spoiling" the identity of individuals (Kallen 1989: 52–55). The "normal" and the "stigmatized" as designations are *perspectives* that reflect social and cultural processes. As such, analysis of stigmatization can be carried out from either a symbolic interactionist perspective (Goffman's approach), or from more of a structural-functionalist perspective in which roles, norms, and motivational structures play a greater part in achieving an understanding of how stigmas are generated as well as maintained (Kallen 1989: 29–30, 51–52, 56–57).

Stigma into Deviance: Perceptions into Actions

Shared social designations are eventually "translated" into actions. That complex of relationships that exists between the human body and the social collectivity constitutes a critical dimension of consciousness in all societies, and provides a basis for action (Comaroff 1985: 6). As Douglas (1970), among others (Bourdieu 1977, Turner 1967, B.S. Turner 1984 and 1992, O'Neill 1985, Frank 1990, Giddens 1991) has noted, the human body as a natural symbol for conceptualizing about social identity provides not only numerous objective physical signs, but is the basis for assigning quite arbitrary subjective values and meanings to it that, over time and space, assume an objective and "true" reality. In fact, the "body" and the "social collectivity" *always* exist in a mutually constitutive relationship. Moreover,

> [T]he body is not merely capable of generating multiple perceptions; it also gives rise to contradictory ones. Thus, within corporeal confines, physical stability coexists with physical transience, stasis with disease and degeneration. It is hardly surprising, then, that as biological metaphors come to represent sociocultural realities, they signify not merely relations and categories but also contradictions in everyday experience; it is very common, for example, for sociocultural conflicts to be apprehended in terms of the arche-

typical metaphor of contradiction, [in this case] physical disease (Comaroff 1985: 8).

Both Sontag's (1978) short but rather insightful study and Turner's (1967) more general approach actually beg the notion of the "duality of the body," which is to say that the body is both the medium and the outcome of social interaction. Its objective physical signs are not only deeply implicated in its production and reproduction, but they have little or no meaning outside of social action (B.S. Turner 1992: 67–73, 85–88). The body as natural symbol may generate contradictory perceptions or confusing and unexpected signs that fall outside of or between existing cognitive categories or types that are not readily interpretable or understood. Their subsequent resolution and interpretation may reflect a transformation of not only society, but of the body and its signs as well.

Sontag draws attention to disease metaphors in political philosophy, citing such analogies between disease and civil disorder or moral decay in the body politic, ethnic groups and cancerous growth or mortal gangrene, radical surgery and repression. Treatment has distinct "military" and repressive overtones. Going even a little further,

> Early capitalism assumes the necessity of regulated spending, saving, accounting, discipline—an economy that depends on the rational limitation of desire. TB [tuberculosis] is described in images that sum up the negative behavior of nineteenth-century *homo economicus*: consumption; wasting; squandering of vitality. Advanced capitalism requires expansion, speculation, the creation of new needs (the problem of satisfaction and dissatisfaction); buying on credit; mobility—an economy that depends on the irrational indulgence of desire. Cancer is described in images that sum up the negative behavior of twentieth-century *homo economicus*: abnormal growth; repression of energy, that is, refusal to consume or spend (Sontag 1978: 63).

People suffer and die from tuberculosis and cancer. Are these metaphors of the time accidental? Foucault's transformation of the health/sickness dualism into the normal/pathological one coincides with the rise of industrial capitalism, representing a changing society and a very different valuation of both body and person. It has been argued that with a growing emphasis on personal initiative and competitiveness, productivity, ability, and achievement (a type of social Darwinism) in the context of the rise of industrial capitalism in the eighteenth and nineteenth centuries, the unemployable such as the sick, injured and the old became defined, *de facto*, as totally unproductive and dependent.

In the context of the rational and depersonalized factory system (see Smelser 1959: 274 ff), in which productivity and efficiency are highly valued, it is the worker who became defined as one of the most important factors of production. Kinloch (1979: 105–24) outlined the process of segmentation and differentiation in the capitalist mode of production, one which over time generated role-specialized minority identities and groups, based on physiological, behavioral and other criteria. Some of these minorities came to be defined as "functionally superfluous," that is, not useful or productive for society (Apter 1971: 87–100, see also Stone 1984: 41–51).

In another version of this perspective, internal regionalization (Giddens's (1985: 120, 182–97) term for sequestration) and the simultaneous creation of deviance as a social and political category is thought to be a part of the growth of state administration, surveillance and direct supervision over an increasingly differentiated society (Giddens 1984: 151–53; 1991: 149–55; Bauman 1987: 45–48), and may be considered part of the solution to problems of system coordination and reproduction, that is, social control. Giddens suggests that concepts like normality and deviance make little sense outside the context of the administrative state, and outside the context of the transformation of urbanism, the development of a mobile labor force and industrial capitalism. This raises the interesting possibility that as the face of capitalism and the relationship between people and technology as factors of production change, so might old stigmas and stereotypes of human frailties disappear.

In Parsons's classic analysis of the sick role and medical practice, illness is a form of deviance and a problem of social control; and the sick role is a tool to maintain the status quo (1951: 428 ff.). In his framework, illness is actually one of several deviant routes that individuals may take in response to the strains they encounter in their social roles. Entrance into the sick role helps individuals cope with their situations, which, Parsons assumed, diffuses the anger, frustration, and dissatisfaction that would otherwise lead to political organization and activism. The sick role, moreover, effectively isolates the deviant and prevents the organization of dissident individuals, while at the same time reintegrates them (Parsons 1951: 312–13).

The physician and the medical profession as a whole are seen by Parsons as integral to the system of social regulation, in that they each have a part to play in controlling access to the sick role (via the clinical definition of illness), and so help to reproduce systemic stratification by virtue of their technical knowledge and expertise. The medical profession as an instrument of the system may serve to rationalize the segregation and control of "deviant" individuals (Conrad 1992: 215–18). Merton (1968: 117) suggests that the sick role serves a latent function by contributing to the system's adaptation in a way that is neither intended nor consciously recognized by those in the sick role (see also Waitzkin and Waterman 1974: 16–24, 36–41, and Gerhardt 1989).

Deviance is not a property inherent in kinds of behavior or in people, but is instead created, constructed and conferred (Becker 1963, Goffman 1963, Schur 1979). A deviant is one who is assumed to transgress or depart, either voluntarily or involuntarily, from behavioral and/or physical norms, which might include physiological and intellectual ideals, religious or secular ideologies, legal codes, cultural definitions of mental health, and cultural ends and/or means. Deviantizing is a process much like stigmatization, and "deviance outcomes" are very much the consequences and products of social interaction, economic, political, and judicial interests, structures and institutional arrangements (Lauderdale 1980, Schur 1980). Defining deviance concerns the issue of constructing stigmatizing classifications. But once an individual is stigmatized by being labelled deviant, a self-fulfilling prophecy is initiated—one that is almost irreversible.

Disabled individuals might be conceptualized as a disadvantaged or minority group in that they are treated and reacted to as a category of people very much like the aged, blacks, women, the poor and other pariah and deviant groups (Sagarin 1971). Blackness, the female gender, advanced age and disability are presumed characteristics of biological inferiority; the disabled are considered less intelligent, incompetent, irresponsible, maladjusted and so are deemed immature, lazy, manipulative, unreliable, corrupt, immoral and so on. Because of the way in which they have been classified, they tend to be avoided, or worse, "put away."

In addition, the disabled occupy the sick role as Parsons described it, which reinforces the presumed pervasive incompetence of the disabled, and relegates them to a state of powerlessness. But to equate sickness with disability is to also generate and perpetuate oppressive traditional stereotypes about the personal and social abilities of disabled people. For example, legitimate exemption from "normal" role obligations changes into an almost permanent exclusion from normal opportunities and responsibilities because disabilities may be long-term or permanent, which leads to the belief that disabled persons will never become capable of leading "normal" social lives.

In the sick role, an individual is generally not held responsible for his or her illness, but in the case of the disabled, this is translated as an inability to attempt self-assertion. By the same token, refusal to behave as a good patient *or as a disabled person* is seen as a lapse of conduct, and as evidence of incorrigible deviance. Finally, playing the role requires active and willing cooperation with "experts"; it is expected and not considered strange that disabled persons should subordinate their personal interests and desires to the therapeutic goals and programs of "professionals" who "know what is best."

The inter-personal as well as inter-group treatment of the disabled continues to be influenced by such attitudes as their assumed helplessness, childlike nature and inability to assume adult responsibilities because of their "sickness." The sick role assumes there is no place in the individual's life for meaningful work, sexuality and intimacy, leadership and community involvement (Vash 1981). One characteristic of modern society is its immense talent for deflecting conflict and shifting issues into different realms. The medicalization of illness, and in particular of disability, has had the effect of transforming real structural issues of politics, law and economics into questions of personal responsibility, behavior, lifestyle and presumed personal and biological deficits (Illich 1976, Bolaria 1988a). The emphasis on the individual in the medicalization of illness and disability is symptomatic of what is called "blaming the victim" syndrome.

The disabled, as individuals and as a collectivity, have not been slow to contest their stigmas, to shrug the blame, to redefine their situations and to reject the roles into which they have been cast. They have recognized that stigmatization and all that the process entails has made it difficult, if not impossible, for them to work together politically. The process of destigmatization, or "coming out" (described by Kallen 1989: Chapter 5) involves attempts by disabled people to *change* negative images of the disabled, and to challenge the continued production, social acceptance and distribution of these images. This is the first part of the process of trying to introduce new behaviors and practices with a view, ultimately, of transforming existing structures and institutions.

The Situation of the Disabled:
Decontextualization and the Transformation of Subjective Reality

Enough studies have been conducted over the years which describe the process of becoming "deviant" inside and outside institutional settings (that is, to become identified as a criminal, mental patient or disabled person). Goffman (1961) demonstrates quite dramatically the connection between defining a problem in a particular way—in this case, seeing dysfunctional behavior and physical or mental impairment as a *medical* issue—and defining, by extension, an entire social system that apparently functions to confirm that definition by ruling out all possible alternative definitions. The efficient operation of any total institution requires that its inmates, or patients, learn the behavioral, symbolic and conceptual parameters of their new social reality.

In institutions, patients are obliged to accept their situation or problem as illness or disease which, from that point forward, dictates the realm of possibilities for them—as interpreted by doctors, health care professionals and others (Safilios-Rothschild 1970: 73–78). Once the "production of patients" has taken place, which involves validating the professionals and invalidating the patients, continued social interaction simply reproduces the inequality, domination and manipulation that is built into practice predicated on the medical model. What takes place in the institution also takes place in the community and in society; the disabled, and other stigmatized minority group members, learn what their positions and roles are. Society, for many pariah groups, is like a total institution. Much of what Goffman writes about what goes on inside institutions holds true for what occurs outside of them (Kallen 1989: 34–39).

At the center of the process of *becoming* disabled (after illness or traumatic injury; for those born with disabilities, the process of "becoming" is their socialization) is what is called decontextualization (Rose and Black 1985: 29). This is defined as the process whereby the individual's subjectivity becomes severed from the objective and historical context that frames everyday human social life. This reduction to an isolated asocial existence is bounded by a particular belief and symbol system that is characterized by medical hegemony and somatic/physical interventions such as surgery, therapies, medication and drug treatments. The decontextualized experiences of daily life—now being recontextualized—become saturated with new language and meaning, a language of illness and disability that contains such concepts as symptoms, regression, decompensation and handicap (Safilios-Rothschild 1970: 54–59, 68–73). This is the language that reduces social reality to a kind of intrapsychic distortion; instead of living life, in whatever limited sense possible, the individual now functions according to a set of rules and standards that actually have no bearing on genuine rehabilitation or reintegration into community living (Sarason 1974: 174 ff).

Interestingly, the behaviors appropriate to the sick (disabled) role and to being a good patient or client are behaviors almost opposite those that are appropriate in ordinary social life. The good "cripple," or patient, is docile, acquiescent, dependent on others and is ignorant of his or her rights and entitlements (Stroman 1982: 52–56). The externally imposed "new social order" becomes internalized and incorporated subjectively over time, and slowly the role and definition of what it means to be disabled is tacitly accepted. But in the process, the individual experiences what is a painful emotional and psychological withdrawal from the norms and forms that gave meaning to "normal" daily life, an experience that is most profound. The person's experience of disorientation and disassociation following illness or injury, and the medical model's rigidly-imposed definition of reality, combine to produce the "disabled" person (Rose and Black 1985: 30). Any efforts at resistance, expressed behaviorally or emotionally, are interpreted as part of the person's problem, and brings about more medical intervention or therapy.

As the now physically and emotionally traumatized individual gains the knowledge and skills to function as a disabled person in the sick role or in rehabilitation, he or she actually loses the important knowledge and skills for living in the community. The individual's potential for independent living becomes compromised due to losing the ability to link subjective experience to objective circumstances, by being mystified by expertise and fulfilling the expectations of what are essentially the power-holders. Personhood is overshadowed by patienthood, and the individual's active participation in and consciousness of social/historical reality is replaced by his or her passive acquiescence or functional adaptation to and acknowledgement of his or her own invalid state. Disabled individuals have described this experience as a sense of being disconnected from ongoing social existence, as if their capacity to engage in the process of living meaningfully has been surgically severed (Goldiamond 1976: 103–118). Precisely this aspect of utter physical and psychological oppression serves to sustain the stigma of disability (Schur 1980: 72–95). The empowering process cannot be understood without fully comprehending these experiences and constraints that disabled people are subjected to.

It is critical to keep in mind, but rather easy to forget, that in the majority of cases disabled individuals, prior to injury or onset of disease or illness, were no different from anyone else. As human and social/historical beings, their needs and interests are those of everyone else, which include income, adequate housing, nutritious foods, comfortable and stylish clothing, friends, intimate relationships, legal protection and the choice to participate in socially meaningful mutual interaction with others. If anything, meeting these needs and interests is probably more important *after* becoming disabled; individuals need these resources as social beings living in the community, and not as patients or clients confined to a hospital or an institution, or otherwise segregated from mainstream life.

There has been a tendency for professional care-givers to define and interpret "universal" needs such as these in light of the assumptions of the medical model, that is, of the inherent defectiveness and deviance of disabled persons. The consequence is that some of their needs might be met, but in ways that sometimes contradict their interests. For example, sheltered housing or workshops have as their basis not some form of care for those who might have difficulty living independently, but the assurance that medical/therapy regimes will be followed. Individual case management and rehabilitation, instead of being built on advocacy or empowerment principles designed to guarantee the essential dignity and benefits needed that focuses on strengths and capabilities, instead concentrates on forging linkages for the disabled to clinics and other treatment outlets, or to services designed especially for them, that is, focusing on needs and inabilities. The socialization to the pattern of dependence is continued (Marlett et al. 1984).

Institutionalized, segregated and ghettoized (Schur 1980: 90–95) disabled individuals cannot be understood apart from their context, and their forms of self-expression used in any other contexts and situations are a crystallization of the distorted social relations into which they have been resocialized. Their individual and collective identities are more of a commentary on that socialization than statements about autonomous living and a quality of life. The individual's behavior and outlook must be understood as both a learned survival and coping strategy, and as a product of regulated social relations that have developed over time. In fact, when the ideological and organizational bases on which theories of mental and physical health are based are considered, the larger context of social control, oppression and domination in which *both* health care workers, themselves restricted to the medical model/paradigm, *and* their products, the disabled, becomes very clear.

The relations between health care professionals and patients or clients are not unlike that of class relations. The disabled collectively endure common economic and political conditions. In addition to the common base of hospitalization, institutionalization, and perpetual rehabilitation and its impact on self-image and self-confidence, there are common social conditions. For example, there is placement in profit-organized care facilities that are regulated, dependence on third-party payments for medical care, services and equipment, and dependence on continued eligibility for different forms of special public assistance programs. Since these are relatively uniformly the case for many disabled people, they combine to form collective subjugation and manipulation (Rose and Black 1985: 33).

The patterns of self-expression supposedly characteristic of disabled persons are understood as reflecting the social, cultural and political forces that dominate their existence, and which further reproduce those forces, the environment and their designated places and roles within it. If certain forms of self-expression, behavior and conduct come into conflict with the accepted roles, norms and values of the larger social and political environment in which the disabled are encapsulated, these are interpreted as threats or challenges, not as self-determining efforts. This subsequently elicits a response from those who have an investment in the structures of control and domination, since there is an unwritten and implicit rule that people must behave appropriately and according to the dictates of the social role structures of society. Berger and Luckmann (1967: 112–13) describe the overall process this way:

> Therapy [read: rehabilitation] entails the application of conceptual machinery to ensure that actual or potential deviants stay within the institutionalized definitions of reality, or, in other words, to prevent the "inhabitants" of a given universe from "emigrating." It does this by applying the legitimating apparatus to individual "cases."
>
> ... Since therapy must concern itself with deviations from the "official" definitions of reality, it must develop a conceptual machinery to account for such deviations and to maintain the realities thus challenged. This requires a body of knowledge that includes a theory of deviance, a diagnostic apparatus, and a conceptual system for the "cure of souls."

The combination of coercive physical manipulation and rearrangement of thought and subjective experience (decontextualization) to comply with a dictated reality effectively extends the medical/rehabilitation model in terms of social control. In other words,

> Such a conceptual machinery [therapy/rehabilitation] permits its therapeutic application by the appropriate specialists and may also be internalized by the individual afflicted with the deviant condition. Internalization itself will have therapeutic efficacy.... Successful therapy establishes *a symmetry between the conceptual machin-*

ery and its subjective appropriation in the individual's consciousness; it resocializes the deviant into the objective reality (Berger and Luckmann 1967: 114). [emphasis added]

In sum, the pervasive influence of this "objective" reality reinforces the demoralized self, which is communicated as disabled identity and self-expression, and so becomes the further focus and rationale of treatment by care and service providers. Furthermore, in identifying the disability with the individual (Goffman's (1963) notion of master status), the health care professionals, indeed, even the doctors, are dissociated from taking responsibility for the consequences of their own activities. Sometimes we forget that the professionals have been socialized into roles, identities and into the conceptual machinery; they become just as disconnected from their real activities as do their "products," the disabled patients or clients. Their efforts are largely directed to reshaping the subjectivity of their patients or clients in order to improve their functioning *within* the disabled/sick role, reaffirming or reproducing exactly those aspects of the individual that society finds most repulsive and unattractive.

Rethinking Disability

Impairments are objective conditions resulting from pathologies and/or accidents. According to Albrecht and Levy (1981: 18), all societies "produce" impairments that are related to their particular levels of social organization and technology. The diseases currently prevalent in modern industrial societies are chronic in nature and produce considerable impairment and socially-defined disability before they finally kill. Chronic degenerative and stress-related diseases like coronary heart disease, carcinomas, stroke, atherosclerosis, and diabetes are closely associated with the industrialization and modernization process. While sophisticated medical intervention and life-sustaining technologies keep impaired people alive who might otherwise die, changes in the causes of death combined with rising life expectancies probably also account for an increased incidence of disability and chronic conditions (Haug and Lavin 1983: 32–33, 36–37).

Regardless of their incidence or prevalence in society, certain impairments are considered disabling only when they interfere with the individual's ability to perform expected social roles, and are formally classified as problematic (Albrecht and Levy 1981: 19). The definition of some physiological conditions as disabilities really refers to the attribution of meanings and the importance of impairment to specific people in society. Albrecht and Levy suggest that the attribution of meaning to impairments is learned, culture-specific and is moderated by the individual's place in society. Attribution of responsibility for the impairment also tends to influence the social definition of disability. The social assignment of responsibility is open to argument, however, because there is a physiological basis for alcoholism and for cancer. Yet, those suffering from problem drinking are frequently judged responsible for their condition, while those incapacitated by cancer may not be (Albrecht and Levy 1981: 20).

Disabilities are subject to moral evaluations and selective social perceptions. The effects of venereal diseases such as syphilis, gonorrhea and even herpes simplex are potentially more harmful than other communicable diseases, yet because of moral and sexual overtones little attention is directed to these problems. By contrast, the severe moral judgements and extreme social repercussions against those individuals with Acquired Immune Deficiency Syndrome and those who are carriers of the HIV virus show the relationship between selective social perceptions and social/cultural role expectations (Weston and Jeffery 1988). In fact, the AIDS/HIV phenomenon is a clear example, though by no means the only one, of how impairment, disablement and handicapping can occur virtually simultaneously.

Disabilities can be seen as socially constructed entities regardless of their physiological bases for other reasons. It is in the interest of medical professionals, hospitals, nursing homes and medical supply companies, for example, to identify treatable, chronic disabilities. Yet, the disabilities that are identified and treated may reflect professional and occupational exigencies rather than actual consumer need. Under the medical model, disabilities are identified specifically as medical problems that require medical treatment. Albrecht and Levy state that the difficulty is that the problem of imminent domain is not easily resolved: Many disabilities are the result of environmental, social and other created conditions that are amenable to social service intervention, or to amelioration of other kinds. Disabled people argue that medical care treatment and rehabilitation services cannot solve the problems of low income, social isolation and architectural barriers that the medical model actually reinforces.

Granted, medical diagnosis does provide a necessary mechanism for controlling the flow of patients or clients in and out of programs and services. The medicalization of disability is positive because people in need can get the quality medical care that might not necessarily be available under, say, a social service model. Even disabled individuals admit this:

> Most people are ill at one point or another of their life and have need of medical help. Disabled people perhaps have a particular need for medical help in as much as disablements generally originate with disease or accident. Some forms of disablement also involve recurring bouts of illness or predictable requirements for medical help at various points during life. In this context the medical [model] and its function of healing is very necessary and valuable to disabled people (Derksen 1980: 15).

Unfortunately, the negative consequences of medicalization include the assumption that medical professionals know best, even for social conditions (Derksen 1980: 16). There is also the tendency to medicalize behavior labelled as deviant, regardless of the origin of the disorder. Part of identifying or designating behavior as deviant consists of accepting the medical perspective of that behavior. According to Conrad and Schneider (1980) and others the medical perspective is used by the profession and ultimately by society to legitimate medical social control over diagnosis, intervention and cure. Social control is achieved through such medical and rehabilitation technologies as behavior-controlling drugs and techniques, surgical techniques, collaboration among health care professionals and regulators that establishes control over a wide range of social behavior, and an ideology that is used to define behaviors as sickness, illness or disability.

What has to be made clear is that disability is an entity, a category and a product of complex ongoing social and political relationships and forces. Similarly, handicap is a social creation, not an objective truth. There is conflict over bureaucratic supremacy between the medical and health care professions, social services and disabled people. The conflict involves ideological differences concerning the nature of the "problem" and the response. Professions and other economic interest groups are powerful forces in constructing disability as a social problem. The struggle for control is contingent on the rewards to be gained by building an industry around a particular problem; thus, the group that controls the construction of the problem most often controls the policy response (Albrecht and Levy 1981: 20–22). It is in this struggle over the definition of the disabled category and the formulation of policy that disabled people want to participate.

Definitions of disabling conditions are often expanded in order to include the involvement and interventions of an ever-increasing number of professionals, specialists, agencies, interest groups and other stake-holders (Stone 1984: Chapters 5 and 6). They compete with each other for power and resources, and it becomes in their best interest to maintain control and defend their interests by making the definition of disability nonnegotiable, and by maintaining or creating dependency. Caught in the middle are disabled people themselves. How the disability category is constructed is determined by who is doing the creating and defining. Disability can be defined as a health issue, a medical issue, a technical issue or as a social issue. That it can be defined in so many ways proves the point that disability is a relative term, and it is its "reality" that is negotiated among all interest groups, including the disabled.

The struggle for control over the definition and creation of the category has produced no winners; control has been wrested away from precisely those in whose "interest" the labelling and expansionistic abuses have been applied. Disabled people have now emerged as the primary stake-holders in the struggle to deconstruct disability, and indeed, to reject and redefine the very context and process that has alienated and manipulated them:

> What will occur if a disabled individual does not accept the arrangements that have been made for him? What will be the result if he demands that the permanent nature of his disability be accepted by those around him and by society; if he says that he is not sick and should not be treated as a sick person? Who can predict the shape of things to be if he will demand to be held responsi-

ble for all the things that adult people are expected to be responsible for in this society; and what will happen when he demands his right to participate in every aspect of society? (Derksen 1980: 2)

The irony is that in order to begin "breaking" from imposed categories and to reconstruct themselves as human beings, disabled people must identify their disabilities and be identified as disabled. In doing so they reaffirm the social roles and the essential validity of the social structure. What they are trying to do is to redefine the social meaning of disability, reject the old disabled role and the behavior expectations that go along with it, and challenge the hegemonic control of the definition process. Disability can never be denied. To get the definition process firmly within their grasp—in order to redefine their social, economic and political position in the larger community—the focus shifts from disability to ability, and from inaction to action.

II

Social Change in Theory and Practice

3

Consumerism and Independent Living
Focusing the Concerns of Disabled People

Disabled individuals who are vocal and active in the disabled community are asserting as their central vision or goal their "reconnection" to social life. This is a pervasive theme expressed time and again in their actions, speeches and position papers, particularly those of the Alberta Committee and COPOH. Integration into social life involves

> ... the ability to live independently and productively in the community and to live with the same freedom of choice as a non-handicapped person. So it's not that you are living on your own but that you control where you live and have the same range of choices as a non-handicapped person (Jill Weiss, COPOH 1987d: 15).

> ... an integrated approach showing us as part and parcel of society instead of different and, therefore, special and deserving of the human interest approach (Standing Committee on the Status of Disabled Persons 1988: 17).

My request for other Canadians is that they make the effort to relate to people with disabilities as they would to anyone else. We may look different on the outside, but we're exactly the same on the inside (Gary MacPherson, Canada, Secretary of State 1989).

A demand of disabled people is that they be understood simply as social beings. The central value of this position is that of validation, meaning that not cripples, not patients, nor clients, but people who happen to be disabled, exist in society as actual or potential producers or participants in their own lives (Rose and Black 1985: 36–37). The idea of validation is communicated through the processes whereby people are "reconnected" to their sociality, and "disconnected" from their objectified status as patients or clients. Existential differences are not denied but are relegated to secondary importance, and commonalities based on class or category position become the significant and essential aspects of daily life that generate such collective action as networking and the formation of self-help groups.

The disabled community's idea of engaging *themselves* as producers/participants in comprehending and acting on their own contextual environments differs quite radically from the medical/rehabilitation model's goal of working to merely improve a disabled individual's functioning—even though the latter claims to improve the quality of life and self-image of the individual (Crewe and Zola 1983). The difference between these two world-views can be understood as the difference between what it means to be a "producer" and a "consumer" of goods and services.

The consumer as producer must undertake to learn how his or her social world is constituted in order to determine in what ways it impinges on his or her life (Derksen 1980). This learning process implies a conscious strategy for action, not an acquiesence to the dictates of others. It also implies a process that is open-ended, constrained only by a temporary lack of motivation, understanding and skills that are necessary to act.

Merely consuming health and/or social services communicates an entirely different outcome than that which is the result of participating in that consumption as a producer. An interesting parallel exists between consuming services and consuming commodities: Both types of consumers are not directly in control of what they consume, both stand outside the framework or the determinants of the production process, both respond to what amounts to a received definition of what their needs are, and, finally, both are passive recipients of interactions which reproduce existing power relations in which they play only a supporting, never a major, role (Gartner and Riessman 1974: 171 ff). This kind of consumption often creates feelings of helplessness and pessimism (Navarro 1983).

Consuming services such as disabled people do is a process in which the disabled consumer is obliged to take on the problem definition of the provider. The process of consuming the service consumes the person. In so doing the possibility of transcending or transforming the given universe of meaning established by the provider is reduced. Even the capacity to develop a critical perspective of society is diminished.

In treatment and rehabilitation programs where people are reduced to disabled patients, where presentation of self or the "disabled identity" and the essence of the person are the same, both the person and the professionals with whom he or she is involved become one-dimensional (in Marcuse's (1964) sense). The world of the possible is reduced or collapsed to stasis and inactivity (Albrecht 1976). Social and personal life is often experienced by disabled people as domination and abuse—it is medicalized. When the person's needs are defined in terms of medical interests, those needs which can be satisfied are often merged with those which cannot, creating either a false universe of satisfaction or, alternatively, producing a "defective" (recalitrant) patient or client.

Consuming health care services free from a conceptual critique of the objective reality of the medical/rehabilitative model can lead to the consumption of a false reality made up of false facts. Consuming this reality (thereby reproducing it) consists of accepting the situation as it is—without grasping the deeper implications of the causes of that reality. Living that false reality reaffirms the disabled role, the role of the professional, as well as the set of institutions and the ideology that creates and sanctions both of them (Kallen 1989: 102–4). Figure 3.1 contrasts some of the features of the medical rehabilitation model with that one constructed and advocated by disabled consumers, that is, the independent living model.

The independent living/disabled consumer movement, in particu-

Figure 3.1 Comparison Between the Medical Rehabilitation and Independent Living Models

MEDICAL MODEL	INDEPENDENT LIVING MODEL
Patient/client role	Consumer role
Acute condition	Chronic condition
Restorative care	Maintenance care
Physical health care	Physical and social health care
Provider direction	Consumer direction
Physician plans treatment	Treatment planned in consultation
Aide recruited by agency	Attendant hired by consumer
Payment to service provider	Payment by consumer to provider

Adapted from Enns 1983: 4, DeJong 1983: 23, Dejong and Wenker 1983: 161–62. See also Haug and Lavin 1983.

lar the development of the independent living model, has as its goal the transformation of people that have been turned into particular types of objects (e.g., patients, clients), who are acted upon in certain ways, and the transformation of the conditions which reproduce their objectification. What the disabled community is individually and collectively involved in is the struggle to transform their social reality, as they perceive and experience it, from often oppressive and exploitative conditions to circumstances where dignity, justice and meaningful interaction can take place. This very much requires their direct involvement in, this, their own social and cultural reproduction.

The Emergence of an Alternative Perspective

Individuals who have become physically disabled, either by traumatic injury at work (Reasons et al. 1981, Dickinson and Stobbe 1988), illness from disease or from birth (for example, the polio epidemic and the thalidimide babies of the 1950s), and whether for the short-term or the long-term, find themselves in a bewildering, new and different world. They are no longer deemed responsible for family, behavior, needs, and indeed, for most of the things they might have been responsible for as "normal" adult persons in society. Gone with these is their freedom of choice as well as their right to expect equal social acceptance as responsible adults, with respect to the rights of political and economic involvement in the community and society, access to public buildings and programs, access to private services and facilities, to travel freely, to choose employment and associates, and to sexual expression. All are gone, or at least are greatly diminished (Derksen 1980).

The disabled individual discovers that he or she is now expected to play a specialized recipient role in relation to charitable givers; in place of the dignity of self-sufficiency, passive gratitude for what others choose to give is expected and, admittedly, often received. The permanent nature of the disability is supposed to be accepted, despite the fact that society and especially the helping professions reinforce the contradictory idea that he or she is "sick" and is expected to get better. The "problem" is remedied by "rehabilitation" and the advice and counsel of a wide variety of professionals is expected to be accepted (Safilios-Rothschild 1970: 68–78, Albrecht 1976: 3–38).

Despite the fact that many of these clients have had many active years of meaningful and gainful employment in the competitive market, they are now assumed to require employment preparation or retraining, and may be placed in a facility specifically for this purpose. If the humiliation of being supervised sorting screws and returnable bottles or similarly dull work is enough to cause them not to perform well enough, they may be judged unready for the job market or unemployable, and might well be assigned to sheltered workshop employment (Derksen 1980: 1, Krause 1976). If they and their families have become sufficiently demoralized by the new situation, residence in a nursing home or special rehabilitation housing project is usually considered as a first alternative and ready solution.

Similarly, if the disabled individuals are not wealthy, and if their self-concept has been sufficiently distorted by negative stereotypes of the disabled so that it is forgotten that their tax dollars have contributed to public transportation and that they have a right to it, they will probably accept, as a substitute, a special trip now and then in a bus operated by some charity-minded service club. In the case of a disabled young person, he or she may find themselves attending a special school, and will learn that their only peers are also disabled, that being disabled means being different, and of the real gap between disabled and able-bodied society.

Disabled persons will find that very often all arrangements are made by assigned social workers in conjunction with other professionals (for example, psychologists, rehabilitation practitioners, therapeutic recreologists, life skills specialists) from a rehabilitative service agency which offers or controls comprehensive diagnostic/evaluative, educational, training, employment, housing, recreational, transportation and social services for the disabled. In short, disabled individuals have no further need of making decisions; when they are not "warehoused" they are rehabilitated from the time they are disabled to when they go to their graves (Derksen 1980: 1–3, Sussman 1976: 223–33, Brown 1977: 159–94).

Many individuals become disabled in their twenties and thirties, often as a result of industrial and recreational accidents. They are aware of what they have lost, and unlike an older generation of disabled persons they are not content to accept the inevitability of a life of dependence. The independent living/disabled consumer movement represents or constitutes a multitude of such individuals who refuse to accept the situation in which they find themselves. They have come to recognize the extent to which the situation has really been defined by others.

The movement's most basic and central objectives from the viewpoint of the physically disabled consumer are *independence* and *integration* with the community. Independence means as nearly as possible the same degree of control and self-determination in the day-to-day living processes as are generally available to nondisabled people. Integration means as nearly as possible the co-mingling in the daily living processes with the rest of the community and society, including the fullest possible use of the comprehensive range of services and facilities that are available and used by nondisabled persons. These goals comprise what is commonly referred to as independent living, also called the independent living paradigm and/or the IL movement.

From the perspective of disabled consumers, rehabilitation is also now redefined to mean "the careful and cogent application of medical and other interventions and/or treatments to remedy only the near-immediate traumatic effects of disablement upon a person" and his or her family (Derksen 1980: 2). While the consumer movement's independent living objectives dictate a mandate for the movement that includes a new view of rehabilitation, it cannot ignore the "environment." This environment includes legislation, public policy, program design, communications media, physical architecture and community structures—in short, all the opportunity structures that prevent or allow disabled persons from participating in the life of society as full members. The distinction between rehabilitation and the other larger environmental dimensions of community life is a critical one for the movement. Only by working to restrict the concept of rehabilitation to a treatment mode can disabled people assert themselves in society as healthy and "normal."

A cornerstone of treatment and rehabilitation efforts as traditionally defined is the medical model of deviance (Gove 1976, Kallen 1989: 27). To get away from that model, rehabilitation has to be redefined as *limited* treatment or medical intervention to achieve a minimum level of basic health (defined as well-being and the capacity to function to potential in any given environment). Beyond that limit, the disabled individual assumes independence and insists on a partnership with medical and rehabilitation professionals in decision-making. The design, funding and delivery of services and programs for disabled people has been carried out largely under the medical model, with the traditional view of medical rehabilitation that has been rejected by disabled consumers (Krause 1976, Brown 1977: 291 ff). Consider the following resolution regarding control of a consumer's own rehabilitation program and examination of the process:

> WHEREAS the disabled consumer is seldom involved in the development of his/her rehabilitation plan; and
> WHEREAS the disabled consumer should be directly involved in the development and review of his or her rehabilitation plan;
> BE IT RESOLVED that COPOH strongly advocates. . . . that any service agency supplying rehabilitation services. . . . be required to develop an individually written rehabilitation plan in consultation with the consumer. . . . (COPOH 1985c: 51).

In addition, traditional approaches to rehabilitation policies, programs and services have been significantly influenced by several "ethics," or world views, which have been obstacles to the achievement of independent living. It is out of the volunteer/charity, medical and professional ethics that the disabled consumer ethic and the goal of independent living has emerged (Derksen 1980: 4–10).

The volunteer/charity ethic has had the greatest impact on the funding and creation of various programs and services, and on the perpetuation of negative stereotypes of disabled people. Charity drives have used disabled children, usually with highly visible neural or muscular-skeletal and motor impairments, to solicit funds from the public. The Jerry Lewis telethons, March of Dimes, Easter and Christmas Seals campaigns, and the Timmy events (originating from the Tiny Tim character of Dickens' *A Christmas Carol*) are notable examples. Until recently and in some cases still, these funds were used to support programs and services for disabled children, at the exclusion of adults.

Even though some of the funding does find its way into programs designed for all ages of disabled people, the public exposure of a fairly narrow range of individuals is considered exploitative, and does little to ameliorate the untrue stereotype of the disabled person as pitied, childlike, asexual, passive, dependent and incapable of responsible participation in society. The Canadian media has been criticized for communicating negative and distorted images of disabled people (Standing Committee on the Status of Disabled Persons, First Report, 1988).

The volunteer/charity ethic magnifies and emphasizes the differences between the able-bodied givers and disabled recipients. There seems to be a direct relationship between the perceived degree of need and poverty of opportunities and resources in the recipient, and the felt sense of magnanimity, self-sacrifice, wealth, health and power of the able-bodied donor and provider. This relationship enhances the "abnormality" of the disabled as perceived by the public mind, and isolates and distances the disabled population even more. The relationship is probably of greater benefit to the able-bodied; guilty feelings are soothed, social status is achieved by giving, and pleasures are derived from community group membership and participation. The publicity generated by charity drives also serves to emphasize, very subtly, the "unthinkable tragedy" of disability and actually encourages collective avoidance and fear reactions. From this perspective of what motivates charity work, charity, apart from the activity of raising money, does not contribute to the goal of independent living and community integration for disabled people.

The medical ethic maintains and even reinforces attitudinal barriers that disabled people encounter in the community. Despite some of the higher ideals claimed in the Hippocratic Oath, the medical ethic has resulted in the perception and subsequent treatment of persons as inert and passive bodies to be worked upon, to be repaired and "fixed." This notion of individuals as passive fields for chemical, surgical and other interventions is, of necessity, some distance from the idea of individuals as whole persons with the right of active participation in decision-making.

As occupants of the sick role, the disabled are expected to regain health and become able-bodied again; the medical ethic persists in focusing solely on the physical body, measuring "ability" against admittedly arbitrary cultural standards of physical integrity, strength, virility, and beauty (Safilios-Rothschild 1970: 126–30, Albrecht 1976: 11–13). When the disabled patient does not respond, or cannot, medical science does not give up. Medical rehabilitation in the traditional sense becomes a permanent feature and burden in his or her life (DeJong 1983: 15–17). In the words of Pat Israel (COPOH 1987d: 21),

> I've been trying for almost a year to find an alternative-health doctor who is wheelchair accessible and also has an accessible attitude towards disabled persons. I just went to one and the first words out of his mouth were, I can cure you of your disability! I said, doctor, I'm not looking to be cured, I'm looking to be a healthy disabled person!

Large growth industries, such as those providing health care, pharmaceuticals, prosthetic devices and equipment, therapies and so forth, have been built up around the problems of the disabled and geared towards maintaining dependence. What is good for an industry may not be good for the individual. Disabled consumers agree that as with rehabilitation, medical, chemical and surgical interventions may be indispensable means to achieve certain ends, but they should not be ends in themselves. Writes Bill Cameron,

> Our great medical system, which is saving lives and therefore, actually increasing the number of disabled people in our population through great medical techniques, is a sickness and injury treatment

phenomenon (Parliamentary Forum on the Status of Disabled Persons 1988: 19).

The medical rehabilitation ethic is based on the professional ethic. The latter is founded on the assumption that professional and technical expertise be accepted without question, and that this knowledge is the property and under the exclusive control of a closed self-governing group of specialists and practitioners. This exclusivity accentuates the distance and difference between the active decision-makers and the passive accepting client, and reinforces the monopoly of knowledge in the field (Coe 1976: 250–51). This cannot help but deepen and reinforce some of the negative stereotypes and the dependency of disabled people. The area of rehabilitation medicine and services has experienced the proliferation of secondary medical professions such as occupational therapy, physiotherapy, rehabilitation psychology and therapeutic recreology (Albrecht and Levy 1981).

Other professionals involved in service provision include the rehabilitation service administrator, the rehabilitation social worker, the professional social service program director—even the professional fund raiser. These professionals and their programs have come to control the widest variety of programs, services and opportunities required by disabled people (Derksen 1980: 6–9, Illich 1976, 1977). These include diagnostic, pre-school, housing, employment preparation, special recreation and special transportation programs, as well as family counselling, technical aids supply and other services. Unfortunately, this specialization has led to the segregation of services to the disabled, and has contributed to the segregation of disabled people.

From the perspective of the disabled consumer, some of these professionals together with their programs and services simply would not function or possibly even exist under a consumer version of rehabilitation (Derksen 1980: 7, Haug and Lavin 1983). While useful in certain circumstances, this over-specialization has become too restrictive. A result of this proliferation of professions has also been the proliferation of separate special programming, some of which work at cross-purposes and which, in any case, continually demand clients in order to justify their existence (Stone 1984: 140 ff). Since the disabled population is fairly "finite," the result is often that the overall rehabilitation process, including treatment, is lengthened far beyond what is necessary (Albrecht and Levy 1981). In addition, "in order to receive private and governmental support, [service and/or rehabilitation] agencies may resort to recycling the same clients over and over again as a way to keep their success statistics high" (Albrecht and Levy 1981: 25).

Despite their value, specialized programs and services as well as the people that design and administer them seem to completely ignore the possibility of expanding or improving *existing* public programs and community services in order to accommodate disabled people in their own communities. Whether this is a result of the mindset of the medical model, or because of the idea that program and service expansion does not pay, or both, there is little here that contributes to the independence and integration of impaired individuals. Professional help is supposed to enable the individual to lead a "normal" social life, but this is unrealizable without including the individual himself or herself in further developing existing community structures. It seems an irony that the success of the medical/rehabilitation model has in effect led to its "failure"; it is precisely this failure that has provided the impetus for the independent living movement.

These ethics or even the medical/rehabilitation model should not be totally abandoned. From the disabled consumer point of view, these features have over time become somewhat constraining, dehumanizing and have generated unintended consequences. There is a fundamental and basic flaw in treating any person as an object of charity. Good will and generosity of self are clearly virtues, and in its appropriate role the charity ethic serves to heighten public awareness of the unique needs and potential contributions of the disabled. A heightened awareness should foster an equal partnership that enhances and not diminishes the image of disabled people, while at the same time produces the needed resources to solve what are undoubtedly common societal problems. Increasing awareness, as well as raising money, was largely the motivation behind the hugely successful Terry Fox, Steve Fonyo and Rick Hansen marathons.

Spokespersons of the disabled consumer movement correctly point out that able-bodiedness, like youth, is at best a temporary condition and that the removal of attitudinal and structural barriers to independent living and integration is, in the long term, in everyone's interests:

> In defiance of [the] subtle denial of disabled people's subjective, persistently real, experience of human limitations and mortality, the disabled consumer movement has generated the term "T.A.B." to

refer to able-bodied people. This is pronounced "TAB" and is an acronym for "temporarily able-bodied" (Derksen 1980: 6).

Most individuals are ill at one point or another in their lives and have need of medical help. Disabled people have a particular need for medical help insofar as impairments generally originate with disease or trauma and sometimes involve recurring bouts of illness. The medical ethic/model and its focus on healing is unquestionably indispensable and legitimate. Where the model seems to have broken down is in its nurturing of the sick role and in taking the idea of physical healing too far. In some cases complete physical healing is simply impossible, and disabled people insist that the medical profession should see this not as defeat or as a failure of the effectiveness of its methods, but as an indication that there is a time when the focus should be shifted elsewhere (Haug and Lavin 1983, Conrad 1992: 224–26).

Similarly, professionals are urged by disabled people to understand the limitations of the expert knowledge they claim to possess and control. Professional practitioners must recognize their need to be accountable to the community which provides them with the resources and the opportunities to practice in the first place. The sharing of expertise in order that disabled individuals may make informed and intelligent decisions does not imply interference by them, or a diminished role for scientific knowledge (Derksen 1980: 16, Haug and Lavin 1983, Conrad 1992: 226). This has led the Coalition of Provincial Organizations of the Handicapped to make the following statement:

> WHEREAS preliminary research indicates many disabled individuals report they encounter a great variety of inconsistent rehabilitation counselling advice and services; and,
> WHEREAS these represent very disruptive and intermittent rehabilitation counselling advice and services,
> BE IT RESOLVED that . . . COPOH . . . examine the need for a comprehensive, consistent rehabilitation process with a minimum of counselling staff on any one individual "case" (COPOH 1985c: 52–53).

Disabled consumers envision a somewhat different distribution of specialized knowledge, and a much closer involvement in the "production" and "consumption" of that knowledge. They are correct in asserting that all of society consumes information, services and products, not just a segment of it. The disabled are also part of a much larger social movement that insists that consumption is not the final stage of the production process or what defines the product, but that it is really its first stage. The goal of independent living, born of a consumer consciousness, is understood as a necessary development from the charity, medical and professional ethics.

The Rise of the Disabled Consumer Ethic

The independent living/disabled consumer movement is better understood in the context of production in advanced capitalist society. In contrast to the industrial phase of industrial-capitalist production, a production characteristic of modern society is that control reaches beyond the productive structure into the areas of consumption, services, exchange and social relations. The mechanisms of accumulation are no longer fed mainly by the use of labor power, but are served instead by the manipulation of organizational systems, information and by intervention in interpersonal relations.

Production no longer consists solely of the transformation of the natural environment into a technical environment, but has become the production of social systems, social relations, cultural orientations and lifestyles and of the biological and personal identities of individuals. Since the personal and social identities of individuals are themselves products of social action, it is the control and orientation of that action that then becomes the "object" of contention in post-industrial society.

What disabled consumers have recognized is the freeing of the concept of production from what it meant in an "older" industrial society, and its reconceptualization in terms of meaning, symbol formation and social relations. Production might be viewed as the formation or transformation of objects, within the framework of certain social relations, by the application of certain means to a primary material. Production is not apart from nature, but is a natural process, technical as well as social. The interlinking analytical components of production, as traditionally defined, are actions, raw materials, means of production and social relations. However, the formation or transformation of objects already takes place within social relations; production is best conceived as the reproduction of social relations in the satisfaction of needs. The relation of the producer to the product is simultaneously the affirmation of an *identity*, that is, there must be a recognition of the product as the result of the work of a producer.

This recognition constitutes a social relationship because it implies a reciprocity of the recognition. Social identity is the attribution of the condition of "belonging to"; social identity emerges out of a situation in which one recognizes and is recognized in turn. Production is the social capacity to recognize one's own work and that of others, and to have one's own recognized in turn. The social capacity also includes the will to appropriate and orient one's own work or production, since to produce means to determine the orientation of production and of the product. Production, recognition, appropriation and orientation are the interlinked analytical components of production conceived in terms of social relationships (Sahlins 1976, Touraine 1977a, 1992: 129–40). What better way, then, to reappropriate and reorient social relationships and identities than by making the disabled consumer a major or central factor in the production process itself?

The consumer movement has become increasingly concerned with the consequences that flow from the way the organization of production changes as the type of production changes. The transition from an economy based on industrial production to one based on high-tech production, information processing and services over the past three or four decades has served to further marginalize those traditionally excluded from the work/production process. Historically, women, the young, the aged, the disabled and others were much less frequently employed in the industrial sector and were less integrated into the work system. Advanced capitalist/post-industrial society is based on a highly advanced productivity in the industrial sector that allows for even larger numbers and kinds of people to remain outside the work force. Many people are threatened to become marginal as far as purely technical production is concerned, but they are not marginal as consumers (Fuchs 1968, Gartner and Riessman 1974). Alternatively, changing forms of work in an information-based economy make it possible for those previously marginalized to now participate more fully. Work is no longer necessarily labor-intensive, that is, involving brute strength or other physical requirements.

It is not coincidental that disabled individuals allied themselves with women, youth, the aged and other alienated minorities during the equal rights movements of the 1960s and 1970s, which included consumer radicalism (Gartner and Riessman 1974). What provided part of the context for the movements of the 1960s and 1970s was the reaction to some of the contradictions generated by increased productivity and the lack of opportunities to participate in that production or the means to consume the products. The independent living/consumer movement of disabled people can be understood as a reaction to yet another contradiction of modern society: The marginalized and dependent condition that disabled people found themselves in and the expectations of the medical model and sick role seemed wholly at odds with the focus on consumer choice in the marketplace, the willingness to take risks and to experiment, and the emphasis on individual initiative in society.

Movements such as the equal rights, youth, gay, black power, and feminist movements were concerned with issues as identity, personal liberation, individual and collective rights, self-actualization and participation (A. Scott 1990). The concerns with rights, entitlements and identity provided the meaningful context for what has since become a major concern: A better quality of life, growth and participation in a consumer/service-oriented society. It is the consumer, not only the worker, who has become the weak link in the post-industrial/advanced capitalist economic structure. Exploitation is also being experienced at the point of consumption, rather than just production.

As taxpayers, clients, patients, customers, welfare recipients, community board members, workers and consumers have turned a rather critical eye on public services, community and government programs (housing, education, health care, welfare), and public institutions (agencies, schools, hospitals, clinics, city councils). Often criticized as ineffective, dehumanizing, insensitive to human needs, unaccountable, and irrelevant or redundant, disabled consumers have been framing their demands to participate in a "new" kind of production. This means making decisions that involve services or programs, and that enables their equal access to all required services and programs in a manner such that there would be no second-class recipients.

The focus of criticisms and political action has been on providing services and administering programs that are less professional, less hierarchical and centralized, less expensive, and that now involve advocacy and self-help. Consumption is now the same as production, that is, the production of services and programs, and so of human and social relations, as consumers exchange their patient or client roles for the consumer role. This increasing consumer/service consciousness, not surprisingly, stemmed from groups largely in consumer roles, e.g., patients, social service clients and service recipients. Out of this emerged a contemporary 1980s-style consumer politics with new tactics, forms, issues and styles—a politics that has insisted on engaging the consumer as a direct factor in service, program and technical production.

Key to a disabled consumer politics has been the identification of the consumer as central in his or her own production, and his or her membership in the larger community. Glen Cave notes,

> I would also like to add that independent living is a consumer issue. Disabled people living in the community have to be good consumers, have to demand good quality products, particularly in the area of technical aids and architectural access. Without those two we lose our mobility and without our mobility we lose our ability to function in the community (COPOH 1987d: 84).

Not surprisingly, a disabled consumer politics is also the result of the emergence of the professional/consumer dialectic (Gartner and Riessman 1974: 154–62). Daniel Bell (1973) suggested that the traditional conflict between worker and capitalist would be replaced by one between the professional and the consumer in post-industrial society. This dialectic has emerged from a set of contradictions that is a consequence of a changing organization and type of production in advanced capitalism. One contradiction is between the purpose of services in providing benefits for people and improving their welfare, health, and education, and the context of a highly individualistic and competitive political/economic framework in which service provision creates and justifies a class of experts, socializes people to the status quo, and maintains class, race, gender and physical/mental differences between people.

A second contradiction is that increasing demands for private, local, community and consumer-based services and programs brings them into conflict with the bureaucratization of these activities at institutional, governmental and other levels. In addition, various bureaucratic dimensions, especially rational-formalism, Taylorism and impersonality are anathema to activities that have humanistic ends and require relational interpersonal processes. The problems of how to plan and organize programs and deliver services for the disabled while at the same time maintaining their effectiveness (that is, their humaneness) and increasing their efficiency persist, and are magnified by the fact that bureaucratization and professionalization often involves the manipulation of services and programs for purposes that may not seem as if they have anything to do with serving people.

Many people in need of services, including the disabled, simply do not get them because of ambiguously-defined eligibility criteria. Those who do receive services do not necessarily benefit by them (e.g., the revolving-door syndrome); many existing services are poorly organized and designed (e.g., misused, wasteful, or worse, inapplicable if in the case of multiple impairments); and, medical and paramedical practice is often inadequate (e.g., sexist, racist, class-based, elitist and unshared). According to Albrecht and Levy (1981: 25–26),

> Social service agencies have an interest in both expanding their services to include more clients and "creaming" the pool of available clients to select those who are easy to process and will be most likely to demonstrate evidence of program success.... Other rehabilitation agencies, like state vocational rehabilitation programs and alcohol rehabilitation programs, also do not want to serve the multiple and seriously disabled because they are difficult cases unlikely to show rapid progress.... For these reasons, many rehabilitation agencies reject clients most in need and foster dependency in those clients they accept.

Impetus for a disabled consumer solution and key to understanding the independent living movement comes from disillusionment with the system. The impetus is derived also from the performance gap and, interestingly enough, an information gap.

Despite the information explosion, and the fact that society and the economy are increasingly information-driven, disabled consumers find themselves, paradoxically, information poor and knowledge poor. Professionals and professional service providers and caregivers often selectively, and perhaps unwittingly, withhold information, assuming disabled consumers to be uneducated and to have no need for expert knowledge. In addition, the disabled may not know precisely what they need to know and where to find or access it. They are sometimes unable to gather information themselves. A very real need exists to develop a means of obtaining information.

Typical of a dialectic relationship, the professional-consumer one is characterized by both unity and the struggle of opposites. There is unity in the sense that both the professional and the consumer are factors in the production of services and programs, and that they both want the quality and coverage to be more effective, efficient and comprehensive. This unity breaks down, however, when questions of control and direction of planning and delivery of programs and services arise. Within the limits and constraints set by some of the societal/systemic contradictions, as well as by the professional/consumer dialectic, the disabled consumer solution has been to create mediating, alternate or interfacing organizations in the quest for an independent living lifestyle. These include consumer-based community boards, consumer-run self-help groups, the use of consultants, advocates and service brokers, and networking.

These empowering solutions, that might be called the revolt of the client, are direct challenges to the social and cultural elitism of the professions and of professional practice and knowledge. The disabled consumer resolution of the dialectic is twofold: Firstly, to place the disabled individual at the center of his or her own production, thereby (re)appropriating and (re)orienting production, and secondly, to bring about the reprofessionalization of the experts, by which means a reciprocal recognition of social and individual identities can be established.

The Means and Outcome of Empowerment: Towards Independent Living

Social movements, such as the independent living/disabled consumer movement, eventually will become further institutionalized. The movement as a particular mode of discourse will find its expression reflected in public policy, professional practice and research, or both. While neither policy nor practice would ever totally embrace all the tenets of a movement's philosophy, an impact on the social order would probably be discernable.

The independent living/disabled consumer movement is more than a social movement or a grassroots effort seeking new rights and entitlements for disabled people; it is also having an impact on disability professionals and on the community (Kallen 1989: 146–49). Not only is it reshaping how the nature and problem of disability has been defined in the past, and so is greatly influencing the thinking of experts and researchers, but it is also shifting the focus of the problem from the individual to the environment. In doing so it is providing new solutions to the disability problem and is redefining the social roles of disabled people. On a practical level, the movement has spawned new program/service planning and delivery models that have come to be protected by legislation and disability policies. The movement—with its discourse of independent living—has come to constitute a new paradigm (Derksen 1980, 1983, Simpson 1980, Enns 1983, COPOH 1985a, 1987d, Crewe and Zola 1983).

The paradigm that has dominated disability policy over the past several decades has been the rehabilitation paradigm, which includes medical and vocational rehabilitation. Within this paradigm, the problems of disabled individuals are generally defined in terms of measured performance in what is called activities of daily living, or in terms of preparation for gainful employment (DeJong 1983, Safilios-Rothschild 1970). The focus is almost exclusively on age, gender, psychological makeup of the individual, his or her impairment, and what bearing these intervening variables have on recovery. From this perspective, the problems of disability are those of the individual; it is the individual that needs to be changed. To overcome the problem of disability, the individual is expected to follow the advice of a physician and a variety of therapists and counsellors, while assuming the role of patient or client (Safilios-Rothschild 1970: 166–76).

The means and ends of the rehabilitation process, which are under the control of professionals, include maximum physical and mental functioning. The success of the programs and services that are part of the process are determined by whether the patient or client complied with the prescribed therapeutic regime. The issue in the rehabilitation process is not whether rehabilitation works, but what kind of therapy or intervention technique works best for an individual or group of clients (DeJong 1983). Science comes first, the individual last.

Over the last several decades, anomalies have appeared that could not be adequately explained or accounted for by the rehabilitation paradigm. Through the examples of a small number of determined physically disabled persons, it was demonstrated that participation in the medically-defined rehabilitation process is not necessary in order to live independently. As early as 1962 in the United States, the University of Illinois at Champaign-Urbana initiated a community living project for disabled students. In 1972 the Berkeley Centre for Independent Living was incorporated, while the Boston Centre for Independent Living was established two years later (Zukas 1979, Coxon 1981, DeJong 1983, Frieden 1983, COPOH 1985a). These centres were managed primarily by the disabled, and provided such services as peer counselling, skills training, transporation, health maintenance and wheelchair repair. Each centre offered its own unique blend of consumer services and advocacy, which eventually included monitoring U.S. federal legislation.*

The independent living (IL) paradigm has emerged as a very definite alternative response by disaffected disabled people worldwide to meet the rapidly growing desire to achieve independence from medical intervention, institutionalization, and external social control mechanisms (Tate and Lee 1983). While some rehabilitation professionals may have introduced IL concepts into their own practice (Symington 1983), the rehabilitation paradigm has not been totally abandoned. Considering the organization of medical rehabilitation and the growth and profitability of health-related industries (chemical, prosthetic) that have, over decades, grown around this model, some

---

* It is interesting to note that in 1973 the U.S. Congress passed a new Rehabilitation Act which has been referred to as the "Civil Rights Act of the Handicapped" (Pub. Law No. 93–112, 87 Stat. 355); an amendment passed into law in 1978 was significant in defining and extending services and funding specifically for independent living. A more comprehensive U.S. piece of legislation covering employment and service delivery in both the private and public sectors is the Americans with Disabilities Act, which became law in July 1990. Canadian legislation will be reviewed in Chapter 7.

opposing interests possibly will remain (Albrecht and Levy 1981).

Nevertheless, the transition is encouraged by redefinitions of rehabilitation initiated by the disabled. Canadian disabled consumer organizations have actively pushed, internationally as well as in Canada, for a much more limited definition—as opposed to the "cradle-to-grave" concept. Thus,

> [R]ehabilitation is a process aimed at enabling a person to reach an optimum physical, mental and/or social functioning level in order to provide that person with the tools to direct his/her own life. Independent living and community services are not, and should not, be part of that process (Disabled Peoples' International, 1980 Charter).

> Rehabilitation means a goal-oriented and time limited process aimed at enabling an impaired person to reach an optimum... functional level, thus providing her or him with the tools to change her or his own life. It can involve measures intended to compensate for a loss of function or a functional limitation (for example by technical aids), and other measures intended to facilitate social adjustment or readjustment (United Nations 1983: 3).

This rethinking of the concept and its subsequent redefinition led the Coalition of Provincial Organizations of the Handicapped to formulate the following statement:

> WHEREAS the involvement by the consumer is a vital part in any system which is responsive to the real needs of the people it serves, THEREFORE BE IT RESOLVED that COPOH endorses the independent living model and direct its efforts to the implementation of the Independent Living Philosophy in all appropriate programs and services related to the disabled in Canada,
> AND FURTHER BE IT RESOLVED that COPOH introduce and advocate the independent living model at the 1980 World Congress as an alternative to traditional open-ended rehabilitation where it has been extended beyond the treatment mode (cited in Enns 1983: 9).

From the point of view of some disabled consumers, the transition to independence and independent living is also a frightening one that requires considerable courage not to resist change. Like "coming out" (Kallen 1989: 40, Chapter 5), independent living is easier said than done. It is easy to accept the dependency prescribed under the sick role as normative, frustrating though it may be, because it removes the obligation to take charge of one's own life and relieves individuals of many of their familial, occupational and civic responsibilities. Moreover, dependency and passivity do not carry with them the possibility and risk of failure; so great in fact is the fear of failure that the phrase "dignity of risk" has become part of independent living vocabulary (Zola 1983b: 352–53). DeJong (1983: 20) noted that,

> The dignity of risk is the heart of the IL movement. Without the possibility of failure, the disabled person lacks true independence and the ultimate mark of humanity, the right to choose for good or evil.

Or in the words of Elizabeth Semkiw,

> Two things are going to have to happen. Firstly, they're going to have to listen, to really listen to what disabled people have to say. Secondly, they have to recognize that when you control your life and make your decisions, you also incorporate a risk and that is part of life. No matter how disabled a person is, they choose to take a certain risk because it gives them certain freedoms. It is their choice and it is not anybody else's right to interfere with that choice. Very often a risk is taken again, for freedom, trading one thing off for the other. That has to be recognized by the community. That is a disabled person's right (COPOH 1987d: 58).

The paradigm shift that each disabled person must undergo or experience for himself or herself involves a learning process undergone in the company of others. In order to learn, individuals have to both disconfirm some proposition in their "practice theory" of everyday life and to experiment; in order to experiment they have to be able to tolerate failure. One of the features of learning is the ability to recognize explicitly that a commitment to experiment does require failing. There are "zones" of failing and "zones" of inability to know, and there are times when failure is not attributable to incompetence but simply to the nature of the environment confronting that individual. For individuals to deal with or tolerate failure, and to learn effectively without destroying their innovativeness, they need to attribute failure to something other than themselves.

According to the independent living perspective, the problem of disability does not lie with the person but in the solution offered by the dependency-inducing consequences of rehabilitation in general and the medical model in particular. The locus of the problem is not the individual but rather the environment that includes not only the rehabilitation process, but the physical environment and the social control mechanisms in society. From this alternative perspective, environmental barriers and constraints are as critical, if not more critical, than the personal characteristics of individuals as "intervening variables" in determining disability outcomes. Key intervening environmental variables would include the social stigma of disability, the hospital/institutional milieu, availability of medical and equipment services, access to educational and vocational facilities, architectural barriers and access to transportation systems, unavailability or loss of financial and social benefits, and lack of legislation and policy (DeJong 1983, Varela 1983).

The independent living paradigm differs significantly from its rehabilitation counterpart in defining outcomes. While self-care, mobility and employment are stressed in the rehabilitation model, independent living stresses a much larger constellation of outcomes, including the importance of living arrangements, intimate relationships, consumer knowledge and assertiveness, and outdoor and out-of-home activities. The IL paradigm represents the emergence of a new value system and an entirely new lifestyle. Consideration of environmental barriers and constraints is key to understanding the thrust and impact of the independent living paradigm in the context of the disabled consumer movement.

Environmental variables can be created, modified, transformed or even abolished—given changed attitudes and political will. The strategies of advocacy, peer interaction, self-help, consumer control and barrier removal are the means as well as the outcome of an independent living lifestyle. From this perspective, full control over one's life is deemed more important than control over one's body. Doing and enjoying some things, to be realistic, may have to be given up by a disabled person, but what is important is whether he or she can determine when and how these things are to be done if helped by others (Zola 1983a).

The traditional rehabilitation methods that belabor the unalterable characteristics of individuals actually also have little policy relevance. Independent living focuses upon the larger institutional and environmental context. Here, policy issues loom large. There is the growing public debate about the extent to which society should shoulder the responsibility of removing environmental constraints, such as inaccessible public transportation, inaccessible or unavailable housing, architectural barriers, unmet personal care needs and skills training. Central to this debate is the difficult issue of income and funding—is it to be public money that pays for these improvements or for personal care services? Ready answers are not available, but the independent living perspective has identified issues that must now be resolved within a political/public policy framework involving the greater community.

By having broadened the problem of disability to include a wider variety of environmental variables and contexts, the idea of independent living has opened up the field of disability policy to other disciplines, as well as the participation of a much wider circle of sympathetic professionals. An emphasis on legal and political rights has encouraged the involvement of legal professionals, the issue of architectural barriers has been taken up by architects, engineers and city planners, and the funding issue has been of concern to economists and public sector finance people. Disabled individuals have sought and achieved professional training to help with what could be termed the "rehabilitation" of society. The problems associated with disability are no longer perceived as strictly those of the disabled. They never really were.

What better way is there to describe community-building than that which characterizes the shift from the rehabilitation to the independent living paradigm, the reciprocal recognition of identity between those who are disabled and those who are not that accompanies that shift, and the achievement of a barrier-free environment?

Independent Living

Independent living is as abstract a concept as the idea of human rights. According to Elizabeth Semkiw, "independent living really is an idea, a concept, a thought process. You apply this thought process to your lifestyle" (COPOH 1987d: 57). This concept is an outgrowth of consumer philosophy that provides a framework for viewing the world, and is a model for the way people want to live. As a framework and model it is not static, but properly should be seen as part of the dynamic empowerment process whereby disabled people learn to take control and to assume responsibility for the management of resources that are required to lead the lifestyle they desire within the constraints faced by everyone else in the community.

Some of the underlying concepts of the model are dignity of risk, taking responsibility, freedom of choice, consumer control and self-determination—to be individually and collectively realized through concerted political action:

> The handicapped consumer movement is the grassroots democratic struggle of self-expression. The goal is to enable every handicapped person to achieve his/her maximum personal independence and full community integration. Modern society has demonstrated time and time again that full social/economic equality and acceptance for any disadvantaged target population *can ultimately only be achieved by the target population itself.* This requires philosophical unity of purpose, public visibility, direct representation, and dynamic political action, preferably of the constructive democratic brand (Simpson 1980: 3). [emphasis added]

The independent living concept does not advocate a particular lifestyle. There is no preset lifestyle that is considered more or less independent than others: "[T]he struggle for independent living and personal determination is something each disabled person must approach in their own way" (Michael Huck, COPOH 1987d: 20). Moreover, the concept of independent living frames the idea of independence in the socio-political sense of the term, rather than in physical/biological terms (COPOH 1987d: 30). Independence is not measured by the number or quality of tasks individuals can perform without assistance, but rather the quality of life they can achieve even with assistance. According to Derksen (1983: 7),

> Many people have confused the IL concept to be a new idea for housing disabled people or delivering residential facilities for them. Many others have confused the IL concept with the provision of personal attendant care services. I believe that though such ideas about housing and care services may be important in working toward full participation for disabled people, they are really not the centre of the IL concept. Rather, the IL concept at its heart has to do with *self-determination and liberation for the individual within his society through collective self-determination and self-help*. . . . [emphasis added]

The dynamics of the independent living concept have not been widely understood and as a result have been misinterpreted. Among disabled people the term actually refers to specific conceptual developments:

> When disabled consumers employ the term independent living they imply much more than what either of these words mean separately in everyday usage. The independent living concept provides consumers with an analytical framework for identifying and solving problems. From this paradigm, consumers frame questions of lifestyle and devise new solutions to lifestyle problems (COPOH 1987d: 26–27).

The notion of self-determination is deeply embedded in the lexicon of the independent living/disabled consumer movement. There is a link between the idea of self-determination and the doctrine of consumer sovereignty in economic theory (Penz 1986), as well as the notion of self-actualization in humanistic psychology (Rogers 1951, 1977). Consumer sovereignty is a central normative principle underlying discussions of optimization and evaluation regarding the design and performance of market economies, and is a core value assumption of welfarian economics (Penz 1986: 1–2, 7–10).

The doctrine asserts "that what is to be produced, how it is to be produced, and how it is to be distributed are to be determined by consumer preferences as revealed through consumer choices in free markets" (Penz 1986: 10, 12–15). The free market is one where there is no single, collective, control over what is produced or over how the output is distributed. Under this ideal model, consumer preference and choice are determined by socially-derived individual wants and interests.

Welfarist interest theory, from which the idea of consumer sovereignty flows, refers to what people desire for themselves, which includes enjoyable mental and physical states. That is, "welfarist interests consist of self-regarding want satisfaction, happiness (or pleasure, enjoyment, or contentment), or whatever is instrumental to one or both of these ends" (Penz 1986: 143). Penz, as do other philosophers of economics, regards the term "interest" as it is used in political theory to be synonymous with "welfare" as it is used in economics. From the consumer point of view, interests for one's own happiness are the determinant of production and distribution, just as in liberal-democratic political philosophy the objective of the political order is the fulfilment of the interests of individuals (Flathman 1966, Benditt 1975).

Disabled persons say that, as consumers, they are the best judges of their own interests, both individually and collectively, and so should have the larger voice in determining what products/services should be provided in the disability services market as well as how they should be distributed. The notion of self-determination is a powerful one, especially when it is linked to independence and the independent living model. The notion is an example of what Penz (1986: 144) calls "essentialist conceptions of human interests." The goal or ideal of self-determination is not only appropriate as an instrumental means by which certain interests can be realized, but is specifically appropriate as an end in itself.

The link between self-determination and "life chances" (as interests) is an obvious one. From a political/human rights perspective,

> Freedom to decide and to determine one's own destiny is [a] fundamental human-rights principle. Indeed, the right to self-determination of all individuals—regardless of their race or class—was one of the earliest of the fundamental human rights to gain universal recognition.... The exercise of this right requires access to political power.... [B]eyond the political process, this right extends into

decision-making in all spheres of life: home and family, work, school, church, club, and choice of life-style. The denial of the right of individual decision-making and self-determination constitutes oppression (Kallen 1989: 7).

The associated idea of sovereignty clearly has political overtones. Indeed, the disabled community sees itself existing under a condition of "internal colonialism" in which it has little or no voice in its own affairs, and must exist under the social, political and economic policies of some "imperial power"—not unlike the experience of other peoples and indigenous populations. As under colonialism, disabled individuals "suffer a spectrum of alienation from blatant neglect to overprotection," and they experience physical isolation, institutional segregation, paternalism and tokenism (Alberta Committee of Citizens With Disabilities 1981b: 24, Krause 1976). When discussing the independent living model the disabled community often invokes the concept of citizenship when making the point that there cannot be grades of citizenship within Canada, that equality of opportunity in all aspects of life must exist for every citizen, disabled or not—"[A]s part of its full citizenship philosophy, COPOH asserts that government should not do things TO and FOR disabled persons, but rather WITH us" (COPOH 1985b: 60–61).

The way disabled consumers use the term "self-determination" (Derksen 1980, 1983, Crewe and Zola 1983) clearly illustrates that they mean it in the specific sense, rather than in the general sense. The means of achieving certain goals and solving particular problems in independent living are as important, if not more so, than the solutions to the problems themselves (Simpson 1980). Yet, even as an end in itself, is self-determination really feasible? As individuals our earliest and probably most fundamental development cannot be self-determined; it is only later choices and interests that may be self-determined.

An important issue is the extent to which later interests are determined by a self that has already been formed by the social environment, and to what extent the social environment still operates on forming people's interests. The vision of self-determination for disabled people involves a conscious un-socializing or un-learning process, the same process that is involved in abandoning the medical/rehabilitation model for the new independent living paradigm.

Self-determination as an intrinsic essentialist conception of human interests and empowerment as a conscious action process are tied together. Self-determination is the means by which new social and personal identities are formed, and new individual and collective self-images developed through the restructuring of motivations.

The idea of self-determination can be linked to the idea of self-actualization, a concept that is central to the humanistic tradition in psychology. The process of self-actualization might be defined as "becoming whatever one can through activities determined by oneself." The fundamental assumption is that the human being, as an organism, has one basic tendency and striving—to actualize, maintain and enhance itself (Rogers 1951). The human being is, in fact, in "a process of becoming." According to Rogers (1951), Maslow (1970) and other motivation theorists, self-actualization is also a directional process. The organism naturally moves towards the goals of maturation, increasing competence, survival, reproduction, self-regulation, autonomy and even community (Plant 1974: 62). From this perspective, not only is individual behavior motivated by a need to realize these goals, but society should be concerned with helping individuals develop their highest potential. This is viewed as their right; the individual has a right to determine his or her personal action in the context of a supportive community (Plant 1974: 61–62).

The assumptions that underlie this perspective are worth noting. Rogers's idea of self-actualization is fully compatible with Penz's essentialist conception of human interests. People are viewed as essentially good and continually strive toward a better state. Rogers suggests that any less-than healthy functioning of the individual is a consequence of the environment, or more correctly, social structures and institutions. People are the best judges of what they want, need and what their interests are. The best vantage point for understanding behavior is from the frame of reference of the individual. The behaviors adopted by individuals must be consistent with notions of the self, which in turn are a result of interaction with the environment and, most important, interaction with others. Maladaptive, self-destructive, incompetent and dependent behavior is the result of conflicting notions of the self, derived from less-than ideal interactions and interactional settings. The cause of humanism is to promote the awareness and the conditions that make it possible for people to become self-responsible, more flexible, make progress in self-actualization, and to become more creatively adaptive.

From the perspectives provided by Penz and Rogers, the independent living model might be described as an operational and prescriptive one (Caws 1974, Holy and Stuchlik 1981). Certainly, it is not incompatible with the doctrine of individual sovereignty in economic philosophy, or the vision of competent and independent action in humanistic psychology. An independent living lifestyle is the outcome of empowerment, that specific developmental and transforming process that is constructed through learning and action by embodying certain assumptions, beliefs and values about the relationship between people in general, and the relation between the disabled community and the rest of society in particular. In turn, the goal of independent living provides disabled people with the rationale for developing the necessary social and political skills useful for playing more conscious and assertive roles in the construction of their own social environments. In fact, the goal of independent living *requires* a more active role on the part of individuals in shaping the social environment and building community.

The independent living/disabled consumer movement has developed and articulated a set of principles that guide both the realization of specific goals and the implementation tactics of consumer policies (Alberta Committee 1981b: 25–29). Embodying the IL philosophy, the principles are basic to the movement's task of improving the quality of lifestyle of disabled people through legislative policy change at all levels of government, information gathering and sharing, research into more viable programs, services and delivery systems, and through monitoring existing legislation and its implementation. Embodied in the principles, derived from Alberta Committee and COPOH sources, is the idea that disabled people have a right to be recognized, to contribute to society; the right to exist likewise implies a right to autonomy.

Principle of Equality: During the past decade disabled Canadians, largely through the efforts of the independent living/disabled consumer movement, have made major strides forward in attaining equality by seeking to secure legal recognition of their community rights in human rights legislation, at both federal and provincial levels. The inclusion of persons with disabilities in legislation and statutes means that discrimination on the basis of disability is prohibited in areas such as employment, housing accommodation, and access to goods, services and facilities. Of particular value to the disabled community is the Charter of Rights and Freedoms, specifically section 15(1) which relates to the equality rights of individuals, and subsection (2) which endorses the development of affirmative action programs that have as their object the amelioration of conditions of disadvantaged individuals and groups.

The movement recognizes that to ensure provision of, and access to, goods, services and facilities, there must be an independently recognized authority to settle disputes. It also recognizes the need for disabled individuals to actively participate in fashioning, advocating and defending a practical interpretation of equality that is in keeping not only with the goals of the movement and the independent living model, but with the needs of the larger community and of all citizens. Equality rights are the cornerstone for empowerment and self-determination for disabled people at both the individual and community level. The notion of "reasonable accommodation" is the operationalization of the disabled citizen's interpretation of equality.

Principle of Full Participation: The disabled community has recognized a tendency for nondisabled persons to speak on behalf of disabled persons in many areas of social and political life. Full participation, or consumer control, includes collective self-representation. The movement is committed to ensuring that all individuals have the opportunity to participate in the planning, monitoring and delivery of all aspects of programs that directly affect them, by such means as meaningful-proportioned representation on advisory councils, research task forces, community service boards, ownership of service-providing organizations and consumer control (e.g., 51%) of all services and managerial structures. The principle most definitely extends to include the process of consultation and joint policy decision-making with different levels of government.

Principle of Integration: The intent of the independent living philosophy and the service delivery models that have developed from it is to enable disabled persons to assume greater control over their lives and to facilitate their integration into Canadian society. To this end, integration is conceived as the desegregation of specialized services for disabled citizens and the eventual establishment of these services as components of mainstream or generic community service delivery systems, in such areas as health care, education and employment. There is recognition and insistence that mainstream community service providers assume a reasonable degree of responsibility for removing architectural barriers that prevent access to public and private buildings, recreational facilities and public transportation systems. In other words, "specialized services if necessary, but not necessarily specialized services."

Principle of Individuality: This principle is derived from an understanding that there are indeed differences between people, that not everyone has the same interests, aspirations and needs, and that not all disabilities can be treated as if there were no differences between them. It is recognized that a theory of formal equality which advocates that all individuals should be treated the same regardless of their differences would wreck havoc on those who possess characteristics which do not conform to dominant or majoritarian standards. The principle endorses a combined theory of substantive and formal equality whose goal is the equality of results for individuals, but whose benefit is felt at the community level. To this end, the idea of special measures, affirmative action and the notion of reasonable accommodation is supported. A balance is sought between tailor-made and mainstream community-based services and programs.

Principle of Accountability: One of the roles of the disabled consumer movement, in the context of the independent living paradigm, is to claim and exercise the right to monitor and evaluate existing public as well as private service and program structures, delivery systems and policies—at local, municipal, provincial and federal levels. In this capacity, the movement seeks to provide the disabled and nondisabled community with evaluations of rehabilitation and other service providers, health professionals and legislators, with respect to adequate benefits, quality services, reasonable costs and qualified personnel. The principle recognizes that medicine stands between biology and social policy, between private bodies and public interpretations. Disabled consumers hold both practitioners and legislators accountable to them, both for their actions and their nonactions.

The Path to Self-Determination

It is not entirely a coincidence that disabled people have opted for an association with the generic consumer movement. From their point of view, they are consumers of services and products, but what they consume and demand are not always ordinary services and products. The issues are not necessarily those related to shoddy workmanship, the promises of false advertising, voided warranties or even the unjustified product safety claims of a manufacturer. They are directly related to physical and mental well-being, the realization of life-chances, physical reproduction, sexuality and intimacy, and intellectual and personal development. These are things that all people, disabled or not, most deeply want and value.

Disabled people are potential or actual users of organizations and institutions—the courts, governments, schools and universities, churches and businesses—those that produce services and products of a qualitatively different sort. As with what they teach or what they produce, these institutions have also been subjected to increasing public scrutiny and skepticism, and so have experienced considerable loss of esteem. Truthfulness of information, relevance and the responsiveness of organizations matter as much to people as product performance and safety.

Consumerism identifies both the generic and the disabled brand of consumer movement that was launched during the 1960s, partly as a result of former U.S. President John F. Kennedy's initiative in establishing the four rights of consumers: to safety, to be informed, to choose, and to be heard (Aaker and Day 1978). Consumerism has since come to encompass the activities of government, business, independent organizations, and professional associations. Significantly, two other consumer rights have developed since the 1960s: The right to recourse and redress, and the right to a physical environment that will enhance people's quality of life. The scope of consumerism has grown to include an active concern with protecting customers and clients whenever there is an exchange relationship with an organization, be it a business firm, government agency, school or hospital.

The disabled community's association with consumerism, its adherance to consumer principles, and the development of a consumer ethic has significance beyond consumption. While the independent living principles are by no means new or unique, they are unique to the disabled consumer movement. They hinge on the concept and practice of an individual's sovereignty and self-reliance. To consume goods and services is not only to "reproduce" oneself but also the social relations within which these goods and services are produced. The disabled insist, as certainly do others who are not physically or mentally impaired, that they be directly engaged and implicated in the production of their own health, learning and growth. People are implicated in their own self-production, while at the same time their fundamental right to self-determination is exercised in the context of community.

Why, then, neglect or take for granted the circumstances and context of this reproduction, by leaving or entrusting it to just anyone? From the perspective of disabled people, the struggle to regain control over the circumstances of one's own reproduction, a control which had been relinquished only gradually and innocently, is the struggle to re-establish and revitalize what is essentially reciprocal in the nature of individual and social (collective) learning in the community-building process. Any kind of control that is reasserted by the disabled community over the context of reproduction, and any successful attempts to reconfirm its participation in the community-building process are at the same time steps toward self-determination and independent living.

Self-determination is part of the larger empowerment process of moving oneself out from under what Foucault calls the clinical gaze, away from the main sources of stigmas and stereotypes. This is so that control over and independence in the circumstances of one's own reproduction can be achieved. Self-determination provides the impetus for individual and collective action. For the disabled consumer movement, breaking from imposed categories means coming up with and initiating new ways in which disabled and nondisabled people can interact with one another. The form as well as the content of interaction must be changed.

4

Beyond Minority Protest
Social Movement and the Meaning of Empowerment

The marginalization and decontextualization of physically disabled and mentally handicapped people is not unlike what is experienced by other stigmatized minorities. Because "handicapping" is essentially the socio-cultural consequence of the translation of perceived physiological, cultural and behavioral differences between people into what become widely shared social designations, it is the "translation process" that must become the focus of change-directed efforts. Similarly, society's normative institutions within which the translation process operates and which reinforce or legitimate the outcome are also not exempt from critical examination. Ameliorating the socio-cultural consequences of the stigmatization process is only one side. The values and beliefs which underlie any kind of social practice and institution that has negative effects on people must be examined, and if necessary, changed or eliminated.

Social designations, categories and even social structures are largely the outcome of patterned interactions as well as learned behavior. "Deviant designations," the disability category and even the medical/rehabilitation model are real only insofar as people consciously as well as unconsciously continue to participate in their creation and maintenance. Accordingly, efforts to eliminate or transform these imposed social categories and the structures that spring from them require two activities. Change and transformation involves mental as well as physical/structural activities. The specific learning process that consciously and strategically combines these mental and physical efforts is referred to as the empowerment process. In order to change those interactions and learned behavior patterns in society that reinforce or perpetuate the negative labels, stereotypes and stigmas, action-oriented disabled people are learning to change attitudes by constructing counter-images. By initiating and learning to engage in new kinds of social and cultural practices, they are also changing current structures.

The more persistant, accepted and unquestioned behaviors that the disabled community wants to eliminate or change are those identified with the medical/rehabilitation model and the disability category, and that are generalized to all disabled people: the sick role, patient or client role expectations, the passive recipient of care, physical segregation, presumed uninvolvement or disinterest, disability as a social problem, presumed social incompetence, and unproductivity in work. Many of the features of everyday life are deeply implicated in the long-term and large-scale reproduction of social institutions and practices; at the same time, macro structural properties of social institutions are implicated in even the most casual of interpersonal interactions. With the proper motivation the goal of disabled people is to consciously and strategically structure their own activities and interactions with those whose care and services they seek. More active intervention even at the interpersonal level will have an impact on larger systems of action in which disabled people are engaged and vice-versa.

At the core of the disabled consumer movement and the movement's independent living philosophy is the idea of empowerment. In her discussion of the protest and rights movements of stigmatized minorities, Kallen (1989) puts forward the idea that,

> Minority protest in pursuit of human rights may be organized around expressive/cultural and/or instrumental/*empowerment* types of goals. When *empowerment* demands take precedence, minority protest may take the form of *contention*, seeking social reforms that will recognize and protect the individual human rights of minority members and will enhance their political, economic, and social opportunities. (p. 45, added emphasis)

Organized minority protest may take the form of contention through reform movements predicated on goals of *empowerment*. . . . In *contention*, the minority protests against its subordinate political, economic, and social status and demands policy and legal changes geared to the collective goal of positional equality (proportionate representation throughout the ranks) within the social order. (p. 157, added emphasis)

Similar statements can be found in an earlier volume that dealt specifically with ethnic minorities (Kallen 1982: 185). Though Kallen's (1982, 1989) discussions are in the context of human rights issues, empowerment is an integral part of her formulation. She has linked it to social movement activity. While social reform, positional equality and human rights constitute empowerment goals and demands, her work does not elaborate what the actual empowerment process entails.

Empowerment as a developmental and transforming process is at the heart of social movement. Implied is that empowerment is not limited to discussions of minority protest activities; it is basic to discussions of social and cultural change and to community-building. From this perspective, reform and equality can only be pursued by empowered individuals who have learned and acquired action skills that enable them to play an ever-more conscious and assertive role in constructing their own social and political environments. The subsequent achievement of reform and positional equality, whether token or really significant, in turn serves to even further empower those who continue to pursue these goals.

Social Movement as a Product of Society: Old Approaches

Older approaches to social movements failed to fully recognize that social movement is reflexive activity and strategic conduct inherent in all levels of social interaction. They tended to reduce social movement or collective action to expressions of radical, deviant and disruptive behavior. But even in some cases, collective action has been characterized as resource mobilizing, identity-seeking or liberating.

This has been the dualistic approach to social movements: The former is portrayed as pathological, irrational, reactionary, noninstitutional, disintegrating and the latter as rational, proactive, institutional and integrating. In both instances the focus of explanation and analysis seems to be on social stability, the sharing and internalization of values, the determinants of behavior and to some extent even on the functional needs of social systems. In both cases, social movements are portrayed as somehow external or extrinsic to society, acting *on* it rather than *in* it. Without a clearer conceptualization of what constitutes action, of what structures and institutions are, how can collective action be properly understood as the production of social practices by knowledgeable, reflective and motivated actors?

Clearly, social movements need to be considered *in* and *of* society, not simply in relation to it. The focus should be primarily on the conditions and circumstances that govern both the continuity and transformation of structures, and the overall reproduction of social systems. What is social movement if it is not reflexive monitoring of action and self-regulation at the level of social structure, and what is social and cultural reproduction if it is not the organization and institutionalization of the results of this learning process?

In *The Constitution of Society* (1984) Giddens wrote that "the study of social movements has been distinctly underrepresented within the social sciences as compared with the vast literature given over to the numerous vying elaborations of 'organization theory'" (p. 203). Giddens distinguishes between social movements and social movement organizations. Giddens argues for a shift of focus just slightly away from the organizational aspects of collective action, towards the "fields" in which they operate. A focus on the former, as has traditionally been the case, tends to result in descriptions of *how* collective action is manifested, but not always *why*. Preoccupation with social movement organizations has tended to portray them as reacting to conflict, crisis or social disruption generated elsewhere in society, or as being the source of conflicts.

In turn, by placing an emphasis on factors of strain, this approach stresses the notion of social system equilibrium and conceptualizes the social system as a natural entity and so fails to recognize its essential artifactual and contingent character. From this perspective it is hard to think of movements as being comprised of individuals embodying the meaning of their own actions or being able to define strategies by themselves. Movements tend to be viewed as consequences of strain, as dysfunctions in the system's integrative mechanisms, or as structural contradiction that disturbs the equilibrium of the system. But movements also are viewed as organized actions whose goal is the restoration of equilibrium and are considered a means of achieving social integration. In both cases, analysis turns on the adaptive reactions in the mechanisms that ensure the smooth functioning of the system (see Coser 1956, Kornhauser 1959, and Smelser 1962).

More sophisticated studies of this structural-functional approach offer explanations which consider social movements as actors who pursue strategies and struggle against other "actors" for the appropriation and control of resources which are assumed to be mutually at stake. Notice here the individualization of collectivities and the assumed homogeneity or unity of movements and of conflicts. One advance is that the social system in which the struggle takes place is understood as socially constructed. Movements are considered social constructions, and an understanding of their strategies is attempted in light of ongoing social and cultural relations, that is, relations of domination, subordination, autonomy and dependence (Wilkinson 1970, Piven and Cloward 1977, Tilly 1978, and especially Touraine 1977a, 1981).

Social movements, rather than being just the consequence of the dysfunctions of the social system, are seen as based on organizational imperatives (McCarthy and Zald 1973). Getting and keeping together individuals and reconciling differences for action requires investing considerable energy and resources in building up and maintaining formal movement organizations. This is known as the resource-mobilization paradigm (Gamson 1968, 1975, McCarthy and Zald 1973, Oberschall 1973; see also Jenkins 1983, and Foss and Larkin 1986).

This rational-system model of social movement activity has the unfortunate effect of turning the study of social movement into the study of strategies. It is as if movements are defined by their goals alone, and as if actors were motivated primarily by the logic of a sort of economic rationality or neo-utilitarianism, e.g., cost-benefit calculations, and little else (Touraine 1985: 769). Resource mobilization does not and cannot occur independently from the social relations of those involved (J. Cohen 1985). It provides at best only partial insights into the meaning of social movement for the reason that the very concept of organization/movement is equated with concepts like strategic action, decision-making and instrumental reasoning (Olson 1965).

Little light is shed on the nature of contemporary collective action, and the approach just described is unable to account for the "new" emerging social movements of the 1980s and 1990s because both the forms of organization that are presupposed and the particular form of rationality that is imputed to individuals do not really fit the new reality (A. Scott 1990). The rational-system model and the resource-mobilization approaches are tied too closely to the conditions of an "older" industrial society. The new social movements occur in post-industrial society, a significantly different context representing a different set of possibilities and constraints for movement actors.

The breakdown/crisis, rational-system and resource-mobilization approaches to social movements are merely close variations on the old structural-functionalist theme. From this perspective, social movements, including social movement organizations, are seen as results or products of systemic dysfunctions, and therefore function to lead the transition to the next social formation. However, the consequence comes to operate as the cause—which is too simplistic an explanation of social movement and social change.

The Duality of Social Movement

There is confusion in these older approaches to social movements about whether movement is exogenous, or whether it comes from within the social system. In the former instance, the interdependence of subsystems and possible structural contradictions arising from their mutual interaction cannot be taken into account. In the latter instance, an account of movement arising within the system is obliged to account for perceived strain by means of the same categories used to account for collective action. To do otherwise is to construct a contradictory explanatory system that is incapable of taking both structure as well as action into consideration.

The chief difficulty with these apparent dualisms (external/internal change; action/structure) is the failure to properly identify social movements as action systems operating in a field of possibilities as well as constraints. Though social movements may be conceived as both a solution and a problem in the creation of a social order, until now there have been no satisfactory models that could explain the process of the definition of the action system, and the process by which individuals and groups recreate their social order. According to Melucci (1985: 792),

> Structural [e.g., breakdown/crisis] theories, based on system analysis, explain *why* but not *how* a movement is set up and maintains its structure, that is, they only hypothesize about potential conflict without accounting for concrete collective action and actors. On the other hand, the resource mobilization approach regards such action as mere data and fails to examine its meaning and orientation. In this case, *how* but not *why*. . . . Action has to be viewed as an interplay of aims, resources, and obstacles, as *a purposive orientation which is set up within a system of opportunities and constraints*. [original emphasis]

Just as any social activity is simultaneously replicative and transformative, so is social movement simultaneously a cause and effect of change, a source of internal as well as external change, and an action and meaning system. Following Giddens's contribution to action theory, social movement is more appropriately regarded as a duality. Social movements are a *cause* of change because the presence of a conflict which is manifested by "deviant" or symbolic forms of activity within asymmetrical social relations must be constantly monitored by those who are in positions of power and domination and, furthermore, obliges them to react, for example, by accommodation, reform or even repression. At the same time social movements are an *effect* because the adaptations made by the system of domination in reponse to them, in turn reflexively monitored by the social movement organizations and individuals involved in them, again generates strategic collective action. And so on in reciprocal fashion following the logic of Giddens's theory of action.

From the perspective of breakdown/crisis theory, collective action always appears peripheral, reactive or defensive to the reproductive logic of the social system. From the perspective of action theory, social movements are the processes through which collective identities are constituted, the means by which a particular version of social reality is contested and reinterpreted, and the means by which the norms and values of a particular system of domination are challenged. Traditional approaches to social movements looked at how social systems produce collective action. Recent approaches, more appropriately, look at how collective action reproduces society.

Society as a Product of Social Movement: New Perspectives

Collective actors and their forms of struggle should be the starting point for an analysis of social change, where society is seen as a field of social action. Power structures are normatively oriented interactions between actual or potential adversaries within a shared cultural field that is open to multiple interpretations. Social movement is synonymous with the contest between competing interests over the control of the work that society performs on itself in constantly forming norms, orientations, practices and institutions (Touraine 1977a, 1981, 1985, 1992).

Giddens (1984: 200) observed that social movements and social movement organizations "are collectivities in which the reflexive regulation of the conditions of system reproduction looms large in the continuity of day-to-day practices" for the purpose of attempting to alter or control the circumstances of reproduction. Significantly, Giddens adds that "reflexive self-regulation, as a property of collectivities, depends upon the collation of information which can be controlled so as to influence the circumstances of social reproduction." Reflexive self-regulation and the information-gathering that is part of this process is essentially a learning process.

In order to transcend the limiting framework of interest theory, resource-mobilization theory and the rational-actor model, and to reintroduce the actions of individuals in the (re)creation of society, it is necessary to focus on the constitution of collective action. This involves a reconstruction of the cultural and normative orientations of contemporary social movements, as well as an inquiry into how social movement organizations order these elements structurally to constitute actions that are collective. In addition, it is important to see what image a social movement has of itself, "who" or "what" it perceives its adversary to be against which reformulated identities are aimed, and what the common field of action is within which struggles over "the control of the development of a socio-cultural life world" take place (J. Cohen 1985: 690, Eder 1982: 11, A. Scott 1990, Carroll 1992).

Earlier views and analyses of social movements were tied to the logic of industrial capitalist development and to a particular kind of economic production. These analyses stressed the primacy of economic contradictions, class relations and systemic crisis (essentially the Marxist view) (J. Cohen 1982, 1983). By contrast, current approaches to contemporary social movements recognize that the logic or identity of the "new" movements does not derive solely from economic "steering mechanisms," because the economic subsystem is no longer isolated from political and administrative mediation. The penetration of the economic subsystem, among other subsystems, by the state has complicated the traditional lines of asymmetry, division and hierarchy by making them multidimensional (J. Cohen 1982: 23, 1985: 691).

In comparison with the industrial phase of capitalism, the production characteristic of advanced capitalist societies, post-industrialist or programmed, in the words of Touraine (1977a), requires that control reach beyond the productive structure and into the areas of *consumption, services* and *social relations* (Melucci 1985: 795–96, Touraine 1992: 129–31). The mechanisms of accumulation are no longer supplied only by the exploitation of a labor force and control over labor-power (Melucci 1981: 179), but by the manipulation of organizational systems, by control over information, over the processes and institutions of symbol-formation and, significantly, by intervention in interpersonal and private relations. The medical/rehabilitation model, against which many disabled people protest as a prime example of an organizational/symbolic system, exercises almost complete control over many aspects of people's lives, including their identities.

Production consists of the transformation of not only social relations and social systems, but the individual's biological and interpersonal identity at the same time. Still controlled by dominant groups, it is only the expropriation of social resources that has changed forms. The struggle for the reappropriation of the control over the resources of society is carried into areas of social and cultural life previously untouched or uncontested (Offe 1985: 834, n.19, A. Scott 1990,

Aronowitz 1992). Modern society has developed the tremendous capacity to intervene in and transform not only social and cultural systems and interpersonal relations, but the very "structures" of individuals, for example, their personality, their unconscious—even their biology (Melucci 1981: 179).

Because the personal and social identity of individuals are a product or outcome of social action, it is not surprising that "identity" is what is at stake in the conflict between the requirements of the power structure and the demands of individuals for the reappropriation of society's resources (Giddens 1991). Melucci (1985: 793, 1988: 248–250) defined identity as a shared definition of a field of opportunities and constraints. What individuals are now claiming collectively is the right to have and maintain their individual identities, that is, in terms of personal creativity and expression, affective relations, and biological and interpersonal existence (van Steenbergen 1983, Foss and Larkin 1986: 137–43).

Techno-bureaucratic domination is characterized by certain controls and manipulation whose effects include an almost complete penetration of many aspects of everyday life, extending to the individual's capacity to use time and space, or even to their procreational/sexual conduct (J. Cohen 1983: 98). In this assault on the individual, there is a simultaneous broadening and deepening of forms of domination and deprivation (Offe 1985: 845). The new social movements, including the disabled consumer movement, are struggling not just for the reappropriation of the material aspects of physical and mental reproduction, but also for the collective control over individual socio-cultural development, that is, for the reappropriation of social, affective and biological relationships and identities.

The central theme in an analysis of the new social movements is that they are "new" precisely because the sources for inequality and forms of domination are far different in modern society from those faced by the "old" movements. Because material goods are produced and consumed with the mediation of largely information and symbolic systems (Melucci 1985: 795), conflict has now moved from the traditional industrial system to cultural grounds (Touraine 1977b: 22–27, 39–42). This deeply affects personal identity, the time and space of everyday life, and the motivation and cultural patterns of individual behavior. Eder (1982: 10) argues that a prime feature of modernity is the possibility of challenging dominant cultural and behavioral orientations.

In post-industrial society, the capacity for cultural production becomes increasingly based on information and knowledge. Control over the production, accumulation and circulation of information depends on rules that organize and make information usable and operational (Melucci 1988: 247–48). This "operational rationality" becomes a source of power for the reason that information/knowledge is not a shared resource accessible to everyone, but is produced and controlled by a few experts (Melucci 1985: 805). Information cannot be separated from the human capability of perceiving it. According to Melucci (1985: 804), research in biology, neuropsychology and in the behavioral and neurosciences provides evidence for the frightening possibility of turning the behavioral and motivational structures of people into an arena through which intervention and struggles for control can take place.

The implications of this are profound not only for the physically disabled and the mentally handicapped, but for everyone: Dominant cultural orientations and values may be concentrated in the "hands of a few" and so may be group-specific, but these values influence virtually every member of society in some way. The flow of information through different social institutions make the effects of dominant values and norms more comprehensive, permeating even areas of private life that used to be outside the realm of explicit social control (Offe 1985: 844).

Disabled citizens insist that "the process of informing is the function of organizations of disabled persons," and that "informing is an ongoing function" (Alberta Committee 1981b). The identification of specific groups that have control over social and cultural production becomes difficult; structural power is dispersed and diffused, and is not always easily attributed to any central or clearly identifiable adversary. Foucault (1980) referred to the source of this power as the "apparatus of power-knowledge," exercised through institutions such as schools, hospitals, clinics, prisons and bureaucracies. Gathering information and informing *oneself* is a means of reasserting control over one's own social and cultural production.

Political and economic regulation, control and power is no longer limited to the manipulation of the *external* constraints of individual behavior. There is an "invasion," in the name of technocratic standards of rationality and coordination, of the symbolic infrastructure of informal and private social systems through the use of legal, educational, medical, chemical, psychiatric and media technologies. In modern post-industrial society there is a shift in social action to the *internal*, where intervention and manipulation occurs at the motivational, indeed, at the unconscious level, and where conflict is at the seam between the system and life-world.

This shift seems to have generated the main conflicts of the 1980s and 1990s and has demanded a redefinition of both the "location" of social movement and its forms of action. As Melucci (1985: 796) noted, conflicts are increasingly likely to occur in those areas of the social system "which are connected to the most intensive informational and symbolic investments and exposed to the greatest pressures for conformity." From the perspective of disabled people, medicine and medical intervention/rehabilitation is precisely one of those areas.

The Role of Empowerment in Social Movement

The new social movements, including the independent living/disabled consumer movement, should be seen in the context of perceived and pervasive threats to precisely those areas of social life that generate meaning and provide a sense of solidarity for individuals. Perhaps this is why individuals are acting collectively and publicly on very private and personal issues, and why they are taking personally broad social problems. Reaction and protest by disabled people against domination and deprivation take the form of contention through social movement organized around the goal of empowerment.

The process of becoming empowered involves learning to overcome internalized expectations and attitudes of bitterness, helplessness, self-denial and alienation. Comments one disabled person who has cerebral palsy,

> I am angry—no, damned mad—most of the time every day. This should not have happened to me—there is no reason, no fairness to the way I am. I have to accept my condition, but nobody's going to make me like it. I hate it, and much of the time I hate everyone:

those more fortunate than me, because they are, and those as badly or worse off, because they remind me of my own state. I am no cheerful Tiny Tim, with a sweet nature developed by affliction, I am bathed in anger almost always (Bill Kiser, in Weinberg 1988: 149–50).

In another context, one individual notes that,

It would never have occurred to me to have expressed an opinion on anything.... It was *inconceivable* that my opinion had any value.... That's lower than powerlessness.... You don't even know the word "power" exists. It applies to *them*.... I didn't question that that's the way the world was.... It was *their* world (Rappaport 1984: 16, original emphasis).

Empowerment is simultaneously the medium and outcome of learned resistance against control and domination at a very personal level, the motivational level. Empowerment is a process of becoming, an enabling process that is achieved and further reinforced through action. To operationalize the empowerment process, it is suggested that the process can be looked at in two ways. Essentially, empowerment has both motivational and relational, or interactional, dimensions.

Empowerment, or power in the motivational sense, refers to a person's intrinsic need for self-determination, and has its base within a person's motivational disposition. Attitude is clearly an important element of the process: "One has to *want* to be independent. When that's established, everything else will come" (Doreen Demas, COPOH 1987d: 61, emphasis added). Anything that strengthens the need of self-efficacy will make a person feel more powerful and "in control." Conversely, anything that weakens this need will increase feelings of powerlessness. Power needs are met when an individual perceives that he or she "has" power or control, and when he or she believes they can adequately cope with events, situations and other people they have to deal with. An individual's power/control needs are frustrated when that person feels powerless or thinks that they are unable to cope with the physical and social demands they face. According to Elizabeth Semkiw,

> Control is a key factor. Any aspect of living in which one chooses the management and organization such as medical supports, banking, or buying groceries, is an avenue of exercising control (COPOH 1987d: 57).

Comments another individual:

> I was thirty-five years old and never knew that I had rights.... It's hard for people to see what's really going on. You spend half your life helping to keep yourself down.... The more that you get involved in making power, the more your understanding of power changes.... The more I'm involved, the more I'm learning (Rappaport 1984: 22).

Empowerment is an enabling process whereby the right circumstances for increasing a person's motivation through the development of a strong sense of personal efficacy are sought. The "right" circumstances, or setting, may also be created when the conditions that foster powerlessness are identified, so that the goal of eventually removing them by various strategic means can be realized.

Empowerment, not unlike power, is also relational or interactional. It can be used to describe the perceived/experienced power or control that individuals can acquire together. Control and power arises when individuals' action outcomes are contingent not only on their own behavior, but on what others do and how they respond. From the perspective of social exchange, mutual interaction, power and control are functions of the interdependence of individuals. Empowerment does not take place in a vacuum:

> ... I would say that if you are thinking about developing something for yourself.... build up some allies and people who are really interested in the type of thing you are doing. You really need other people for input.... You can't build something for disabled people and be the only one interested in it. You have to look around for people (Connie Oxelgren, in COPOH 1987d: 65).

> I think disabled people should put some energies into developing their own personal support network. It is really tough to go from a

very controlled environment like an institution to full blown independent living. You are all of a sudden put in the position of having to make every decision for yourself. It's a real learning process. Not having a well developed personal support network can be disastrous [sic] (Rick Laird, in COPOH 1987d: 87).

At the interpersonal and intergroup levels, the resources that can enable individuals and groups to have control over their own circumstances might be the personal characteristics of the persons, their access to material resources, as well as their expertise, knowledge and access to information. This focus on resources leads to a consideration of strategies and tactics to obtain further resources to increase one's own power and control. From this perspective, the empowerment process entails the decentralization and sharing of community resources. This would include decision-making powers.

Individuals can empower others, have others empower them, or they can try to empower themselves. Regardless of who is "doing" the empowering, it is the belief in one's self-efficacy and self-worth that must be strengthened while at the same time one's belief in personal powerlessness is weakened. A person's motivation to increase his or her power and control depends on expectations that their efforts are going to result in controlling more resources. The expectation is that by controlling or having access to more resources, certain other desired outcomes can be achieved.

What is most important in empowerment is that the person's need for self-determination or self-efficacy is met, not necessarily that his or her outcome expectations are always met. The motivational dimension of the empowerment process is stressed. Even under conditions of failure to achieve certain outcomes individuals may feel empowered if their efficacy beliefs are reinforced and if their motivation persists. Individuals convinced of their powerlessness may be inclined to behave in ineffectual ways, just as their perceived self-efficacy will weaken the impact of direct experiences of failure by sustaining their actions in the face of difficulty or failure.

Empowerment has a great deal to do with reversing the internalization of the assumptions and expectations of the so-called medical/rehabilitation model, that is, recontextualizing the disabled individual in social life and "revalidating" him or her. This has to be accomplished first at the motivational level, and only later at the level of pursuing reform, equality and rights. However, the motivational and interactional dimensions of the process cannot be separated from each other. The links between motivated action and social interaction are made possible by such empowering devices as open communication and networking between peers, the creation of opportunities for participation in collective decision-making, and autonomy from professional and bureaucratic interference. Simpson (1980: 8, 27) writes,

> So few organizations in society realize that each problem-solving and sharing process is and should be a vital learning growth experience for every individual involved. This author firmly believes and contends that how the self-determination and involvement process of solving any societal problems is carried out can be actually as important as the solution itself.... Motivation can be achieved through group sharing, learning, and goal setting....

The feeling of empowerment for the disabled person comes from experiencing *ability* in the performance of tasks and in making decisions. It comes from observing and interacting with peers going through the same process in a group setting and observing those who have progressed, from verbal interaction, and from receiving strong emotional support that reduces feelings of anxiety, fear and helplessness. Communicating, networking, organizing and participating are the principal means by which action is motivated and sustained. What is empowerment if it is not the melding of the motivational and relational dimensions of human interaction? What is social movement, implicated in the empowerment process, if it does not also have motivational and relational dimensions?

The empowerment process provides the thrust, or underpinning, for the independent living/disabled consumer movement. An independent living lifestyle presupposes a belief and a confidence in one's own ability to act, to take risks, to make decisions and to live by them. Individual action and decision-making have an impact on larger action systems, which in turn can motivate or enable future action. Knowledge and skills are constructed largely through actions; experience is at the core of empowered learning, and the building up of skills progresses through a repetition of cycles of action and self-reflection.

This is what Giddens calls the duality of structure.

> You've got to live it. You've got to *do* it. It's like, you can take an instruction course on how to do sex best, but if you don't go do sex, if you don't go and try it, then all you know is the hypothesis. . . . It's the same way with going through the experience of community organizing. . . . You have to *build* it up (Rappaport 1984: 26, original emphasis).

While empowerment is a labor-intensive individual learning experience, it is sustained and nurtured by the effects of collective effort. Grassroots organizing and organizations best serve as the locus of support and learning. The various support organizations and networks built up by disabled people not only enable independent and community living, but, more importantly, are recognized as the means and outcome of the empowerment process.

Defining Features of the New Social Movements

New social movements address problems that are located on the motivational level, with the "life-world" as the arena and the "public" realm as the systemic field. It is at the motivational level that techno-bureaucratic domination operates, and so it is at the motivational level that resistance and challenge must take place. The movements also are concerned with organizational and technological over-complexity that accompanies severe cultural and psychic impoverishment. The new contemporary social movements should be seen in the context of real and perceived threats to those "spaces" which generate meaning and a sense of community for individuals (Melucci 1988). In the developmental frameworks of Habermas and Touraine (A. Scott 1990: 60–80, Carroll 1992), there is an emphasis on reflexivity, an expansion of the public realm, and the reestablishment of more familiar everyday discourses.

For Touraine, reproduction based on the activity of socio-cultural production gives rise to a "more evolved" action system, in which struggles over the direction and orientation of social and cultural life occur. The basic assumption is that human societies have an evolutionary capacity to develop themselves through learning processes, and so obtain the capability to generate their own normative orientations by increased self-reflection.

From Touraine's perspective the new social movements articulate conflicts within a field of possible experiences that seek the institutionalization of new competing cultural and moral competencies. Unfortunately, Touraine does not offer a clear means to determine how individuals actually translate ideas about values and meaning into intentional or strategic action. Touraine's (1981) *The Voice and the Eye* emphasizes the usefulness of intervention by objective outsiders, e.g., action sociologists, in helping social movement actors define their strategies and, indeed, their movement.

Habermas's (1979, 1984, 1987) framework complements Touraine's, by elaborating on the ideas of cognitive and moral development, and focusing especially on the role of knowledge and communicative interaction with respect to social action. For Habermas, language is the medium of social interaction. Human society has the capacity to invent more effective ways of discursively dealing with conflicts and contradictions. In his communications-theoretic foundation for a critical theory, Habermas sees different societies, or systems of historical action, as characterized by different types of collective discourse. Societies have their own logic of justifying and rationalizing the interpretation of particular values and norms, which is achieved through socialization processes and specific forms of communication.

Socialization processes are motive-forming: As individuals are socialized and as their identities are formed *via* the "kinds" of languages they speak, certain kinds of social relations—asymmetrical, autonomous, dependent, dominant, and subordinate—are going to be reproduced *at* the motivational level (McCarthy 1978: 337–53). Individuals learn their "places" in society. The reproduction of society is achieved by the normative self-understanding of communicatively-socialized actors (Honneth 1987: 372–76). Habermas argues that an increasing reflexivity *via* the new creation and institutionalization of norms and values is achieved through social learning in the dimension of moral-practical insight (J. Cohen 1983, Thompson 1984: 297–99). Habermas suggests that societies, much like the cognitive development pattern of individuals, progressively move from a preoccupation with their immediate needs towards an expanding awareness of the world and the needs of others.

An expanding awareness and sense of community carries with it the possibility of separate social action-realms, a growing capacity for purposive and strategic action, and the potential for increased reflexivity. Habermas argues for a conception of society in which differently organized spheres of action, each distinguished by separate forms of rationalization and discourse, emerge. In modern society, two spheres or systems of action—economic production (the market economy) and political administration (the state), and the life-world—have become separated. The market/state and life-world undergo a progressive uncoupling and alienation from each other, where the life-world—that collectively shared private symbolic space of interests, values and beliefs within which cultural traditions and personal identities are reproduced and sustained (Melucci 1988: 258–59)—attains the status of just another subsystem among others.

The different action spheres, however, still have to be somehow anchored to the life-world in order to maintain moral and authoritative domination, and to ensure the participation, commitment and loyalty of all individuals. Anchoring is achieved by the intrusion into the life-world (its colonization) of a purposive-rational mode of discourse. The result is that the life-world itself, or community, becomes increasingly rationalized and instrumentalized (Honneth 1987: 375–76, Thompson 1984: 289–93). Domination in modern society depends on a homogeneous culture, mass literacy and on a monolithic and uniform education system. The life-world, in which cultural transmission and socialization takes place, and in which an individual's personal identity is structured, takes on the instrumental and functional values of the greater market/state system. The denial of meaning, feeling, identity, individual autonomy and the appropriation and commodification of the behavioral and motivational structures of individuals that accompanies this uncoupling and colonization process has been described as the "determining pathology of our times" (Honneth 1987: 376).

The penetration of these "steering mechanisms" (economic and political administration) into people's private and personal lives triggers conflict between the normative/motivational structures that constitute people's social identities. Serious controversy arises over "what" and "whose" norms, interests and goals take priority. As the life-world becomes saturated with the rationalizing values of the larger system, society is increasingly seen as a system capable of producing and generating its own normative and motivational guidelines—for everyone. The truly *social* and *cultural* struggle between power/knowledge apparatuses and their users or clients over the control of the production of society occurs.

Habermas is correct to have linked the administrative penetration of the socialization and cultural reproduction processes to the emergence of social movements as well as to the identity and autonomy crises of individuals. Both Touraine and Habermas have provided a framework by which it is possible to understand contemporary social movement as a crucial element in the social/collective learning process, and as a vital means to reassert the viability of the life-world and the re-creation of community. It is not simply an issue of life-world/community *versus* the market/state, but of a range of possible discourses and action types that can bridge or link the two.

The process of decolonizing the life-world (and rebuilding community) and resisting an ever-expanding instrumental rationalism involves the creation of new solidarities and new "public spaces" whose purpose might be to try to reintroduce the normative dimension of social interaction back into political life (what Melucci has termed the democratization of everyday life). Touraine and Habermas see contemporary social movements as structured by cultural tradition and as the "learning mechanisms" that link the creative reinterpretation of existing norms and values, and the institutionalization of new discourses. This means developing new structures that involve organized social interaction, the formal articulation of new associational forms, and the establishment of "legitimate" channels of communication (J. Cohen 1983: 110, Simpson 1980: 36). What is at issue is not necessarily the replacement of existing institutions or structures, but changing the meaning of existing relations and interaction.

Does not the defense of society against an alienating rationality, an attempt to revitalize basic institutions and subsystems, and a bid to participate more fully imply an affirmation and a general acceptance of the system as a whole? J. Cohen (1982, 1983) has interpreted the new social movements to be essentially institutional reform movements that seek the continuity, albeit with some modification, of present structures. Changes are sought within the existing social order and social formation.

Habermas sees the desire to work within the existing system as evidence of how deeply the life-world (community) has already been colonized. His position is that people have become so integrated that they can no longer conceive of truly alternative ideas and values. Giddens (1985: 201–2), however, argues convincingly that an expansion of the administrative reach of the system (i.e., the state) actually *increases* the possibility of reciprocal relations between dominant and subordinate groups, because "the more reciprocity is involved, the greater the possibilities the dialectic of control offers subordinate groups to influence the rulers." Even within constraints there are choices, from Giddens's perspective:

> Independent living really is an idea, a concept, a thought process. You apply this thought process to your lifestyle. I would think that even if a person were in prison and the only choice that they could make would be whether they would eat their food when they first got it, or eat it an hour later, they would still be practicing independent living (Elizabeth Semkiw, COPOH 1987d: 57).

An interesting feature of the new social movements is that conflict is not necessarily confined to the actions of any single social group that can be identified by a particular culture, lifestyle or class. In what is often described as mass society, in which cultural models and ways of life tend to become homogeneous, conflicts mobilize those categories, groups and individuals that find themselves directly and immediately manipulated and affected by the forces of socio-cultural production. There is no central leading collective actor and no clearly defined opponent. A challenge facing the new movements is to determine against whom, in what direction and to what degree "unitary" strategic action should be aimed. Coalition-building and establishing working relationships with "natural allies" are two possible strategies.

A second feature is the blurring of public and private spheres and the appearance of conflict at the "seam" between the market/state and life-world/community (J. Cohen 1982: 29, 1983: 102–4). Those areas which were previously fields of private exchanges, for example, sexual relations and biological identity, have become stakes in conflict situations and are the scene of public collective action (Frank 1990). Concurrently, the public field and the political arena are subjected to the pressure of individual needs and demands. Birth and sex, health and illness, aging and death have become critical points around which collective action is expressed. These are now in the realm of public conflict, and are the "objects" being reclaimed by various groups. Similarly, sexuality and the body, leisure and consumer goods, and relationships with nature (van Steenbergen 1983: 121–22) are no longer simply the *loci* for private pleasure, use or consumption, but have become areas of collective resistance and demands raised in opposition against those who have appropriated them for entirely their own use.

A third important feature is the tendency for some collective actions to be identified with nonconformity and deviance, and for some individuals to be treated as deviants, or worse, as victims (Melucci 1981: 176). But the fact remains that when a particular form of socio-cultural domination permeates daily life and impinges on everyday existence, opposition will be interpreted as a form of marginality and deviance. Derksen (1980: 13) remarks on the reaction of rehabilitation service providers to disabled consumer activity:

> [One] reaction, which was most unsuccessful, has been to use covert influence these providers have on governmental and private funding sources to deny resources to emerging consumer groups. This was often accompanied by offers of assistance and resources to disabled consumer activists and/or their organizations.... When these offers were refused, there were often charges that disabled consumer leaders were maladjusted, un-accepting of their disability, or even mentally and psychologically unbalanced or ill because of their disability. Consumer movement activists were accused of being radical or militant.

A consequence is that there has been a proliferation of public agencies whose primary task is to process and monitor social demands and needs that potentially are conflict generating. This "public intervention" is designed to reduce conflict and deny the legitimacy of demands and needs by relegating them to the status of pathology, by removing them from the political arena, thereby depoliticizing the issues, and by subjecting those who voice them to counselling, therapy or rehabilitation (Eder 1982: 18). Because of the power structure's increased capacity for surveillance, *via* control over the production and dissemination of information through its agencies, it becomes relatively easy to stigmatize and label all unacceptable or conflict-based behavior as deviant.

Since what is at stake is the reappropriation of individual identity and autonomy, collective action often centres on the issue of individual as well as group identity. A fourth feature that may be considered characteristic of contemporary social movements is that solidarity is a primary objective. It is a means by which a "diffused" or anonymous adversary can be confronted (Melucci 1981: 176). In some cases, ascriptive membership based on gender, race, age, physical and mental ability, and sexual orientation (i.e., focus on the body) becomes intrinsic to the formation of both the individual's and the group's identity and sense of solidarity (Habermas 1981: 36). Particularism of identity and issue becomes the specific forms of resistance against power and domination that is itself generalized.

The formation of a collective identity or group image also involves, on a slightly different level, the "exposure" of the contents of the motivational level of consciousness. Since the actions of individuals are motivated, rationalized and reflexively monitored, any penetration of the individuals' motivational structures by the system of domination will influence how action eventually will be carried out. Since people's motivations are structurally integrated through a common learning process and are an integral part of their identity, individuals seek to "restructure" their motivations with the aim of reformulating, redefining and confirming their new identities.

Interestingly, in some cases this entails an emphasis on direct participation in the political process and a concomitant rejection of third-party representation.* The refusal to accept political mediation is

---

* Melucci (1988: 258–59) noted that participation means taking part in promoting one's self-interest. Participation entails belonging to a system, and this belonging is the enjoyment of the benefits of an identity. Representation, by contrast, means remaining different and never being heard entirely; the enjoyment of the benefits of one's identity is deferred or prevented.

based on the notion that the mechanisms of control and manipulation against which the struggle is directed in the first place will simply be reproduced, albeit on a smaller scale (Offe 1985: 829). It has been argued that the core institutions and mechanisms of the political system, e.g., the parties, parliaments, elections and unions have simply lost some of their capacity to provide collective identities and solidarities (J. Cohen 1983: 99). Direct action and direct participation, and the need for spontaneous, anti-authoritarian and anti-hierarchical forms of organization is important. Some form of political representation and some level of participation is essential for a movement's credibility and viability (Melucci 1985: 815, A. Scott 1990: Chapter 6).

Finally, another feature of some of the new movements is that they are not necessarily always focused on the political system. Characteristically, the movements are not oriented towards taking political power or taking over the state (Melucci 1981: 180), but towards expanding an individual's or group's autonomy and independence from different technical and professional systems of domination. In those instances where a movement might be politically oriented, the goal is to increase the possibilities for direct political participation by trying to open new channels for the expression of demands and needs, and to create new forms of participation in policy-making areas.

The goal of new social movement actors is to try to "revitalize" the life-world by deflecting the often hard-felt impact of the economic and political/administrative subsystems. Participation in the larger social system is based on interaction that might presuppose a particular type of discourse and way of communicating, but whose rationality consciously is rejected. Deflecting the impact of this rationality entails monitoring and trying to change not only the process or means of communication, but also the ways people interact and deal with each other. All these are elements and important aspects of the community-building process.

Social Movement as Learning and Becoming

The independent living/disabled consumer movement should not be regarded just as a social reform movement or just as a minority rights movement. Rather, the movement is first and foremost a *process* by which "rehabilitated" bodies and minds, "spoiled" identities and the deeply "colonized" behavioral and motivational structures of disabled individuals are being reclaimed and reappropriated (Giddens 1991: 99–103).

The independent living/disabled consumer movement is contentionist in approach and its goals essentially integrationist. The meaning of the movement is best understood in terms that make explicit reference to the structuring of personal and collective identity, autonomy and interests. Handicapping based on widely shared social designations, the category of disability and even acquiesence to the medical/rehabilitation model all constitute *learned* behavior patterns. Simply stated, domination and subordination is learned behavior, and this behavior is embedded in the consciousness of disabled as well as nondisabled individuals, and becomes an integral part of their motivational patterns. Empowerment in its motivational and relational dimensions constitutes an unlearning and then a relearning process.

In modern society systems of domination have come to operate by manipulating and embedding specific needs, desires, values and a particular world-view into the motivational patterns of individuals. Successful domination is sustained by carefully perpetuating and reinforcing these internalized dominant values, beliefs and interests. The persistence of deviant designations and of social categories is testimony to the power of meaning and the role it plays in the reproduction and maintenance of interactions, relations and structures. The effect of this "internal colonization" is that the participatory competence of individuals is curtailed severely. The marginalization, isolation, dependency and powerlessness that is directly experienced by disabled people can be understood as the structural outcome of both *externally* and *self-imposed* physical and psychological constraints.

The whole point of the independent living/disabled consumer movement and the struggle to regain control over the setting, context and circumstances of disabled people's self-production is to increase the awareness of the conditions imposed on their actions in order to act upon them. The empowerment of disabled individuals involves not only the restructuring of motivation and a relearning of interaction skills, but their resocialization into beliefs, needs and interests that are different from those held by others. Empowered individuals must become capable of "sensing" how their wants, interests and options in life are limited and reinforced by their very articulation. What is important in the empowerment process and in social movement is that they eventually act, individually and collectively, on the knowledge they have acquired (Gadacz 1987).

Empowerment is a process of becoming, an enabling and transforming process that is constructed and achieved through action and practice. It is movement from a feeling or actual position of powerlessness to one where control and power can be exercised. The process is not directly observable, but its effects or results are. This "emergence" is a learning process, involving a necessarily progressive development of participatory skills and political understandings. Individuals are not just acquiring new skills in becoming empowered, rather, they are reorienting deeply engrained systems of relations with those who claim to "know better." Remarkably, disabled people often are involved in this process in precisely the same environments and contexts which enforce their oppression, and which continue active and implicit attempts to maintain that oppression.

The learning and becoming process subsequently extends to the more conscious and active development of peer support relationships within a caring community of peers and friends. Over time, and through ongoing efforts, individuals will be able to construct more viable strategies for action, come up with more effective mechanisms for collective expression and support, and develop more sophisticated capacities for resource development. The eventual development of a grassroots organizational setting with peers is considered vital in cultivating social and political skills (Berger and Neuhaus 1977). A grassroots organization provides individuals with a sense of strength in numbers and an organizational setting in which individuals can collaborate in mutually supportive problem-solving.

More effective coping skills and technical organizing and leadership skills are eventually developed. Participatory competence is realized only in the context of direct action, which means the creation of new situations and contexts for further action by combining acquired knowledge with other kinds of resources. New situations for direct action that might be called empowering solutions include the formation of consumer groups, self-help service groups, networks and the development of service brokerage models and independent living centres.

III
Implementing Change

5

Organizing for Empowerment
The Disabled Consumer Organization

The independent living/disabled consumer movement as a social movement is a particular means of reappropriating and restructuring a people's social reality. Social movement must be seen in terms of what it is, not only what it does. The activities of movements, including the independent living/disabled consumer movement, are part of what are called autopoieses, that is, self-creation (Zolo 1990). Self-creation in the disabled consumer movement refers to the practice of independent living in self-made contexts. This is a crucial aspect of the ongoing community-building process because community structures and institutions are self-made. Anything less than participation in the process would mean imposed structures, segregated community living and second-class citizenship.

According to Melucci (1985), a social movement is an action system operating within a systemic field of opportunities as well as constraints. The ways individuals build or constitute their actions, that is, their organizations, serves to establish links between meaning, orientation and the systemic field. The way the movement is structured and organized is an important factor in understanding its meaning within the larger community and the social order. Without being structured, collective action probably would not be possible; action would have neither unity nor would it be continuous. At the same time, any attempts to define or create structures by disabled people requires that they consciously shape and define their action.

The organization of social movement does not necessarily have to be identified with any particular formal structure. While the empirical forms of collective action might be legitimate objects of inquiry, they have no meaning apart from the movement and so constitute only one level of inquiry (Touraine 1981, Tilly 1984: 305–15, 1985: 731–37). The empirical forms also would not make sense without accounting for the mobilization of resources (the allocation of material, funds, capabilities, values, decisions) and leadership and membership issues. However, these are not the "causes" of collective action, movement or community-building, and so cannot solely be considered points of departure for analysis.

Social movement is the struggle for change and innovation in community life and the struggle to participate actively in that change. On a practical level, disabled consumers must face society in ways in which they can sustain their demands and actions. Struggling against particular systems of domination and presenting conflictual demands means that action must also be strategic, consistent and continuous. The development of a movement is not the consequence of any internal logic of a particular organization or group's development. Rather, it corresponds to a continuous two-way process by which the system of domination the movement is trying to transform checks, absorbs and deals with the challenges and innovations the movement members have come up with. In this process, the movement and the community influence and change each other.

For action-oriented disabled individuals, this means that they have to choose a certain logic of action. They have to select one sense or kind of action among a number of possibilities—while leaving room for improvisation and innovation (Tilly 1984: 307–8). They also have to fulfill all the instrumental and mundane requirements of organized action. Community-building must "oscillate" between the level of pure demands or pure expressive action and the level of group or institutionalized action. The spirit and vision of integrated community living for the movement would be sacrificed were action to be located at either of these extremes. Instead, it is only when a position somewhere midway between the two extremes is taken that fruitful interaction is possible.

For the independent living/disabled consumer movement, the logic of the community-building process that is adopted is determined by what it means to be a consumer and by what it means to be living independently. Consumerism from the point of view of disabled people involves making the disabled consumer the central factor in the "production" process. Production is the transformation of people as objects into subjects within a framework of social relations; it involves the re-creation of social and community relations, as well as the biological and personal identities of individuals. In reorienting social relationships, in form and in content, the production/consumption process is best conceived as the reorganization and reorientation of community relations for the satisfaction of individual and collective needs.

The empowering solutions adopted by some disabled people are the instrumental means by which their independent living needs and those of other members of the community can be satisfied. At the same time, the structures created by disabled people represent the challenge of "pure expressive action" in articulated form. The empirical forms of the disabled consumer movement are the context in which the process of organizing and strategic community-building can be looked at systematically.

From Objects to Subjects: Empowerment and Agency

Guided by the independent living philosophy, the disabled community and its members must recognize the dialectic between objective conditions and subjectivity. The subjective aspect exists only in relation to the objective aspect. "Subjectivity and objectivity thus join in a dialectical unity producing knowledge in solidarity with action and vice-versa," according to Freire (1984: 22). A raised consciousness is based on a growing solidarity between people as subjects. As Freire states, subjects know and act, while objects are known and acted upon. Subjects know their social world and continually act to transform it, while objects merely consume aspects of their social world and exist to reproduce it. Disabled persons within the medical model would not be unlike commodities, "things" manufactured to maintain and reproduce a certain social reality. By contrast, subjects are dynamic and are participants as well as consumers and producers. The transformation of objects into subjects, of clients or patients into producers/consumers is what Freire calls *praxis*.

Freire suggests that oppressed people, perhaps more than others, have a direct interest in transforming their world, that their interest, premised on ideas of justice and freedom, inherently is part of their humanity. The oppressed have what Freire calls an ontological vocation, that is, they are immersed in a natural struggle "to recover their lost humanity." They may not completely be unaware that they are downtrodden, but only that their perception of themselves is impaired by the reality in which they are submerged. They have the feeling that they are being judged and held accountable for "the way they are."

> I also had to deal with the way other people felt. What happens to people with hidden disabilities is that others are very angry at them. The anger is not shown directly because this is not socially acceptable. Each disability has a different social situation. For a person with a hidden disability it can be very hard because people don't see you as trying, they see you as giving up (Jill Weiss, COPOH 1987d: 16).

Championing the work of Paulo Freire, disabled individuals recognize that changes in themselves or in society will never take place without their own direct involvement in changing the conditions and circumstances of their oppression (Henry Enns, speech at the 1986 Alberta Committee's annual general meeting; see also Simpson 1980: 3). Some action-oriented disabled people have come to learn and understand that they have internalized their oppression that is now part of their identities, and so catch glimpses of themselves submerged in a reality not of their own making.

In order to prepare themselves for the struggle to reconnect to social/historical reality, "they must perceive the reality of oppression, not as a closed-world from which there is no exit, but as a limiting situation which they can transform" (Freire 1984: 34, Ortner 1984: 152–53). Many disabled people have come to realize that injustice, domination and oppression are mutable historical facts, and are not aspects of an underlying and immutable natural order. With respect to social and physical barriers to independence and integration, "a corollary of the barrier-free environment is that social and cultural settings *can effectively be changed*" (Alberta Committee 1981b: 20, emphasis added).

Disabled persons recognize their domination as having two dimensions. First, objectively, there is the power relation and structure between doctors, rehabilitation health care professionals, service providers, agency personnel and the disabled community. Second, subjectively and reflexively, they see that the way they express and present themselves as disabled people as a category of people is a reflection of this asymmetrical relation (Zola 1983a). The latter refers to the continuous communication of pathology or illness, inability, incompetence, deviance and fault. Writes Irving Zola (1983a: 57),

> [W]e who have chronic diseases and disabilities must see to our own interests. We must free ourselves from the physicality of our conditions and the domination of medical professionals. . . . In particular, I refer to the number of times we think of ourselves, and are thought of by others, in terms of our specific conditions. . . . Whatever else this does, this distracts our attention from our common social disenfranchisement. Our forms of loss may be different, but the resulting invalidity is the same.

The primary theoretical model or paradigm that is imposed on disabled people is the medical/rehabilitation one. This model is seen, especially by those disabled individuals who have become empowered, as essentially closed-ended and static; the world of the disabled person seems to revolve around an axis having diagnosis and medication/therapy as its endpoints. In this circle of certainty, as Freire describes it, there is nowhere for the disabled person to go. The disabled person merely becomes a "better" disabled person or patient, and so less of a whole human being. It is exactly this world, this circle, that the disabled individual must see critically and from which his or her "escape" must be planned.

Part of recognizing the experiential dimension of submergence requires that its omnipotence be grasped fully. Enmeshed in the medical/rehabilitation approach, disabled people must learn that their behaviors and their very consciousness is shaped by role expectations; they recognize that the circle of behavior-consciousness-behavior is fixed and closed—it goes nowhere, except back to reinforce itself and the social context that created it. Transformation requires reconnection to an objective world where oppression might be of a different order, but that can probably be dealt with directly. In a sense, the oppression of the closed world of the medical model has to be exchanged for the discrimination and oppression of the larger community. Zola (1983b: 352–53) states:

> The world in which we live is not always safe, secure, and predictable. It does not always say "please" or "excuse me." Every day there is a possibility of being thrown up against a situation where we may have to risk everything, even our lives. This is the REAL world. We must work to develop every human resource within us in order to prepare for these days. To deny any retarded [physically disabled] person his fair share of risk experience is to further cripple him for healthy living. . . . An environment or device that prevents any kind of risk produces not a real life but a mirage of one. There is human dignity in risk. There can be dehumanizing indignity in safety.

Subjective revalidation is possible only through a process of rehumanization, of becoming an actual participant in producing the complete social world. This is a learning process that can only be begun by disabled persons who are not so submerged, who have had the opportunity to reflect critically about their domination and oppression or that of their fellows. Their leadership and work in the wider disabled community revolves around the efforts of identifying aspects of the no-exit reality, in order to show how it is a product of the manipulation of resources, rules and so of interactions between people. The focus of this limit-setting activity by individuals, as Freire calls it, is to learn to see reality as permeable.

> I suddenly hated all the manhandling—being lowered into the water by someone else with everyone on the beach looking on. All of my plumbing (catheter and leg bag) were exposed. I became

acutely aware that I did not have the beautiful body that you see on T.V.

Yeah, there are big bodies, little bodies, straight bodies, and not so straight bodies. With us the old locker room concerns about penis size and breast size become very insignificant.

We both laughed and proceeded to compare notes on experiences we have had as persons with disabilities. Many sessions followed where we talked about and experimented with various coping mechanisms we used, to deal with everyday problems. . . . I realized how important it was for a person with a disability to have the experience of meeting and talking with another person with a disability (Patricia Sisco, COPOH 1987d: 105).

Reflection on reality and the disabled person's experience in it is initiated through what Freire calls dialogue and what disabled consumers call peer counselling—the mutual identification of specific problems, complaints and issues by involvement with peers. How and why do things happen as they do? Who benefits the most from current arrangements? In this process, the disabled individual is legitimated and validated as a critical commentator about his or her own situation, while at the same time his or her own questions and concerns are elevated to a more general, collective, level where action might be contemplated.

Part of the process of empowerment involves examining the relationship between the situations people find themselves in, and their perceptions of themselves in those situations. Considering that the "situations" by and large constitute the therapy/service/consuming activities of the disabled individual, it is precisely these that become the focus of inquiry. What the professionals and experts of the health care/health service industry want "obscured" now becomes the focal point for reflexive observation and the starting point for critical debate and purposive action. What previously was immutable and inevitable now becomes alterable. The next step might be to locate these consuming activities in the larger contexts of law and legislation, policy decisions, regulations, court decisions and program funding. These are targeted for reflexive monitoring and strategic intervention.

Those within the disabled community who are committed to an empowerment action orientation probably would agree that one of the most critical needs of human beings is the need to be a creative and effective participant in one's environment (Rose and Black 1985: 57–60). To act upon the social world and to transform it, thereby creating new possibilities for expressing one's individual and collective interests invokes Giddens's idea of the dialectic of control. An empowerment action orientation sees disabled human beings as potentially capable of critical intervention into their own realities.

In direct contrast to the unidirectional or unilateral aspect of rehabilitation practice, empowerment and independent living involves coming up with different strategies that are designed to address the independent and community living needs of disabled people in both the objective/social and subjective/emotional dimensions. These strategies should focus on the development and implementation of service programs, specialized and accessible community housing, accessible transportation, attendant care and daily living skills training. Successful implementation would generate a measure of validation, support and legitimacy for disabled individuals, on both an individual and collective basis. In turn, validation and legitimacy not only alter self-concept, but also influence the ability to exercise control over the objective conditions thrust upon and endured by disabled people.

"A Voice of Our Own": The Disabled Consumer Organization

Disabled organizers emphasize that consumer organizations, groups or group coalitions are essentially modelled after the major political structures of the community and of society. Disabled consumers insist that some degree of parallelism is essential in providing an effective consumer balance to existing structures. This is in keeping with the independent living/disabled consumer movement's contentionist orientation and its integrationist stance. Comments Allan Simpson (1980: 23),

> It is essential for consumers to gain an appreciation of how group dynamics, consensus building, group sharing and internal decision-

making procedures are evolved and implemented at the political/bureaucratic levels. The individual must learn how the political system works. . . .

Disabled consumer advocacy organizations do not directly provide hard or technical services (for example, equipment and devices, prosthetics, pharmaceuticals, transport systems, career training or housing). Instead, they provide *information* about these and other things such as consumer education, ongoing research into developing technology, and available programs and policies. They do so in order to empower disabled individuals to participate in the community and in society, and to become partners in policy decision-making processes at all levels.

Despite the historically activist profiles of some disabled organizations in Alberta and other provinces, their goal and purpose has never been to take political power or to usurp state power. On the contrary, the disabled community seeks institutional reform and revision, not revolution: "Confrontation tactics and absolutist ideologies will be avoided by the Canadian Disabled Consumer Movement" (Derksen 1980: 18). The disabled consumer movement can best be described as an institutional reform movement. This implies the continuity of present structures: "Consultation and cooperation, not confrontation" became a key action phrase by the end of the 1970s.

To link disabled people effectively to each other as well as to the larger system, parallel/alternative and cross-disability consumer organizations are the most successful in operationalizing the goals of the independent living model. Cross-disability representation is essentially a 1980s phenomenon; until then almost all organizations of the disabled were single-disability in orientation, with the disabled population as a whole largely unorganized and without a collective consciousness (Kallen 1989: 146–47). Disabled persons have found it increasingly necessary to work within the framework of parallel organizational structures in order to learn about organizational dynamics and to develop skills transferable to and useful in the general community. Similarly, the disabled and nondisabled need to work through shared and familiar structures in order to understand their mutual needs. How else could community be achieved anyway?

A more formal consumer organizational model consists of the

authority and organizational structure that typically is centralized around a president, an executive director, an elected board of directors, committees (executive, finance/budget) and hired staff. The membership component consists of paid-up active individual and associate members and with representation from other organizations. Membership policy directions are generally established at meetings, conferences and at the annual general meeting. Board members and appointed executive officers are authorized to coordinate the members' policies and resources, and to implement detailed strategies for specific approaches to the political level. The general membership can become involved directly through research committees or specific action sub-groups.

In addition to office business, the executive director, administration staff and office assistants may carry out actual research, gather information and disseminate it on the request of members as well as the public. They may also produce a newsletter and manage a working library. An association usually operates under established procedures including published by-laws and/or a charter, and detailed policy/job descriptions; it provides an excellent context for individuals to learn basic and essential administrative skills, and to gain some democratic decision-making experience.

Alternatively, local consumer action groups usually have a more dynamic informal structure, one that is coordinated by a few experienced individuals rather than formally structured. Under this model, all members are encouraged to unite and concentrate on one or two fundamental issues at any one point in time. At conferences, open assemblies or similar such forums, issues or organizational goals are presented for discussion and adoption by the membership. Efforts are directed at involving the entire membership in planning as well as implementing strategies. The assembled membership modifies and approves position statements and plans of action; both the statements and the strategies can be drafted first by a research committee and elected board members, or they can be the outcome of workshops held at conferences. Tasks can be assigned by the assembly to various sub-groups, who in turn work within agreed upon time frames.

This type of flexible organization provides a context for total involvement, sharing and a means of producing "a broad group of informed leaders" within and across the entire membership. Consequently, greater internal accountability reflects the enabling process of empowerment in which the whole organizational membership is involved. Members work closely with one another, and develop strong sensitivities to the needs and interests of others in different disability groups.

Cross-disability involvement and focus is significant because it is a direct effort to counteract and overcome the fragmenting consequences of the medical/rehabilitation model. The focus on disability and on the patient results not only in the decontextualization of individuals but in the creation of categories of individuals and their social separation or alienation from each other. The movement's cross-disability focus and its coalition structure serves to unite and integrate what has in essence been a fragmented community. This process of integration in the context of organizational involvement has consequences for the empowerment of those involved, and signals the beginning of the community-building process.

In the more formal organizational model there is a greater tendency to rely more on the formal leadership to approve a plan or strategy, and on an office staff to do the technical work. Being left out or not knowing one's role in the organization can often be the result of this type of arrangement. Central staff, separate from the group's members, could conceivably become a competitive force within the organization. In the formal model, impatience can develop on the part of the board and other elected officers to get consensus and have issues resolved quickly as they often work against timetables set by others over which they have minimum control. Individual empowerment may not be possible under these circumstances, and more formal structures are probably useful in some cases.

In reality, consumer groups find it desirable to utilize a combination of these two organizational approaches. Formalized board representative elections through annual meetings, combined with administrative coordination by a board executive and hired staff, allow for special meetings to plan, initiate, adopt or implement new policy resolutions. The more informal structure, clearly an effective and motivating form of membership involvement, allows for greater grassroots participation and the articulation of issues of immediate concern.

With this combination, members are more motivated and derive greater meaning from the process of learning how to cooperate in the decision-making process. Individuals share in the creative process of organizing themselves. This process is simultaneously a vital part of community-building because it is an ongoing organizing activity.

Members of the consumer group depend not so much on their elected officers for leadership, but look to *themselves* as "leaders in the larger community." Integral to the empowerment process, as a social and cultural process, is dialogue or mutual communication. Members recognize that they share concerns in common, that joint action promises more benefits than working apart, that the means to accomplish resolution and consensus-building ensures their participation that is required to move on issue positions, and, finally, that each member has a part to play in the creative process.

Combinations of these organizational types may be found at the various levels of consumer organization, though the structures tend towards the more formal at the provincial, national and international levels, and towards the more informal at the local or community level. The local consumer group serves as a setting for individual self-development, growth and confidence-building, and as a vehicle for leadership development. It also could be seen as a low-level communications system that links the smallest elements of the disabled community to one another and provides a means of linking or bridging the disabled to other communities.

From the point of view of action theory, a small local consumer group is a coordinating action network for individuals and other uni-disability advocacy and semi-service/self-help groups. There are over 700 of these small local uni-disability groups in Alberta, including Cleft Lip and Palate Clinic, Deaf and Hard of Hearing Services, Multiple Sclerosis Society, and Arthritis Society. The coalition is "the most important implementation structure" in the independent living/disabled consumer movement (Simpson 1980: 16). At this level, practical community service delivery systems and benefits for individuals can be realized through local action. The local consumer coalition group often demonstrates on specific issues, lobbies elected and appointed officials, and directly negotiates with various community and political leaders who are responsible for delivering specific public and private services.

A provincial consumer group is a "coordinating action structure/coalition" comprised of individuals and numerous local-issue/uni- and cross-disability consumer groups as well as semi-service organizations. The Alberta Committee of Citizens With Disabilities includes Employment Services for the Physically Disabled, Handicapped Housing Society, and Alberta Association for the Deaf. Provincial consumer groups are necessarily more formally structured. The provincial coalition is "the most effective and important strategy coordinating arm" of the independent living/disabled consumer movement, since it has both the geographic and jurisdictional scope to involve fully individual members in the region, and the technical/funding means to support and mobilize local and small groups, even in rural areas. The provincial organization also organizes marches and demonstrations, and conducts extensive consultation, political lobbying and monitoring activities at the provincial level.

At the national level, the Coalition of Provincial Organizations of the Handicapped is comprised of all the provincial consumer organizations and also enjoys the cooperation of well established national organizations and associations including the Canadian Paraplegic Association, Canadian National Institute for the Blind, the Muscular Dystrophy Association of Canada, the Canadian Cancer Society, and the Canadian Down Syndrome Society. The purpose of the national coalition is to focus on major national human rights legislation, and legislation covering the direction and funding of vital and major policy areas as transportation, housing, education, employment, social security, rehabilitation services and independent living support systems.

As a national voice of the disabled, the coalition's goal includes acting as a representative (cross-disability) body at the federal level. COPOH, for example, works closely and directly with the Canadian Association of Independent Living Centres (CAILC), the federal government's Standing Committee on Human Rights and the Status of Disabled Persons, the Public Service Commission, numerous federal government ministries and departments (for example, Canada Employment and Immigration, Health and Welfare, Treasury Board), the Canadian Labor Congress, and other bodies.

Beyond the national level, Disabled Peoples' International (DPI) is an international cross-disability coalition of people with both mental and physical disabilities (COPOH is part of that coalition). Conceived in Winnipeg at the 1980 World Congress of Rehabilitation International, DPI was established formally in Singapore one year later at its first World Congress. The first World Council was also elected DPI there. It now holds Congresses every four years. In 1982 a delegation from DPI made a presentation concerning world-wide human rights abuses of disabled people to the United Nations Subcommission on Discrimination and Protection of Minorities in Geneva. The result was that in 1983 the United Nations Economic and Social Council recommended, and agreed to, consultative status for DPI within the U.N. framework. The Head Secretariat is in Stockholm and its Development Office is in Winnipeg. This office's development program organizes leadership training seminars in Africa, Asia, Latin America and the Caribbean (Driedger 1989).

Organizations of disabled people from almost seventy countries are represented on the World Council; DPI has divided the world into five regions and is working to develop an infrastructure of regional assemblies and councils. DPI's interest is in mobilizing disabled people in North America and Europe in order to raise awareness of, strengthen support for, and empower their brothers and sisters in Third World and developing countries. There is considerable interest in the treatment programs and medical systems that exist or that might be lacking and could be developed in these countries and how they impact on the disabled. Also on the international scene, the first-ever International Conference of Ministers Responsible for the Status of Persons with Disabilities was held in Montreal in 1992. A result of this was the establishment of a permanent Conference of Ministers, charged to help the United Nations' World Program of Action concerning Disabled Persons (Canadian Human Rights Commission 1992: 39).

Whether at the local, provincial, national or international level of organization, disabled consumers make an important distinction: Their organizations are "of," rather than "for" disabled people. A group "of" disabled persons is made up and controlled by disabled persons, with respect to structure, policy and program decisions, and external representation. "For" implies control by nondisabled persons or disabled persons who are not consumers, with externally produced policies and programs/services aimed at disabled individuals without their input. Precisely this is an aspect of the medical model that disabled people reject outright. COPOH's national coordinator to the Standing Committee on Justice and Legal Affairs in 1982 stated:

> We are an organization OF disabled persons as opposed to FOR disabled persons. We are based on the philosophy of citizen participation and self-representation. We believe in our society there has been a tendency for nondisabled persons to speak on behalf of disabled persons, and essentially what we are saying is that disabled persons have the right to represent themselves (Minutes of the Proceedings and Evidence of the Standing Committee, 1982, Issue No. 115: 9, op. cit. in COPOH n.d., page 7).

Alberta Committee of Citizens With Disabilities

In Alberta the disabled consumer movement came under the leadership of a well organized and tough-minded provincial alliance organization that had been active since the early 1970s. Founded in 1973 under the name Alberta Committee of Action Groups of the Disabled, it was a merger of two local organizations, the Edmonton Action Group, and Disabled on the Move from the city of Lethbridge. Percy Wickman, one-time president of the Committee in its formative years, past national chairperson of COPOH, an Edmonton alderman, and a Liberal MLA, remembers the decision to form an action group:

> Frustrated by the failure of established agencies to bring about necesary change, this group was determined to do it for themselves. Why not—what the hell—it's our lives that are affected—why shouldn't we determine our own course?

According to the Alberta Committee's (1980a) historical notes,

> The Alberta Committee was the first group in Canada adopting the philosophy of groups of disabled people working towards improving the lifestyles of disabled people. For a number of years, it was the only organization in Canada intervening on behalf of disabled people.... The Committee is one of the leaders in self-advocacy.

The movement gained significant momentum when, later in 1975, the Alberta Committee played a key role in forming a unique body, the MLA/Handicapped Joint Committee.

In particular the MLA/Handicapped Joint Committee has provided a forum for the exchange of ideas as well as an important communication link between the disabled and the legislators. That Committee was formed as a direct result of a luncheon held in November, sponsored by the Edmonton Action Group of the Disabled and attended by forty members of the Legislative Assembly (statement by [former] Alberta Premier Peter Lougheed, February 12, 1979, cited in Alberta Committee 1980a).

This committee consisted of five disabled consumers, and included the Ministers of Labor, Advanced Education, Social Services and Community Health, as well as the Leader of the Official Opposition and the Leader of the New Democratic Party. They met approximately four times a year, from 1975 until the Joint Committee disbanded in 1979, to discuss and implement policies, services and programs relevant to persons with disabilities.

Consultation led to the successful implementation of programs, services and amending legislation that included Assured Income for the Severely Handicapped (AISH), Alberta Aids to Daily Living (AADL), Alberta Home Adaptations Program (AHAP) and even the Alberta Human Rights Protection Act. It was this cooperation and success that helped establish the credibility of both the Alberta Committee and of the greater independent living/disabled consumer movement.

By 1980 the Alberta Committee had accomplished even more. It was one of three founding groups of COPOH, the Coalition of Provincial Organizations of the Handicapped, with which almost every other local and provincial organization in the ten provinces and territories eventually became affiliated. Five years of consultations, two major provincial conferences, dozens of briefs to the Alberta Legislative Assembly, the Premier, various legislative committees, the Alberta and Canadian Human Rights Commissions and other federal and provincial bodies resulted in the acceptance of the Alberta Committee's suggestions for amending the Alberta Individual Rights Protection Act (the IRPA became law on September 1, 1980) to include the rights of physically disabled individuals. However, not until 1990 did the rights of mentally handicapped individuals become protected under Alberta legislation.

By early 1981 the Alberta Committee was faced with a number of issues that led it to question its future policy orientation and activities. Was the organization to tie its policies to wider human rights and consumer issues, or was it to continue as an action-oriented group concerned solely with solving the problems of individual consumers as they arose? Having established strong community and government ties and having accomplished many of its original goals, the Alberta Committee was forced to prioritize its concerns and objectives, lest it offend a friendly government and an enlightened citizenry. As a sign of the organization's maturity and prominent place among the province's policy communities, and most certainly in recognition of the importance of maintaining image, it changed its name that year to the Alberta Committee of Consumer Groups of Disabled Persons.

Under the new name and entering its twelfth year of operation, a great deal more was being accomplished. Between 1984 and 1986 the Committee made submissions and oral presentations to the Alberta Committee on Tolerance and Understanding (under authority of the province's Minister of Education), the Special Committee on Participation of Visible Minorities in Canadian Society (which produced the report *Equality Now*), Judge Abella's Royal Commission of Inquiry on Equality in Employment, the (federal) Sub-Committee on Equality Rights of the Standing Committee on Justice and Legal Affairs (*Equality for All*) and, finally, to the Royal Commission on the Economic Union and Development Prospects for Canada (known as the Macdonald Commission).

The Committee's slogan "from grassroots to full participation" was given a second interpretation, which was to mean the participation of disabled and nondisabled individuals in the independent living/disabled consumer movement. By 1985 participation and board as well as executive membership had been extended to include nondisabled people as well as the continued representation of a cross-section of disabilities (the deaf, hearing impaired, blind, visually impaired, amputees, mobility disabled, and those with mental and emotional disabilities). The board maintains a two-thirds majority in favor of disabled persons. The eventual inclusion of the nondisabled—or the "temporarily able-bodied" (TABS) as they are referred to by the disabled—was described by Committee members as a clear sign of greater maturity and independence on the part of the organization. Independence might better be understood to mean interdependence; hence the invited involvement, full cooperation and separate but equal partnership of the temporarily able-bodied. The Alberta Committee made it clear that control of the organization would always rest solely with the disabled.

In late 1985 the organization once again changed its name to the Alberta Committee of Disabled Citizens, reflecting its politics, its empowered position and the spirit of cooperation established in the community and province. Significant developments in Alberta in the late 1980s included the establishment in March 1986 of the Edmonton City Council Citizens Task Force For Physically Disabled Persons, and the final formation of a Premier's Council on the Status of Disabled Persons in 1989.

The Committee's logo depicts a solitary oak tree, profiled above and below the surface of the ground. The roots are the strongest part of the tree: This is representative of the disabled consumer movement where its strength lies in the grassroots participation of individual members. Shown as tall and sturdy with leaves even though the limbs are missing on one side, the suggestion is that disabled people who have impairments are able to contribute and participate in society, and that they are growing stronger—as the consumer movement is. Finally, the single acorn on the tree depicts the new growth and the small groups which have given birth to other, larger, ones.

The structure of the Committee includes a maximum 17-member (minimum of 7) volunteer, but elected, board of directors that collectively represents a cross-section of disabilities including the deaf and hearing disabled, blind and visually disabled, amputees, mobility disabled, and those with hidden physical, mental and emotional disabilities. This is essentially the Committee's policy-making body. One-third of this board can be made up of TABS (for example, spouses, immediate family, close friends and others, including health care and social service professionals), provided that their personal philosophy is compatible with the Committee's. The board elects an executive committee consisting of a president, vice-president, a secretary and a treasurer, and is also responsible for the formation of sub-committees including finance and budget, fundraising, the AGM committee, public relations and membership, building standards, independent living, human rights, transportation, disabled natives and disabled women and others. Each board member serves on at least one sub-committee, with the membership involved on a volunteer basis.

Core hired staff include an office administrator, a managing director that carries out the daily business of the Alberta Committee between meetings and takes policy statements from the minutes of board meetings, and a research/communications officer who collects and disseminates information as requested by the membership and others. All are accountable directly to the board of directors. In addition, disabled consumers and others may be hired on a casual basis to do paper work, envelope-stuffing, photocopying, or on a seasonal basis (for example, summer students).

The goals of the Alberta Committee are to improve the quality of life of the disabled community through educational, legislative and policy change at all levels of government, using as the basis the philosophy of consumerism as articulated through the principles of independent living. The Committee acts as an empowering tool for individuals who join it and those who wish to form their own action groups. Since 1986, the Alberta Committee has helped to open small "affiliate" offices elsewhere in Alberta. It sees its role as developing informed consumers, who can be the best judge as to what their barriers to independence might be, and what solutions and services are needed and might be developed.

In its advocacy role, defined as representing the rights and interests of oneself and/or other individuals, and speaking on one's own or others' behalf, the Alberta Committee does not offer any services such as equipment or residential options. It fulfills its mandate through the following set of soft service objectives. These are the building blocks or resources of community-building and empowerment:

(1) Information Production and Distribution

According to the Alberta Committee, "the process of informing is the function of organizations of disabled persons." The Alberta Committee handles a wide variety and large volume of requests for information from service agencies, private as well as public, government offices, the general public and disabled individuals. Information that is requested ranges from employment equity legislation, different sources of income, specific service providers and their quality, availability of technical aides, social support services, access to transportation, to finding out which local restaurants and office buildings are accessible to the mobility impaired. To make intelligent and relevant decisions, disabled consumers clearly need current accurate information; office staff endeavor to provide it. In interviews with the press and other media, policy positions formulated by the membership and by the board are explained in detail.

Information and the knowledge that is gained is recognized as crucial to the elimination or reduction of barriers that "wedge themselves" between independence and integration. The focus on information as a community resource for empowerment is stressed, for the reason that choices and decisions made with regards to services and lifestyles otherwise would not be informed ones.

> Information is a consumer product just as food is a consumer product. Information is also a consumer conditioner in the same analogous way as food is a consumer conditioner. Information, like food, can be either nourishing or debilitating, depending on what it is composed of and how it is prepared. It seems quite natural to pay careful attention to what foods we consumer and demand that those who produce and provide our food pay careful attention to its production and that they be accountable for their actions as regards food production.
>
> It is important that the same considerations be observed in the production, distribution and exchange of information. The quality of any product can be ensured directly by the participation in the production of the products; and/or indirectly by monitoring the production of the products preferably in cooperation with a responsive and accountable producer/provider (cited from the "Spokesman," in Alberta Committee 1981b: 20–21).

In its role as information broker or information "clearinghouse," the Committee publishes a quarterly newsletter ("Awareness is the Key" to 1991, "Alberta Citizen" since 1991) which it circulates around the province, emphasizing distribution in the rural and northern areas of Alberta. Used as an information/networking tool, the purpose is to keep the grassroots informed on many topic issues and up-coming social and political events. The Edmonton office maintains an active and specialized resource library of books, background research reports and briefs (government, private, and self-produced), legislation and newspaper articles which members and the public are free to use.

The Committee is an affiliate of the DISC network (Disability Information Services of Canada), operated from the Walter Dinsdale Centre (Calgary) and the University of Calgary, which is managed by staff, a management team and a national advisory committee. DISC is a national electronic information and communication network system that can be accessed by modem, upon subscription, either privately or from libraries, drop-in centres or other organizations/facilities. Through the use of electronic bulletin boards, ever-developing databases, electronic mailing and conferencing, individual consumers, or those involved in outreach programs, rehabilitation, independent living and employment centres, government agencies, small businesses, physicians, bioengineers and other professionals can communicate with each other, and importantly, with consumers as well. Extensive use is made of this network by many individuals; networking is an obvious empowering tool in the community-building process.

(2) Public Awareness and Consumer Education

As part of its community-building efforts, the Alberta Committee seeks to raise relevant issues at all levels of government through the process of ongoing research and written and oral presentations to elected and appointed officials, including school board representatives, municipal government representatives, local business-Chamber of Commerce people, service club officers and many others. It initiates, conducts and organizes workshops, seminars, public speaking events and public awareness campaigns on an annual or ongoing basis in order to increase the profile and visibility of the disabled community and the consumer movement, as well as to identify the physical and attitudinal barriers in issues including housing, employment, transportation, recreation, education and public facilities. The Committee's AGM is organized usually around a theme featuring a keynote speaker from a relevant policy area, and includes a series of session workshops. One popular theme was "Families in Transition—Dealing with Disabilities"; sessions were organized on family violence, sexual abuse of children and on the role of spouses and caregivers.

The Committee is clearly an image-building tool for the disabled community. Public awareness campaigns involve mall displays, posters, the preparation of audio-visual materials for loan purposes, "open house" on various organization premises which include group homes and co-op housing projects, public service announcements and press conferences. These are prepared, organized and conducted by disabled individuals. The goal is to at all times portray disabled individuals positively, living and working in the same variety of life circumstances as anyone else. Two prime examples of strategies for creating positive images of disabled people are the Positive Attitudes Towards the Handicapped (PATH) display and National Access Awareness Week (NAAW). The PATH display is a set of mural-posters, audio-visual and other educational materials organized by a group of agencies in Edmonton (since 1982), whose coordinating committee is chaired by the Alberta Committee. This educational display makes its annual rounds one or two days a year in shopping malls, community colleges and other post-secondary educational institutions.

The Alberta Comittee is also the Edmonton/northern Alberta regional National Access Awareness Week coordinating committee. A federal government initiative in recognition of Rick Hansen's "Man in Motion Tour," a national week of recognition and awareness for people with disabilities was declared in 1987 and organized by national, provincial and community-level committees. Since 1989, extensive awareness campaigns are presented, together with social and cultural events and sports activities, in all major Canadian cities in June. Part of the planning and coordinating network of committees, the Alberta Committee facilitates the flow of information from the national level to local communities, and helps establish steering/planning committees in smaller centres so individuals may further organize activities. The Alberta Committee also helps people to develop action plans that enable them to identify barriers that isolate disabled persons from full participation in community life (Secretary of State of Canada 1988a, 1988b, 1989–92).

A significant NAAW strategy adopted since 1988 by many communities has been the creation of the Five Star Community: This monitoring program is conducted by the disabled and nondisabled, who are called "partners in community action." In a Five Star community, the five essential elements of community life—housing, employment, transportation, recreation and education—are rated in terms of availability/accessibility. Since these may mean something different to each person, the community as a whole attempts to identify the range of options that would encompass the needs of all its citizens.

Because there is no one system that possibly can provide access to all individuals, it is necessary to look at several options within each area. For example, accessible housing does not mean only houses or apartment buildings with ramps and wide doorways, but can also mean group homes and co-op housing that includes attendant care. Workplaces should be barrier-free and technical aids should be available. Employment equity programs should be available so that the disabled can successfully compete for nontraditional jobs on an equal basis with the nondisabled. Accessible transportation includes better access to the regular transportation system (taxis, buses, planes, trains), not just a separate or parallel one.

In education, classes could be integrated or specialized to meet the needs of a particular group of students, teacher's aides might be made available, and adapted transportation to and from school could be organized if it is needed and does not already exist. Similarly, specialized sports activities or "buddy" programs would ensure the participation of disabled children and adults in community leisure and recreation activities. These are all clearly means to community integration.

The task of the Alberta Committee is to sensitize and educate the public and other disabled people to the needs of the disabled who may live, sometimes isolated, right next door, and to make them aware of *who* the disabled are. The process of raising awareness, or image-building, on a wider community level includes efforts to change the way people talk about disability and refer to disabled persons. The Committee recognizes that language is a powerful tool; it can evoke images and ideas that strongly affect perceptions. Language use is clearly critical in changing attitudes about disability (see the Standing Committee on the Status of Disabled Persons, 1st Report, 1988). The whole range of human emotions, characteristics, and attributes that are applied to nondisabled persons should be shown to apply equally to disabled persons.

Disabled people should be treated with respect and dignity, and language that arouses fear, guilt, pity, suffering or abnormality should be avoided. An impairment or disability is a fact of life, and so should be recognized and referred to without embarrassment. Disabled people object strongly to using euphemisms to describe disabilities. The term "partially sighted," for example, implies avoiding the acceptance of blindness. Terms like "mentally different," "handicapable," or "differently able" are considered condescending. Other examples are (Secretary of State of Canada 1988b: 33–36):

INAPPROPRIATE	APPROPRIATE
the handicapped	disabled person(s)
cripple	physically challenged
spastic (noun)	person with cerebral palsy
deaf-and-dumb	person with impaired hearing
lame	mobility limited or impaired

Medical language should be avoided altogether, unless its use is appropriate to the topic of conversation. Reference to disease is acceptable only in the case of chronic diseases, such as arthritis, multiple sclerosis, cerebral palsy or Parkinson's and Alzheimer's. Disability that results from anatomical or physiological damage (for example, cerebral palsy and spina bifida) should be referred to directly. As well:

UNACCEPTABLE	ACCEPTABLE
invalid; infirm	person with...
patient; case	person with...
suffering from MS	person with MS
afflicted	caused by...
deformed	born with...

Technical aids should be referred to in a matter-of-fact way, rather than in emotional terms:

UNACCEPTABLE	ACCEPTABLE
confined to a wheelchair	wheelchair user
wheelchair-bound	"wheelie" (acceptable slang!)
gibbles around	person who uses crutches
home-bound	limited mobility

Finally, language should not pick out differences or make odious comparisons with nondisabled people; the living and working activities and circumstances of disabled people should be emphasized, rather than their impairments or disabilities. People should be mentioned first, rather than their particular functional limitation:

blind lawyer	lawyer with a visual impairment
disabled manager	manager with . . . an impairment
mentally retarded worker	worker with a mental handicap or who is developmentally disabled
sick; defective	person with a disability

In the Committee's research briefs, press releases, oral and written presentations and submissions, and brochures the emphasis on appropriate language use is evident. In the process of redefining just who disabled people are, specific language is utilized to show that particular impairments or disabilities do not in fact measure ability, that mental and physical disabilities really occur along continua, not unlike abilities, that disabled people do not constitute a homogenous group, and that functional impairments do not necessarily limit all other life functions. For example, blindness is a problem for driving, but not for playing the piano or practicing law. Attitudinal and perceptual barriers have just as great a negative effect on disabled people as physical and architectural ones. The removal of both kinds of barriers clearly contributes to the integration of disabled people and to their recognition as *persons*.

(3) Research

Research is the principal means by which information is gathered and processed. The research the Alberta Committee undertakes is determined as often by the needs expressed by its grassroots membership as by requests for input and consultation with the provincial and federal government, service providers and rehabilitation professionals. The most crucial topic areas include transportation, housing, employment, education and recreation. Research is conducted on the possible implications of existing legislation, services and programs on the well-being of disabled persons; as well, solicited and sometimes unsolicited research input might form the basis for the future development of proposed or pending programs, services and laws.

The research process usually is conducted by the research officer in cooperation with the information officer, library technician and the Committee's communications officer. The researcher officer's responsibilities include collecting studies relating to specific issues, drafting briefs as requested by the board and keeping the group up-to-date on developments regarding changes in legislation, programs and services. The information officer's job is to initiate and maintain personal contact with government, and to liaise with other local action groups as well as agencies regarding desirable legislative and policy changes related to the interests of disabled people. The communications person coordinates material on local and provincial concerns for the membership, and deals with the media. He or she also assists local actions groups research and write their own materials, and prepares press releases.

In this integrated process, these individuals have a very close working relationship with subcommittee members, who are in direct contact with the grassroots membership. The orientation and specific wording of briefs and other research items are reviewed and endorsed by the subcommittee, who may then submit the final product to board members for approval, adoption and presentation. In this way, briefs and reports to agencies, commissions of inquiry and task forces are considered to be "as close to representative of the points of view of the coalition membership as possible."

Research that the Alberta Committee has conducted since the 1970s has ranged from vocation and education integration, job adaptations, taxicab service, barriers to domestic air travel, voting in elections, income security, local architectural barriers and housing options. The results were presented to such bodies as the Alberta and Canadian Human Rights Commissions, Alberta Legislative Assemby, various legislative committees and ministers, task forces, the Canada Transport Commission and to such federal government appointed groups such as Judge Abella's Commission on Equality in Employment and the Macdonald Commission on Economic Union and Development. The pay-off is the Committee's ability to provide accurate and critical information when needed, the reputation it has earned for providing balanced perspectives on emotionally-charged issues, and its acknowledged leadership role among disabled people.

Over the past decade, the research briefs and reports the Committee prepared and submitted to the provincial government have led to specific programs that impacted positively on the quality of life of disabled Albertans. Examples of programs which have been implemented in Alberta since 1980 which reflect consumer input include Assured Income for the Severely Handicapped (AISH), Alberta Aids to Daily Living (AADL), and Alberta Home Adaptations Program (AHAP). Input that found its way into specific Alberta legislation, including amendments to existing laws, are the Individual Rights Protection Act, the Dependent Adult Act, the Social Development Act and the Incapacitated Voting Act.

An interesting example of the Committee's impact was Bill 27 which became Alberta's School Act [1988]. Uproar and controversy was raised by a specific clause in Bill 27 that would have had the effect of denying universal access to education to an individual deemed "noneducable," because of "a severe lack in intellectual functioning or severe medical fragility" (*Edmonton Journal*, May 7, 11, 1988). The Alberta Committee, in conjunction with other groups and individuals (e.g., Severe Handicaps Alliance for Public Education, the Liberal/New Democrat education critics, and students and staff in the Rehabilitation Studies program at the University of Calgary) prepared and submitted extensive documentation detailing the practical, legal, moral and political implications of the clause containing the phrase "noneducable." A persuaded minister of education subsequently rewrote the Act so that it would guarantee handicapped children universal access to programs and services to meet their education needs by way of a Special Needs Tribunal that would be established to facilitate the assessment process.

(4) Advocacy and Monitoring

Advocacy is considered an underlying theme of empowerment and of the independent living/disabled consumer movement, and is defined as providing individuals with assistance in presenting their situation to others who are often not supportive of their needs or position (Wolfensberger 1983). The primary focus of the Alberta Committee is to foster support for the establishment of local consumer-controlled initiatives by working directly with action groups, independent living and support groups and by representing them. The purpose of the advocacy process is to ensure that the needs of disabled persons are met through consultations with them, and with their cooperation and ongoing participation; the process involves a variety of actions and decision-making techniques, depending on what is being advocated. The rights and best interests of the disabled can be directly represented in actual service planning and provision processes. Professionals, paraprofessionals and other service providers can be advised, on behalf of the disabled person and his or her family, about specific needs-meeting strategies that might help that person achieve certain goals.

The idea of advocacy means the self-representation of individuals and speaking or acting on one's own or another's behalf. This is very much a reflexive activity. Ideally, disabled persons learn to eventually reassert control over their own particular concerns and aspects of their lives; this is the purpose behind the skills training workshops, conferences, seminars and research activities of the Committee. Self-representation is facilitated by and is the result of working relationships with government officials, service providers, the business community and the general public. Without a positive self-image of the abilities and contributions of disabled persons communicated through the advocacy process and the responsiveness of society, the empowerment/community-building process could never unfold or evolve.

The advocacy and monitoring process cannot be considered separately from each other, or from such needs-meeting strategies as natural support networks, brokerage, individual program planning (IPPs), and peer counselling. With some of these strategic solutions in place and a sensitized and informed public, the Committee may withdraw gradually from the advocacy role. Monitoring the services and programs with which an individual or small group of individuals is involved continues, ensuring their continued reciprocal involvement with those whose services have been contracted.

> We expect equal recognition and participation at all levels of government.... Alongside this expectation, the consumer organizations and their members must also be recognized as monitors, evaluators and creative critics of existing programs, services and policy models. Without such recognition, at least in terms of financial and manpower resources, research and innovative programs, policies and services cannot occur (Alberta Committee 1981b: 40).

Since late 1987, the Alberta Committee stepped up its monitoring and advocacy activities on three emerging critical areas: the concerns of northern/rural disabled citizens, women with disabilities and disabled Native Canadians. While all disabled people are disadvantaged in education, employment and income, these groups are significantly more disadvantaged and face additional unique problems. Not the least of these include physical isolation, total lack of resources and facilities, physical and sexual abuse, and lack of access to such generic facilities as women's programs and shelters.

As a result, the Committee has taken steps to prepare research reports on these issues, to liaise with Native organizations on and off reserves, and with such bodies as the Alberta Advisory Council on Women's Issues, the Alberta Status of Women Action Committee, establish contacts within generic agencies, organize co-joint workshops and consumer courses, and to encourage participation in and growth, for example, of such young national networks as DAWN (Disabled Women's Network) (Stone and Doucette 1988; Fine and Asch 1988; Lonsdale 1990). The formation of DAWN was in fact precipitated by disabled women breaking away from COPOH. Disabled women argued that COPOH did not adequately represent their interests and concerns. In May 1988, as part of its general awareness raising strategy, the Alberta Committee together with the National Film Board presented "The Impossible Takes a Little Longer" in Edmonton, a film about disabled women. This premiere was followed by a forum, moderated by the vice-president of the Standing Committee on the Status of Disabled Persons, on the topics of women and employment, and work and family responsibilities.

Coalition of Provincial Organizations of the Handicapped

A Disabled Persons Conference held by the Canadian Rehabilitation Council for the Disabled (CRCD) in Toronto in 1973 provided the vehicle for disabled people to meet from across the country for the first time. At this conference disabled people learned that people with disabilities in Alberta (the Alberta Committee) and Saskatchewan (Voice of the Handicapped) had organized in order to lobby for transportation and accessibility needs. The result was that organizations were quickly formed in other provinces. In 1975 the Manitoba League of the Physically Handicapped was formed. That Fall a conference was organized by the Manitoba League inviting the Alberta and Saskatchewan groups to discuss the possibility of creating a national organization. Following a series of meetings throughout 1976, a national cross-disability coalition structure was consolidated, with groups from the western provinces forming the core of the organization. The goal was to build the coalition from coast to coast (Driedger 1986).

COPOH gained provincial affiliates with the help of six national coordinators, and by the late 1970s almost all provinces were represented on COPOH's elected National Council. COPOH organized annual Open National Forums to discuss national issues and pass resolutions. COPOH's major provincial affiliates are comprised of over 85 local groups and are accountable to an active membership of approximately 30,000 individuals. Each major provincial affiliate, which is independent and autonomous, appoints two representatives and two alternates to the Council. This system in conjunction with the Open National conferences ensures a fair population-balanced delegate system for ratifying organizational and policy resolutions. In addition to its provincial affiliates, COPOH has developed links and liaisons with the Yukon and Northwest Territories, and with disabled Canadians of Native ancestry throughout Canada.

The National Council of Representatives is responsible administratively for electing National Executive Committee officers, which include the Chairperson, Past Chairperson, Vice Chairs (External and Internal), Treasurer and Secretary. The Chairperson serves as the senior spokesperson of the organization and ensures the coordination of national policy decisions. COPOH's central office in Winnipeg is run by a staff consisting of a National Coordinator, research analyst, development education officer, comptroller and administrative assistants. The office provides the research and communication vehicle for information to members and the coordination and processing of grant applications for funding. COPOH's Ottawa Information Officer, part of the staff, maintains the Coalition's profile in Ottawa by meeting with public servants, private sector representatives and other organizations. The National Coordinator assists Executive officers and committee chairpersons to communicate the policy resolutions of the membership to the appropriate federal authorities. The Coordinator is also in direct touch with provincial consumer organizations, and assists them in strengthening their structures and consumer-oriented influences.

COPOH's mandate as a national coalition "of" disabled consumer organizations is articulated clearly: To improve the status of disabled persons through their full participation and integration in Canadian society; to encourage and promote the idea of self-help; to provide a national democratic structure whereby individuals can voice their concerns on issues that affect their lifestyle; to act as a monitoring body; to promote strategies and policies to ensure improvements in the status of disabled persons in the community and at all levels of politics; and, by acting as an educational and motivational force, to create awareness of disabled Canadians' concerns and establish an altogether different image of "ability" in the public mind.

To fulfill its mandate, COPOH's National Council creates various committees, appoints chairpersons and approves their action plans. The Telecommunications committee has worked on a number of projects in cooperation with the federal government's Department of Communications, including the implementation of a communications system for COPOH designed to improve the communications network linking the national and provincial consumer groups' offices. Modern communications systems encourage information-sharing, and have important and obvious implications for subsequent social policy development (Dobell and Mansbridge 1986). Perhaps more significantly, the committee is engaged in monitoring print, television and radio media with respect to negative images and stereotypes of disabled people. Other concerns are with the financing of consumer-based publications, closed captioned television, publicity guidelines for charity telethons, and access to government information for the print and hearing impaired.

The Human and Equality Rights committee has over the years developed a comprehensive and "battle tested" plan of action. This plan includes lobbying for the introduction and passage of human rights laws, evaluating the impact of case law on persons with disabilities, monitoring policies and programs to ensure they are in compliance with laws, and pursuing legal challenges of disabled persons in the courts.

Through the efforts of COPOH and its committees, including the Human Rights committee, disabled Canadians finally have gained legal protection—through several years of intense lobbying and public demonstrations—under an amended Human Rights Act in 1983 and the Charter of Rights and Freedoms in 1982, with the important equality rights section (section 15(1)(2)) finally becoming law in 1985. In advocating human rights, media campaigns, public speaking, rallies and protests are undertaken by the committee and its supporters.

The Rights committee, following COPOH policy, also liaises with other political and advocacy organizations, including labor, women's groups, anti-poverty organizations and ethno-cultural organizations. The Coalition established the following resolution as a matter of policy:

> WHEREAS the goals and objectives of the labour movement and the disabled consumer movement in Canada are similar;
> BE IT RESOLVED that COPOH approach the labour movement, the business community and other similar bodies in the general community in order to set up a formal network of cooperation (COPOH 1985c: 57).

In the words of Jim Derksen, COPOH's national chairperson in 1986,

> I believe we are at a very important stage in the evolution of our movement in as much as we need to develop new attitudes toward the boundaries of our organization and our activities. Firstly, I believe COPOH should move toward a more open coalition mode, similar to that of the National Action Committee on the Status of Women (NAC) and the Council of Aboriginal Peoples.... Secondly, we should also improve alliances with organizations representing various disadvantaged sectors which have much in common with disabled people in Canada. Such coalition building must be done in a careful and skillful manner to minimize any philosophical, policy, and/or strategic compromises which may be called for, and to maximize advances in the status of disabled persons in this country (COPOH 1986 *Annual Report*: 2).

Other active committees in COPOH include Transportation Implementation, Parking, Income Security, Housing and the COPOH/DPI International Coordinating Committee (ICC). While accountable to the Council, the ICC's mandate is to stimulate interest in international disability issues in Canada and abroad, and to provide leadership to coordinate Canadian efforts internationally in the disability field in conjunction with organizations including the National Institute for Medical Rehabilitation and the Canadian International Development Agency. The committee also makes recommendations to the federal government to take action on international documents (Standing Committee on Human Rights and the Status of Disabled Persons 1990b).

The ICC's development education staff officer helps prepare and coordinate resource material on disability issues in the developing world for ICC representatives drawn from provincial affiliates. Moreover, COPOH Council and the ICC appoint the committee's representatives, taking into consideration regional representation, women, language and various disability categories, who participate directly in Disabled Peoples' International activities.

As with other consumer organizations, COPOH does not provide direct hard services but works to make certain that information about services, programs and facilities, as determined and demanded by the disabled community, are provided and made available. By far the most effective means by which COPOH realizes its goals and objectives is through its established committee system, its consultation unit and its Open Forums.

COPOH's first forum on employment was in Winnipeg in 1978. Disabled people affirmed that employment was not only a right, but that working in the community with all other citizens was the best option for them. At the time, 19 resolutions were passed, ranging from job training programs, funding for job/business creation programs, contract compliance legislation, provision of work-site aids and equipment, to awareness training for Public Service Commission recruiters. Subsequent forums since 1978 resulted in additional resolutions dealing with employment that were the bases for strategic action (e.g., protests, media campaigns and monitoring programs). These forums have also established the beginnings of an active two-way process of consultations with federal as well as provincial governments in employment equity, reasonable accommodation and contract compliance issues.

One consequence of the developing two-way communication process was that COPOH set up a consultation unit that functions separately from the regular staff, and whose membership and activities may change with the issues. This group of disabled individuals has worked closely, on a fee-for-service basis, with those federal government departments, equipment manufacturers, service planners and builders who require the expertise of COPOH in the formulation and development of plans, bills and devices in areas including equipment testing, company/business staff training procedures, communication devices, and building/structural design.

Consultation is an ever-developing process that need not always involve teams or units, though they are valued as a means by which the process is facilitated. Presence on advisory boards, councils, research task forces and participation in joint committees is recognized as appropriate, indeed necessary, in bringing about a mode of discourse that best mediates between "society" and certain of its members. The greater the presence and participation of disabled persons in the consultation process, the less need there may be for formal structures of representation.

In 1979, COPOH's second forum on Accessibility of Transportation (Ottawa) that coincided with the Canadian Transportation Commission's public hearings resulted in a National Policy on Transportation of Disabled Persons (Department of Transportation) and greater accessibility of such carriers as Air Canada and VIA Rail. Action on resolutions ranging from tri-level government cost-sharing, liability waivers, employee awareness training, installation and use of wheelchair lifts, power batteries and safety, research and development as well as labor union support has been the priority of the Transportation committee.

Rulings in favor of the consumer against such carriers as VIA Rail and others helped establish key principles in transportation policy for disabled people: Self-Determination, One Person/One Fare, Equality of Access and Service, Dignity of Risk and Dignified Travel. These principles serve as the basis upon which equitable access to transportation through the removal of environmental and attitudinal obstacles can be achieved; disabled travellers recognize neither cost as a justification for not providing access, nor do they consider routine assistance in boarding, moving about and deboarding as an "extraordinary" effort by carrier personnel. The 1985 Canadian Transport Commission decision in the Clarris Kelly case is regarded by COPOH as a major milestone in its efforts to secure equal access to transportation. Kelly was initially denied transport by VIA Rail because she was not travelling with an attendant. The CTC ruled in her favor. In 1989–90 Air Canada was unsuccessfully challenged on the issue of self-reliance (travel without being required to be accompanied by a fare-paying attendant). In 1991, the Federal Minister of Transport was presented with draft regulations prepared by the National Transportation Agency (replacing the CTC in 1988) that would amend the National Transportation Act to improve accessibility of any federally regulated transportation system, including the airlines (Canadian Human Rights Commission *Annual Report* 1991: 26). Regulations on the Terms and Conditions of Carriage of Persons with Disabilities came into effect January 1994. These new regulations, published by the National Transportation, will put to rest the long-standing issue of whether a disabled person who requires an attendant should pay an additional charge. Issues of cost, charges, medical proof, and who chooses the attendant are however still being debated (Canadian Human Rights Commission *Annual Report* 1993: 32–33).

Other forums were organized to address such issues as Rehabilitation, Consumerism, Income Security and Employment, and Independent Living and Transportation. The forum on Rehabilitation resulted in the redefinition of rehabilitation, the formulation of the philosophy of independent living and the start of the independent living movement in Canada. COPOH has indicated, in agreement with its provincial affiliates, that future forums are likely to continue to focus on two of the most pressing issues facing the disabled community, that of employment and integrated community living.

The issues of employment and integration are at the heart of independent living: to earn or receive an income in order to exercise one's choice in having one's own accommodation, getting an education, marrying and having children, and going to theatres and restaurants. COPOH does not believe that just because disabled people have had medical intervention, or rehabilitation, that it is necessary to persist in classifying them in a "health" category when issues of rights or living life to the fullest in the community is concerned.

New Relationships, New Structures

Empowerment involves a transformation that disabled people, individually and collectively, go through. This is their transformation from objects into subjects. The process does not, and will not, stop with independence or community integration, for these are unending states of being. Organizational structures and the means of organizing themselves (for examples the Alberta Committee and COPOH) enable this transformation process.

Disabled consumer groups (1) facilitate disabled persons in discovering, formulating and defining the problem of powerlessness, (2) provide the setting in which alternative explanations regarding the causes and dynamics of powerlessness are generated, (3) facilitate the decision-making process with respect to the identification and removal of obstacles to learning, growth and participation, (4) facilitate the implementation of individual as well as group action decisions, and (5) enable individuals to monitor or get feedback of the results of their own actions and the reactions from other parts of the social system.

The purpose of consumer organizations is to enable individuals to perceive themselves as causal agents in achieving their own solutions to independent living and community integration. They also help them recognize that other disabled and nondisabled persons have useful knowledge and skills as peer-collaborators in the problem-solving/community-building effort. The more important "action principles" that guide the operation and organization of disabled consumer groups including the Alberta Committee and COPOH as empowering settings are (adapted from Simpson 1980: 24–32):

1. An open membership is maintained to ensure that all citizens, of whatever disability, and whether disabled or not, can participate in open discussion and open assembly conferences to raise issues and voice their concerns. This is regarded as a basic citizenship right and responsibility.
2. The group endeavors to communicate regularly with its member-

ship, in a variety of ways, taking care to respond to specific needs and communication disabilities. The primary purpose of the group is to coordinate member's views and concerns.
3. The organization is founded on a democratic constitutional basis, operating with reference to clearly outlined job descriptions, in order to motivate members through maximum involvement in all fundamental internal policy decisions, and to encourage individual involvement in related community policy- and decision-making systems.
4. The consumer organization is considered autonomous and operates on the basis of maximum self-help. It is not controlled or influenced by any external force, large or small, other than its membership.
5. General funding is accepted only from philosophically supportive sources, "without strings attached." Few "true" consumer organizations will accept funds from service agencies who have raised their public funds through the traditional charity-sympathy appeals or who otherwise have unacceptable public fund-raising images. By the same token, because consumer monitoring and research efforts benefit the entire community, serving as an important social feedback mechanism to the public sector, it is considered appropriate to accept "core" government funding where such is openly negotiated for a specific purpose. Consumer groups are nonpartisan, however, and are above party politics as a matter of principle, despite government funding.
6. All consumer action projects, whatever their initial goal, attempt to fulfill two additional consumer goals, namely, building cross-disability cooperation, experience and trust, and establishing greater public/political credibility for the consumer group as a responsible force serving the whole society, not just the disabled community.
7. Consumer groups, at whatever level of organization (local, provincial or national), avoid becoming professional or permanent service organizations, or owning a direct service, other than providing information or consumer research data to members, agencies, and the general public. At the same time, groups avoid the image that disabled people want segregated services or special/favorable treatment. Only essential support systems with the necessary and

appropriate modifications are requested, preferably provided through regular and established community delivery systems.

8. Internally, staff domination is avoided by ensuring the hired staff are committed to providing a strong information and administrative base. They are to build cooperation and facilitate communication, and do not take sides on internal political issues.

9. Externally, consumer organizations try to develop strong in-depth working relationships with what are considered three "natural" allies of the consumer movement, namely, labor unions, the business community, and inter-faith community religious organizations.

10. Consumer organizations try to establish a clear policy understanding, internally and externally, that only they, through their policies and elected representatives, have legitimate authority to be their own spokespersons and negotiators. Organized disabled persons avoid communicating through "handicapped advisory committees" that are appointed by government or others to coordinate and represent the views of disabled people. Such is considered a direct contradiction and challenge to the right of people to organize in order to represent themselves. It is more appropriate for a Minister or a department to invite consumer groups to name their own representatives to a specific, time-limited, study advisory group or council (for example, the MLA/Handicapped Joint Committee in Alberta with which the Alberta Committee was involved [1975 to 1981], Alberta's Premier's Council on the Status of Disabled Persons, and Alberta's Premier's Commission on Future Health Care for Albertans).

Disabled consumer groups are only one of other forms of "strategic" organization that enable disabled people to empower themselves and to begin the long process of community-building. Consumer organizations such as the Alberta Committee of Disabled Citizens and COPOH have adopted a basic operating philosophy to ensure that the powerlessness experienced by disabled individuals is either reduced or eliminated altogether. Open membership, cross-disability representation, and direct participation as elements of community-building would ensure that at least the opportunities for developing skills and understandings are available.

Indeed, the powerlessness that disabled people feel and exhibit probably is due more to power absence rather than to power failure. Integral to empowerment as an element of the community-building process is the identification of the power blocks, or power structures, that contribute to this absence. The development and implementation of specific strategies aimed at reducing or eliminating the effects of what might be called indirect and direct power blocks is also important.

Indirect power blocks might be those that are incorporated into the developmental and learning experiences of the disabled individual as mediated by those with whom that person is in close contact and with whom he or she interacts (e.g., family members, therapists and doctors). Negative valuations or stigmas attached to the meaning of disability become incorporated into the person's motivational structure, preventing full development of such personal resources and skills as positive self-concept, cognitive skills, physical and mental competence. This lack of development further limits the growth of interpersonal interaction/relational skills, which can affect the performance of valued social and community roles.

Direct power blocks might be experienced by disabled people; these are the ones that are "applied" by some agent of society's major social institutions, or they may be inherent in the way community institutions are set up or structured. For example, a power block exists when well-intentioned but no longer relevant health care services become an obstacle to the normal development of other aspects of a person's mental and physical well-being. On another level, though an individual may have the personal resources required to use his or her interpersonal and other social/technical skills, blocked educational, employment and other opportunities limit or deny that person the right or chance to access or use those resources, to develop them further or to learn new ones.

Finally, either valued social and community roles are denied or some material resources that are important for the effective performance of social roles are withheld (e.g., adequate income for the performance of the parental role; accessible transportation or worksites to perform as an employee). Power blocks on all of these levels have to be recognized, understood and the capacity for dealing with them learned and developed, by the process of empowerment—at the individual and group levels. Integrated community living requires the dismantling of power blocks on a number of levels. Consumer organizations such as ACCD and COPOH are set up uniquely to initiate this dismantling and rebuilding process.

Powerlessness in the individual is the inability to obtain and utilize social and other valued resources to achieve such personal goals as independent/integrated community living. Powerlessness on the group or the comunity level may be defined as the inability to get and use resources to pursue and achieve collective goals. Powerlessness refers to the inability to manage emotions, knowledge, skills and material resources in ways that make possible the effective performance of valued social and community roles. Part of the process of becoming reconnected to and recontextualized in social life involves reclaiming previously denied social and community roles.

Individuals within the disabled population are often prevented from achieving a goal due to power deficiencies that may be a direct or indirect consequence of a negative group identity or image. The consequence is indirect when it is related to underdeveloped personal resources and interpersonal/relational skills of individual group members. It is direct when these individuals, as a group, cannot obtain such necessary resources as funding and legal or political sanction to accomplish their collective goals. Consumer groups work to rectify the disabled population's image problem, and try to provide the means of obtaining the necessary resources needed for integrated community living.

It is far from the truth that all disabled persons are powerless. Despite negative valuations and images, individual (direct) and institutional and systemic (indirect) discrimination, many disabled persons are able to obtain and utilize a broad range of personal, interpersonal and social-technical resources to pursue and achieve their goal of independent living (with reference to Giddens's dialectic of control). The whole point of empowerment is to clearly expose why power absences occur in the first place and what effects power blocks that derive from discrimination can have on individuals, not to reinforce the stereotyping of a total group on the basis of characteristics of only some of its members.

The idea of empowerment is a goal for self-intervention at the individual, group and community level; as a process, it deals with a very particular power block, namely that imposed by the external society by virtue of a stigmatized collective identity. Empowerment is, in a sense, a culture/social-specific process, since it assumes the experience of membership in a socially stigmatized category, the experience of non-membership or exclusion from community life, and the experience of trying to transform both. Empowerment as a transforming process entails developing different specific support systems and action strategies by those disabled people who have been "blocked" from achieving individual or collective goals because of the complexity and degree of discrimination they have suffered.

The consumer group may help individuals perceive the power structure as multidimensional and multipolar, not as monolithic, thereby indicating that some parts of this structure are indeed "open to influence." This could encourage creative solutions to the problems of independent living and community integration. The overall goal of this type of organization is to enable disabled individuals who have been subjected to systematic and pervasive negative valuations to perceive themselves as causal forces capable of exerting influence in a world of other people, and capable of bringing about some desired effect.

This is not to deny the power and significance of external forces in creating obstacles, but it does place a greater emphasis on the latent potential in disabled individuals. This emphasis on individuals as causal forces focuses away from the medical model of finding "a cure." The idea of the individual as a causal force instead emphasizes the forces effecting change or solving problems, rather than the inimical forces which contribute to the creation of the situation in which the individual may find himself or herself.

A consumer organization such as the Alberta Committee or COPOH as a cross-disability coalition structure is probably the most effective means of coordinating and structuring relationships for monitoring and influencing public policy. Given the social reform and contentionist goals of the independent living/disabled consumer movement, the consumer organization is a vital tool in the reform process. Reform is integral to community-building. As Dobell and Mansbridge (1986: 20–22) note:

Impact upon policy development is greatest when these different levels and arms [various kinds of NGOs] form a consensus, coalition, or alliance around specific themes, policies or programs. While most networking and coalitions in the social policy field are formed in response to government agendas and funding decisions, a number of recent liaisons and networks have been forming around non-government agendas. The reason for this is that NGOs are searching for solutions that existing government institutions seem unable to offer.... The most visible linkages between groups and sectors are the established coalitions.... Since most issues and programs in the social policy field involve federal and provincial jurisdictions, and can include municipal implementation, coalitions often develop locally and in each province. Alliances and networks are most easily and quickly coordinated at a community level to meet emerging current needs.

Disabled consumer groups as a specific category of nongovernmental organization play an important role within the social policy/community-building process. The networks they establish provide important channels for information-sharing and the building up of formal relationships, not only between a number of similar-interest and local/issue groups but also between professional organizations, service organizations and government-related institutions and agencies. Networking is a rather important means of sharing and relaying information.

Coalitions such as COPOH, on the other hand, serve to structure relationships between different kinds of smaller regional and local organizations that then allows them to work together, yet enables them to develop and operate separately. Self-reliance and autonomy within a formal partnership arrangement is, moreover, demanded, ensuring the integration of micro and macro policy and planning initiatives. In this way, independent local or regional groups provide valuable data and program/service evaluations about unmet needs that need to be embodied in macro policy formulation. Since it is acknowledged that no service, program or policy evaluation is value neutral, the independence with which this "social reporting" is conducted is a significant feature of this process.

6

New Solutions and Innovations for Empowerment and Community Building

One assumption of the process of self-actualization is that people know best what their needs and wants are, and what is in their best interest. Individual behavior is motivated by a need to mature, gain competence and to have some degree of autonomy. Freire calls this our ontological vocation. According to Carl Rogers, any less-than healthy functioning of individuals is a direct consequence of their social environment. Behavior that is *not* self-actualizing is a result of constraining and inhibiting social practices, interactions and structures. Unfortunately, Rogers's account does not take into consideration the possibility that self-actualization can be achieved by, or is an integral part of, an intentional and conscious (re)structuring of one's own social environment apart from intervention by experts.

A shortcoming of Rogers's theory is that people are somehow separate from the structures within which they interact. They have little or no influence on them, or are always interacting in situations that are structured by others, never themselves. By contrast, Giddens's (1984) approach to action is that it accounts for the possibility that individuals can participate directly in the structuring of their own interactions. Not only are structures the outcome of patterned and reciprocal interactions between people, but they are the intentional and directly motivated outcomes of purposive and conscious actions.

The idea of self-actualization as originally conceived by Rogers would be incomplete if it did not include a view of social structures and society as constituted by and contingent on the actions of knowledgeable agents. From Giddens's theoretical perspective, the ability to transform the less-than ideal social environments and interactional settings that foster maladaptive and dependent behavior is entirely within the power of those affected by them once individuals have come to understand how and why certain interactions, structures and institutions prevent self-actualization.

Indeed, empowerment is best conceived as a learning process at the level of personal, organizational and community interaction. The alternative and innovative organizational structures developed by action-oriented disabled people in the context of their movement would not make sense without a more dynamic view of the relationship between structure and individual action. That innovative organizations are being developed at all is proof that the constraining nature of existing imposed structures is recognized by disabled people, and they understand the reciprocal relationship between self-actualization/self-determination and enabling structures.

The consumer coalition structure with its research/monitoring organizations is not the only structural context through which disabled persons can empower themselves to achieve independent living. Consumer groups are not the only possible mediators situated between the segregated rehabilitation world and integrated community living. As one node in the network, it is the consumer organization that is instrumental in focusing, translating and communicating the needs of disabled consumers in a language that is comprehensible to both the wider disabled and nondisabled communities. The disabled consumer organization is first and foremost a vehicle for consumer and public education and lobbying and a means of evaluating and monitoring existing legislation, policies, programs and services. By providing in part an organizational setting in which the evaluation and reflexive monitoring process can take place, a consumer group tries to provide education, encourages the establishment of support networks, gathers information, diagnoses consumer needs and engages in action planning. It also attempts to integrate and diffuse the results of its activities within the overall coalition or network, out to disabled individuals generally, and out to the community in particular.

Disabled consumers have built other structures that enable them to pursue the goal of independent and integrated community living. Organized according to the principles of independent living, the purpose of these structures is to provide viable and workable alternatives to existing agency arrangements and/or service approaches. For example, in independent service brokerage an entirely new consumer empowering solution may be initiated. Because of the radical nature of the shift in philosophy and approach that service brokerage represents, there is concern that traditional agencies, services and government policies have no way of assessing the approach's value or effectiveness (Marlett 1988). The consequence is that public support and legitimacy as well as government funding may not be granted for initiatives that might be "too new." While it is important to innovate, innovation may be constrained. The limiting power of existing social and community structures cannot be underestimated.

These new structures redefine ways in which people interact with one another. The very basis of their interaction represents a significant departure from what is expected of members of a stigmatized minority. Contrary to the expectations set up by the medical model, disabled individuals are not incapable of critical reflective rationality, are not dependent, are not unable to form and articulate their own beliefs and desires. Nor are they unable to act with others in a common world. Disabled people as persons are indeed "self-legislatively, self-defining creatures" and, within limits, are fully capable of defining and shaping their own lives (Rorty 1987).

The notion of personhood implicit in the definition of self-actualization or self-determination is a significant one: The imposition of handicap or any social designation, whether physical, mental, gender or age-based reflects a lack of agreement over and denial of some fundamental presuppositions of personhood. Presuppositions for what would constitute a "person" would include a capacity for reflective rationality, autonomy, decision-making, forming beliefs and entering into mutually affective relationships (Rorty 1987, passim). The creation, structuring and organization of new ways of interacting involves both asserting the positive aspects of the presuppositions that constitute personhood, and showing that the negative ones are unfounded or illegitimate. By developing structures that form the context of their social and political reproduction, disabled people prove participatory competence, responsibility, autonomy, creativity and world-making. They demonstrate a full capacity for independence and integration.

"Taking Charge": Experiments and Innovations in Independence

Many related factors have contributed to the development of the independent living model and to the articulation of an independent living philosophy. First, there has been an increasing disillusionment and growing impatience with the expansion of the medical service model over the past two decades, particularly with the rising costs of services, increased professional control and impenetrable bureaucratic structures. Second, there has occurred a steady demedicalization of disability, a shift from a strictly medical approach to more of a political economy critique of disability as a social phenomenon.

Significantly, these two developments also have been accompanied by an extremely strong opposition to institutionalization. Although the movement of people from institutions back to the community is neither systematic nor wide-spread in Canada, most would agree that institutionalization represents loss of self-determination and isolation from the rest of society. The dehumanizing consequences that this brings are no longer tolerated; furthermore, institutionalization or hospitalization has been likened to "arbitrary detention or imprisonment," *viz* section 9 of the Charter of Rights. In particular,

> Institutionalization dehumanizes because personal liberty and self-determination are exchanged for the care that is received and the institutionalized person is isolated from mainstream society.... Despite these negative characteristics, a large number of citizens with disabilities in Canada live segregated from the community in institutions, not by choice but *because of the paucity of community supports* (COPOH 1987d: 41, emphasis added).

Rejection of the service model and forced institutional living has encouraged the disabled community to stress the principle or process of "normalization." The emphasis in normalization is on the value of people with disabilities able to have ordinary life experiences, and the focus of attention is on the ways that language, images and programs can enhance autonomy or maintain people in dependent social roles. Proponents of normalization strongly support community integration and the exposure of people with disabilities to culturally and normatively valued experiences "in order to establish and/or maintain personal behaviors and characteristics which are as culturally [and socially] normative as possible" (Wolfensberger 1973, Brown 1977, Kallen 1989: 159–66).

Rather than segregating individuals in residential institutions or placing them in specialized service care in attempts to make them "normal," efforts are focused on bringing these individuals into lifestyles and conditions that are as close as possible to typical, or normal, living patterns. Following deinstitutionalization, this means re-integrating the disabled individual into as many facets of family and/or community life as possible. What this process does *not* try to do is make that person "normal" in any physical or mental sense. Normalization is often misinterpreted as precisely this (see Kallen 1989: 164–65). Reintegration into family and community life is key, because

> Deinstitutionalization [alone] does not address the question of individual empowerment. Peer counselling, advocacy and information and referral are not components of deinstitutionalization. Deinstitutionalization does not address direct consumer control or the involvement of disabled people in service delivery (COPOH 1987d: 41).

Together with self-help, consumerism, the push for deinstitutionalization and the idea of normalization, the overall concept or philosophy of independent living has generated strategies for community-building, including revitalizing and re-establishing links between disabled individuals and various generic education, employment, transportation, housing, recreation and other services. The most viable alternative to institutionalization that has been developed is the independent living service delivery model. This model has two components, namely IL *programs* and IL *centres* (Alberta Committee

1987b, 1987c, Coxon 1981, Lord and Osborne-Way 1987). Independent living programs improve the life conditions of disabled persons by providing them with the ability and means to make their own decisions and to be self-sufficient. These are the tangible programs and support services often available through IL centres. These support programs and services are developed according to the underlying ideas that the focus of the services is on environmental changes and that the disabled person know his or her own needs best.

Independent living programs include residential, transitional and service provider programs. These would involve the further development of very specific or individualized services including such as live-in personal attendant care, daily living skills training, physical environment modification and/or adaptive/technical aides, mobility training, social and other functional skills development, time management, sexuality and family support counselling. Specific needs not only are determined by the disabled person, but are met either by the individual or by their peers (for example, through peer counselling, by selecting, hiring, training their own personal support attendants, or by directly negotiating with their own physicians, therapists, counsellors or other service providers). Flexibility, availability and variety are the key to successful programs. While the services provided by a community/independent living program may vary considerably from community to community depending on the needs of disabled individuals, the overall goal of most IL programs is to ensure the maximum independence and participation of disabled persons in their own affairs.

To this end, IL programs are based on implicit operating principles which are called community living principles (Alberta Committee 1987c). First, services are designed according to specific individual needs, choices, strengths and, to be realistic, with available and appropriate resources in mind. Second, services are always flexible and responsive to the changing needs of the individual. Here, the focus is also on choice—the decisions that are made and the actions taken should be directed by the individual himself or herself, with full knowledge of the possibilities and information necessary to make an informed choice. Third, the disabled person should be able to have a personal network of committed individuals, for example, family, guardian, friends, that can assist in program and service decision-making, and who could challenge decisions made by others that might adversely affect the disabled person. This means that the disabled individual's personal network must have access to that person's service system.

Fourth, and finally, there has to be a "fixed point of responsibility," that is, a single group of people, or a sole individual to whom the disabled person can go to get assistance in coordinating required services. The responsible group or individual develops and helps maintain program linkages and ensures the continuity of care from all involved service providers. Coordination is the key, since it is the gaps in services primarily due to the lack of coordination that can translate into tragedies.

Overall program and service coordination and delivery, reflective of these four operating principles, is achieved through different mechanisms which can be organized or actually provided through what is called an Independent Living Centre.

Independent Living Centres

The comprehensive definition of "independent living centre" that has been adopted by the independent living/disabled consumer movement is:

> An independent living centre promotes and enables the progressive process of disabled citizens taking responsibilities for the development and management of personal and community resources. A centre, while reflecting each community's unique character will be: consumer controlled, community based (local ownership), cross-disability, nonprofit, advocates of independent living, promoters of integration and full participation (via use of existing services). Essential program components are information and referral, advocacy, peer counselling, service development capacity (via research and planning, demonstration programs, service delivery and coordination, service networking, consumer monitoring), and including such direct services as housing assistance, attendant care, transportation, vacation relief, and technical aid loans (COPOH 1985a: 3–4, 1987d: 92–93, see also COPOH 1985c).

Independent living centres are of crucial importance to the independent living service delivery model because they facilitate the effective operation of various programs. They form the bridge between the independent living/consumer movement and the new service delivery model that the movement has inspired and created. The IL centre is a transition between rehabilitation and integration into the community where, increasingly, the growth of generic services is stimulated and utilized. Without the IL centre the other cluster of independent living programs and soft services such as peer counselling, individual advocacy, information and referral, and personal support services would be difficult if not impossible to put into practice. In addition to providing services, independent living centres are also an extension of the self-help ideal of the independent living movement. The centre is governed and controlled by disabled people themselves; IL centres represent a "bottom up" rather than a "top down" approach.

The unique aspect of independent living centres is not just the individual services it provides, but the delivery approach which is flexible and open to new ideas as the needs of individuals are identified. An IL centre is open to persons with any type of disability and its staff will deal with any area of concern including housing, transportation, employment, sexuality and access to available social services. The centre seeks to fill gaps in service that are identified by disabled consumers by implementing pilot projects which can be continued by other, more appropriate, organizations or individuals. A centre acts largely as a distributor of information about services offered by other social agencies, while providing only limited direct soft services. These services are provided by volunteer participants interested in the self-help approach, by the coordination of cross-disability information, by facilitating access to services that already exist in the community, and by stimulating the development of new ones. The ultimate goal of independent living is community integration, not the creation of separate services that would further isolate disabled people.

Examples of prototypes, or forerunners, of the larger and more well-known independent living centres include the Disabled Living Resource Centre (opened in 1980 in Vancouver), Ten Ten Sinclair (Winnipeg), the Community Enrichment Project (started in 1975 in Edmonton by the Alberta Rehabilitation Council for the Disabled, and since 1980 based at Edmonton's Grant MacEwan Community

College), and the Residential Aide Programme (based at Grant MacEwan Community College). These centres range from being "a one-stop shopping centre for visual and specific information," an apartment complex for tenants exhibiting varying degrees of disability (severe to nondisabled), to college-based daily living skills courses involving nutrition, money management, apartment and household management and personal care attendant training.

These initiatives, while certainly responsive to local needs, were developed largely by outside agencies and not at all through consumer action. Not all of them are or were managed or controlled by disabled people, nor are they organized or implemented according to the four community living principles (Lord and Osborne-Way 1987: passim). Despite all good intentions, these prototypes remained accessible to only a small segment of the disabled community, and the different programs and services were not coordinated in any significant way. The development of centres owned and operated (though not necessarily founded) by persons with disabilities who are aware of local community needs and the extent of available community services is the logical next step.

The first independent living centre in Canada was started in 1982 in the twin cities of Kitchener-Waterloo, Ontario. This IL centre was conceived and funded by the Mennonite Central Committee (MCC) in response to the International Year for the Disabled (1981). The IL centre board of directors is made up of disabled and nondisabled persons, with broad representation from the Mennonite community (Lord and Osborne-Way 1987: 10–11). The MCC constitution apparently continues to guide the Kitchener IL centre structure, though over the years plans have been underway to make the centre more autonomous. By 1985, the IL centre consisted of a ten-unit integrated apartment project, a downtown resource centre and office, and eight community-based locations where satellite or outreach support systems were provided to the area's 260,000 people. Staff included a director, three program coordinators and several administrative assistants.

The independent living centre's major initiative during its first three years of operations was an apartment project with in-house attendants, with funding obtained from such sources as the MCC, the Ontario government, federal grants and donations. Information and referral capabilities, a peer support program, individual advocacy and consultations in housing design were developed subsequently. In mid-1985, peer support, advocacy, and consultations were not yet official programs at the Centre.

In 1984 Winnipeg's Independent Living Resource Centre (ILRC) grew out of a joint initiative involving the Handicap Concerns Program of the city's Mennonite Central Committee and the Manitoba League of the Physically Handicapped. It was called a resource centre so that it would not be confused with a residential independent living program. The primary goal of this IL centre was the establishment of information and referral services, an advocacy support program (handling employment problems, disability insurance questions and home-care complaints), an attendant care support service and vacation relief (the provision of attendant care services for disabled persons while on vacation, or while primary care givers are away).

Since 1984 Winnipeg's ILRC established further projects and services, such as a Peer Counselling Training and Support program, a self-managed attendant care training program, independent living skills training seminars, a registry of accessible housing and apartments, a leisure education demonstration project and sponsorship of a technical aids and equipment display centre.

Funding by operating grants for these various consumer-initiated and controlled projects that are part of Winnipeg's ILRC has come largely from both private (United Way) and public sectors (Health and Welfare Canada, Canada Works, Secretary of State). Consumer control is emphasized here, as the ILRC is staffed by disabled individuals, specifically a managing director, program coordinators, administrative personnel, researchers and volunteers; as outlined in the centre's by-laws, the majority of ILRC's board and its several program advisory committees are made up of disabled consumers. Cross-disability consumer representation and involvement also is sought.

After over three years of preparatory work the Calgary Association for Independent Living (CAIL) opened its doors to the community in 1984. Similar to other independent living centres, CAIL grew out of an active national and provincial consumer movement, but also received support from the Mennonite Central Committee. Part of the Walter Dinsdale Centre for the Empowerment of Canadians with Disabilities (a.k.a. the Dinsdale Disability Information Service Centre), CAIL subsequently developed strong links with the University of Calgary's Rehabilitation Studies and Social Work programs. During the first year of operations the Calgary centre chose to concentrate on education, that is, information and referral. Other IL centres focused on education early in their developmental history because an essential first step is the coordination of information about available community services and programs for those disabled people who need it. By 1986 CAIL had developed its referral capacity, a year-round vacation relief program, as well as advocacy and various support and self-help functions. Importantly, all board members of the Calgary Association are persons with disabilities; however, open board meetings and an annual general meeting may be attended by both disabled and nondisabled consumers and citizens.

CAIL has led the independent living/disabled consumer movement in developing innovations in individualized services. For example, CAIL, with the University of Calgary, developed the Disability Information Brokerage System (DIBS) line, which is a computer accessed data base containing extensive listings of services for disabled people. Three registries are provided on this data base: Services, Attendant Care and Jobs. The DIBS line allows people with different disabilities to choose what is appropriate to them, according to their own particular service, personal one-on-one care, and employment or work needs. Other important innovations that clearly distinguish the Calgary centre from other independent living centres is the establishment of service brokerage, and the Joshua Committee.

Service brokerage and Joshua committees are unique as service development innovations and market-based alternatives to professionally dominated public sector services. Both promote the principles of independent living, and provide empowering alternatives to traditional services. They ensure that disabled consumers have direct access to funding and the ability to choose the support services they want, not necessarily the traditional services that agencies or government feel are appropriate. Moreover, the disabled consumer secures and purchases the services, allocates his or her own resources and is accountable directly for any funding assistance received. This represents a significant departure from the traditional "balance of power" between professionals, agencies and the client. As MacLean et al. (1987b: 5) stated,

Are we also intimidated by the professional monopoly—an entrenched labour force created to operate human services under the societal assumption that the disadvantaged groups require servicing? Independent Living challenges the traditional power balance, in that it asserts that disabled persons best know their own needs. This does not mean that there is no role for professionals and social welfare officials, but that current roles would be realigned in a partnership.

The Formation, Organization and Structure of IL Centres

The independent living centre as a service delivery model and a means of community-building are clearly a necessary development of the independent living/disabled consumer movement. An important feature that distinguishes the independent living approach in the core functions of independent living centres is the clear separation of hard service provision, and individual or collective advocacy (soft services). Organizations, including the Coalition of Provincial Organizations of the Handicapped and the Canadian Association for Independent Living (CAILC), have taken the position that service agencies cannot be free of their own service objectives. In order for *any* consumer organization to be an effective voice of disabled citizens, it must be free from the vested interests of service provision:

> Disabled consumers have determined that service delivery is not an appropriate role for the consumer movement. The consumer movement has been mandated to monitor service provision, not engage in it. If an organization is providing a service it cannot effectively monitor that same service. A conflict of interest arises (COPOH 1987d: 33).

The emphasis is on stimulating and encouraging the development of generic community services and programs, and on avoiding situations where the drive for innovation, flexibility and change may be compromised. Independent living centres obviously serve a unique purpose in the community-building process, and should be more than just another form of service organization or agency.

Several key common and inter-related elements can be identified in the historical development of independent living centres. They include: leadership from and cooperation between disabled and nondisabled people, sensitivity to, awareness of, and direct response to local and community needs, and support and backing from the community as a whole. From the information available about the founding and establishment of independent living centres it is evident that a core group of disabled individuals provided the initial impetus. Much of the leadership and vision for the actual development of the first centres came from Henry Enns of Winnipeg. Mr. Enns was consultant to the Mennonite Central Committees of Kitchener and Winnipeg, and acting director of the Kitchener-Waterloo centre and Winnipeg's ILRC. Mr. Enns was also Disabled Peoples' International's chairperson in 1988–89.

In Kitchener, Winnipeg and Calgary core groups came from the independent living/disabled consumer movement to staff the emerging centres (Kitchener's Action League of Physically Handicapped Adults, Winnipeg's Manitoba League of the Physically Handicapped and Calgary's Action Group). Leadership plays a critical role in articulating vision and commitment, demonstrating the competence of disabled people and in ensuring that the consumer perspective does not become lost in the shuffle.

The process of empowerment is best facilitated by disabled people. This is not to say that nondisabled people have not been intimately involved in this process. Only at CAIL, however, have nondisabled persons never served as board members, though they provide support in technical, service, research, informational and "political" areas. Consumer direction and control is important, but the independent living/disabled consumer movement also recognizes the critical support and collaboration provided by the nondisabled, and the importance of establishing legitimizing links with the wider community. Writes Jim Derksen (1980: 16–17),

> It is important, in my view, that disabled consumers recognize society at large and the able-bodied people in it have interests in common with disabled consumers; that in a sense all of society consumes or is impacted upon by the way services are provided for disabled people.... This means that the membership requirements

of disabled consumer organizations will in many cases need to be modified so as to allow participation by able-bodied people . . .

Collaboration with select community groups, including regional planning councils, human service agencies, clubs and even neighborhoods, is an effective and necessary way of gaining public endorsement of the independent living philosophy and acceptance of disabled people as fellow citizens.

Data suggest that despite some community support, it has not been easy for the independent living centres within their respective communities (Lord and Osborne-Way 1987, Kallen 1989: 163–64). They have often been criticized as "inappropriate, unnecessary and irrelevant" by municipal planning councils and traditional human service organizations, but, as disabled consumers have remarked, conflict is inevitable and legitimacy is achieved only with persistent effort and work, a function of time and communication. In fact, it is as much a question of effort and sheer presence in the community as it is of dealing with different perceptions of the centres. As with the early stages of any organizational innovation—considering how innovative the centres are—reactions of uncertainty and skepticism as to purpose and role are bound to occur.

To overcome these uncertainties, to establish the centres' legitimacy and to act as mediating structures between disabled people's formerly segregated lifestyles and a participating community lifestyle, systematic ways of supporting individuals to being part of the community have to be developed. This is why links with community groups and associations that serve all citizens must be forged, and why image is important. IL centres cannot be islands unto themselves; just as with disabled consumer organizations, a correct balance between independence and cooperation—interdependence—is sought.

The way independent living centres are organized and managed also is significant because centres are part of a movement that itself places a high value on *process*. The organizational structures of ILC's are expected to be consistent with the philosophy and goals of independent living, though there may be "stylistic" differences between structures and management. These differences simply attest to the unique influence of the respective communities, and the flexibility with which centres have responded to the needs and idiosyncracies of their settings. No style or method of operating is said to be better than another; they are simply different. In terms of organizational style, the Calgary and Kitchener-Waterloo centres are virtually opposite in their degree of structure (Lord and Osborne-Way 1987: passim).

In Calgary (CAIL), the word "association" is used rather than "centre," and the title of director is not used at all. This is apparently consistent with the group's desire to avoid language and behavior that infers bureaucracy, hierarchy or formality. In this way, CAIL tries to communicate its desire to be an association of people, rather than a place denoted by the term centre. CAIL's spokespersons refer to this structure as "organic," that is, as horizontal rather than vertical, and as open (Lord and Osborne-Way 1987: 62, 64). The strengths of this structure, according to CAIL participants, are that CAIL can be responsive and flexible to emerging individual and community needs. The acknowledged weaknesses of a loose structure, however, include some disorganization, and the possibility that other groups may perceive CAIL as not having clearly defined goals or a specific focus.

By contrast, the Kitchener-Waterloo independent living centre has the greatest degree of structure. Characterized by clear, formalized positions and lines of authority, the staff include an executive director, administrative assistant, several key project coordinators and a full-time bookkeeper. There are bi-weekly staff meetings, and the coordinators are required to submit written reports to the director; in addition, the administrative assistant attends and takes minutes at all staff, board and committee meetings. Again to contrast, staff at the Calgary centre are responsible for job areas that necessarily overlap (such as information and education, brokerage, and peer support), rather than for specific positions or roles; at the same time each person can also be a member of one of several advisory committees. There is nothing to suggest that such differences in approach reduce the overall effectiveness of each centre's core functions.

The organization and management of independent living centres also involves the interplay between each centre's staff and its board, especially in planning and decision-making. Ideas for new initiatives and approaches usually come from the experience of working directly with disabled people in the community, and are brought to the attention of the centre's board of directors by the staff. Details of new initiatives are examined by a program committee which subsequently seeks board input as potential projects get closer to implementation. Decisions relating to the allocation of resources that pertain to projects usually are made by the board or one of its sub-committees. In order for this decision-making format to work effectively, lines of communication must exist and be maintained between those individuals that consume the services, front line staff and those who are responsible for planning and administration (i.e., board members). This is much easier said than done:

> Our Committee has not had a whole lot of time to look at the future. . . . There seems to be an overwhelming response from the community right now. . . . Our Centre is still evolving. . . . Opportunities for Centre staff to share their learnings and experience with board members is an important part of decision-making . . . (Lord and Osborne-Way 1987: 65–66).

A means of communicating feedback to those responsible for organizing and coordinating programs are clearly important for the recipients of services, and for ensuring that program or service strengths are enhanced and that weaknesses can be identified and remedied. Interestingly, part of the solution to communication difficulties is in ensuring that board members are disabled consumers; presumably, being able to share experiences facilitates understanding what other disabled persons want or need.

Planning and decision-making depend a great deal on sharing and communicating information at all levels of a centre's structure; staff will attend board meetings (Calgary), or they can meet on a regular basis with the centre's director who then takes information to the board (Kitchener and Winnipeg). Still, boards and staff at these IL centres are concerned about the lack of effective short-term planning and the need for long-range planning. There is concern that much of the activity of the centres has been reactive rather than proactive, particularly the role of the independent living centre in the community-building process. Among the issues related to planning and decision-making are the degree to which IL centres can best serve cross-disability populations, how the more severely disabled and physically isolated can be reached, and whether the growing population of elderly people should be made a target for IL centre activity.

There has been a questioning of the relationship between the centres' ability to stimulate or encourage consumer direction and individualization beyond their front doors and existing service agencies. Some staff and board members perceive a danger in slipping into a social work mentality in the advocacy role or becoming human service bureaucracies, and in losing consumer and grassroots control when generic services take over. The difficulty lies in the fact that outside the centre, in the community, consumer direction and control may become lost.

Long-range planning must include the training of competent disabled people who can monitor generic service delivery and reach "back" to the independent living centre from the community. It must include educating the public. Independent living centres face the additional challenge of impacting on the consciousness of the larger community. A formidable task, this probably cannot be achieved outside the context of the cross-disability coalition structure or network of consumer organizations.

Independent Living Centres as a Social Innovation

For developing and emerging IL centres, it is important to focus on their planned functions, services and approaches that are consistent with the independent living philosophy, with the community context in which the centres are located, and with a coalition structure that is in place or is developing. The interplay of philosophy, context and structure helps create the necessary environment in which further individual and collective empowerment can take place. At the same time, independent living centres are an initial outcome of the empowerment process, as well as a further means of empowering people. The IL centre is in reality only one vehicle of several for enhancing the quality of life of disabled people.

The ongoing development of IL centres clearly represents an innovation in community-building. For innovative concepts and practices to be adopted, they must be understood and accepted by potential adopters—for disabled as well as nondisabled people. Effective communication is key to the subsequent diffusion of the independent living concept and model that underlies this innovation. While written and published materials will help disseminate knowledge of both the IL concept and the idea of "centre," innovations are evaluated not only on the basis of research but through the subjective evaluations of peers who have adopted the innovation. Face-to-face dialogue between disabled people and supportive individuals, including those from other agencies, serves to expand the understanding and acceptance of the concept and the practice, and give them legitimacy in the larger community.

Yet, acceptance of any innovation involves more than just effective communication. Potential adopters also must see a relative advantage to the concept, and they must feel that it is compatible with their own values and approaches. In addition, acceptance of innovative ideas in the general community takes time and usually requires a trial period during which time people can observe and reflect on the process "in action" and the results. An important implication for the establishment of new independent living centres is that they might consider starting with a small number of program and service initiatives, to gradually add others as the ideas become generally more accepted. This requires some planning and a more proactive approach to individual and community needs.

As with all social and/or technical innovations, changes will occur as those individuals involved in the emerging independent living centres continue to experiment with the concepts and the principles. Disabled consumers stress that the idea of independent living is not sufficient, but that compliance with the principles and functions of independent living (cross-disability, consumer-controlled, promotion of integration and community-based) are of greater importance and consequence. While innovation is a constructive ongoing process, there is always the danger that people trying to adopt new ideas might lose sight of the original vision.

The Canadian Association of Independent Living Centres (CAILC) was established at the 1985 COPOH national conference in Montreal to monitor the IL philosophy and practice, to ensure the effectiveness and integrity of programs, services and the centres across the country.

Prior to the 1985 COPOH conference, representatives from independent living centres across Canada held a national symposium which launched the Canadian Association of Independent Living

Centres, a national coordinating body for centres. This organization was officially recognized and endorsed by delegates to the COPOH conference in Montreal (COPOH 1987d: 49).

CAILC did not hold its first annual meeting until March 1988. Primarily a consumer directed organization, the Association was formed to act as a national coordinating body that would create and develop coherent overall guidelines for policy planning, strategic development of core functions and for achieving consensus over definitions and goals as additional independent living centres are created across the country. Existing centres apparently see themselves in a positive light in relation to the guidelines established by CAILC.

According to CAILC no single centre has achieved status as a full independent living centre according to the essential program components (information and referral, peer counselling, advocacy, research and planning, demonstration programs, service delivery coordination, and service/consumer networking in areas as housing assistance, attendant care, transportation, vacation relief and technical aid loans). Lack of uniformity or consensus between centres, and the "tension" between independent living/disabled consumer movement goals and the need to innovate, is attributed to the complexities of local situations and the need to be wholly responsive to the needs of local disabled consumers.

CAILC envisions a clearly defined role for independent living centres, in their functions and in their relationship to the independent living/disabled consumer movement *and* consumer organizations. Consumer organizations have important advocacy and monitoring roles with government and community. As COPOH has argued on all of these points,

> In Canada the consumer movement has consistently maintained that a distinction must be maintained between monitoring organizations and those which provide services. Canadian consumers insist that COPOH should retain its role as an independent monitor of all services affecting disabled citizens including independent living centres.... In Canada, the consumer movement engages in group advocacy and centres concentrate on individual advocacy (COPOH 1987d: 49).

Both CAILC and the Coalition of Provincial Organizations of the Handicapped have insisted that IL centres focus their advocacy efforts on individuals leaving broader monitoring and advocacy efforts to the consumer groups. CAILC and COPOH have suggested that the two approaches are complementary, but they caution that groups and centres must not attempt to define the same activity to avoid a conflict of interest. CAILC and COPOH maintain that the independent living/disabled consumer movement does not have the resources to advocate on behalf of individuals.

Individualized advocacy is a logical and natural extension of the individualized support services that IL centres provide, but potential conflict of interest with consumer action groups that are also part of the larger disabled consumer coalition structure arises when funding for core service functions is sought. Private and public sector funding is available for programs and services that reach the largest number of people, but not for *individuals* with their own individualized mixed services requirements. Since it is the *programs* that get the dollars, it is then up to individuals to figure out how to get services from them.

Because the idea of direct and individualized funding was a relatively new one in most provinces by the mid-1980s, IL centres were obliged to pursue block funding (Alberta Committee 1987c: Appendix B, Attendant Care Action Coalition 1986: 6–9). In some cases this has meant that IL centre staff and boards of directors have had to deal with government and service providers "on behalf" of disabled people as a category of individual, something that is obviously antithetical to the independent living model and the IL philosophy. On a positive note, this situation encouraged the development at CAIL of a constellation of unique service delivery/personal empowerment mechanisms unified under one model that made possible customized or personalized funding and services.

The Idea of Supported Independence

The most significant cluster of interrelated innovations that provide empowering alternatives to traditional services available to disabled people are those that have been developed by CAIL. The supported independence (SI) model, a self-help model that combines the idea of ecological intervention with the principles of the independent living movement, was developed by CAIL (Marlett and MacLean 1987, 1988, MacLean et al. 1987a, Marlett 1988: 28 ff).

The independent living approach to community integration stresses consumer control and choice. The individual, no matter how disabled, is assumed to know best his or her own needs and be able to make decisions. This is very different from the more traditional service models that allow control only when the individual has demonstrated competence. Moreover,

> [I]ndependent living [is] a *process* whereby disabled citizens achieve their desired individual lifestyle by assuming responsibility for the development and management of personal and community resources. The central underlying concepts are risk, responsibility, choice, control, freedom, and self-determination . . . [I]f an individual has chosen a particular lifestyle for some management reason then it can be considered an independent lifestyle. An individual requiring attendant care may opt to live in a nursing home where these services are provided so that he/she can devote his/her energies elsewhere. . . . Some have referred to I.L. as a liberation philosophy (COPOH 1987d: 29–30).

As Irving Zola noted, "independence is not the quality of tasks we can perform without assistance, but the quality of life we can live with help." In the words of Connie Oxelgren,

> An immediate plan is to move away from home again. In all probability I will be moving into a nursing home. Though I am not particularly looking forward to this move, it does have an advantage. I will be relieved of attendant hiring and management tasks. This will allow me to put all my energy towards completing my university degree (COPOH 1987d: 64).

Under the supported independence model, control by the individual over his or her own situation is assumed *a priori* and once the decision is made to take it, actual competence is assumed to follow. Obviously, participatory competence can only be learned and acquired through action and activity; from this perspective, the process has to start somewhere and at some point. The material and social environments are adapted to support the disabled individual in his or her activities, not the other way around. The person's disability is accepted as a given and is regarded as secondary. Changing rules and procedures, equipment and technical aides, and even the people with whom a disabled person interacts, is more effective in the disabled individual's self-determination than any attempts at behavioral and physical (clinical) intervention.

The key to the SI model, according to Marlett and MacLean, is that the disabled person is in the "driver's seat," and is in control, and with the help of his or her support team focuses on building supportive and enabling environments. This involves encouraging self-advocacy, developing peer or natural support networks, accessing individualized funds and developing "resource safety nets" that permit the individual to manage his or her own staff, including personal care attendants, agency workers, rehabilitation and/or community development professionals, and guardians.

For the SI model to work, support or enabling systems should be in place that disabled persons can use to realize his or her independent living/lifestyle goals and, hopefully, achieve greater participation in mainstream community life. As the means and the outcome of empowerment, they include a consumer-controlled independent living centre with trained staff, the commitment of family and friends, a personal support staff who work in cooperation with funders as well as service providers, an open-minded and flexible local social services management, a service broker and a volunteer brokerage advisory team of rehabilitation and other professionals who are committed to the principles of independent living. Of particular interest is CAIL's development and use of both nonprofessionalized personal support groups (Joshua Committee) and independent service brokerage.

The Joshua Committee:
A New Initiative in Personal Support Networks

Many valuable soft services are delivered to disabled people through independent living centres. One unique aspect of these centres is that they are controlled by disabled people at both the board and staff levels; another unique feature is the use of volunteer persons who may or may not be disabled. A significant part of IL programming involves disabled people sharing disability-related information, knowledge and skills with each other. Disabled individuals who are consumers of health services can become disconnected from the intricate web of relationships that, as a whole, constitute community. These individuals experience difficulty re-establishing their lives outside the service system into which they have been socialized. This "disconnection" is especially marked for those individuals who have been institutionalized.

However, neither institutions, programs nor professional service providers can totally recreate the experience of community or respond to the need for meaningful work, income, support services or even reciprocal relationships. The solutions to these problems call for radical change in the nature of the social relationships of disabled persons, and this change must occur first at the grassroots level. Independent living and the idea of independent living centres is one solution. The Joshua Committee is an integral part of it (the name is derived from the biblical character Joshua who caused the walls of Jericho to crumble).

A Joshua Committee is a personal network of support or a group of volunteers (see also Powell 1987, Stone and Doucette 1988, Warren 1981) that have been established, either at the request of the disabled person or at the suggestion of a friend, to assist a disabled person lead a lifestyle of his or her own choosing. These committees are unique to the disabled persons around whom they have been developed (one person = one committee), and their members are active in supervising service staff, coordinating personal care attendants and distributing funds (Hicks 1985, Lord and Osborne-Way 1987: 51–54). The first Joshua Committee was formed in Toronto in 1980 through the efforts of a disabled woman and her peers.

By the end of 1985, 35 committees had been formed in Calgary, coordinated by a CAIL staff person specifically assigned to the task. CAIL alone has taken the concept and developed it further; other IL centres have nothing similar. Joshua committees can be made up of a wide range of individuals, including disabled and nondisabled peers, friends, relatives or family, neighbours and personal care attendants. Medical, health care or other kinds of social service professionals also may be invited to participate, but their involvement is strictly on a personal basis. Commented a CAIL staff person,

> The biggest strength of Joshua Committees is that of personal commitment. I think a lot of people get disheartened because although people are there to support them, if they are not paid, they don't come around anymore. These are citizens who are respected in the community and who are coming together and saying "I support you." Just that (effect) in itself, on the person, and on the way society views the person, is really positive (op. cit. in Lord and Osborne-Way 1987: 52).

The strengths of the committees are the personal commitment of its participating members, and their flexibility. This is why the Joshua Committee is referred to as a natural support system. The committee helps the disabled person make decisions for himself or herself; its function and role is not to make decisions for the disabled person, but to respond to the demand for information with which decisions can be made. The focus is on choice: Decisions are made and actions are taken by the disabled person based on information and knowledge that is provided and shared by committee members. The idea is clearly to encourage and assist the disabled person learn, first, how to even ask for information, and then how to process it, to understand the importance of perceiving alternative choices, and to gain skills in the decision-making process.

The committee's effectiveness is determined primarily by its ability to act as a safety net whose very existence encourages and inspires the disabled individual to experiment, take risks, and deal with failure. The committee provides a means of bridging the lack of knowledge and the "zone" of failure by providing knowledge, and by helping the person learn to tolerate failure without destroying his or her innovativeness. The member's moral support is often sufficient; indeed, because community living is not restricted to the hours of "nine-to-five," this support has to be very flexible, and to be effective, supporting individuals must be available and accessible nearly all the time.

As disabled individuals begin to realize their own potential, the likelihood increases that the choices and decisions they will make will be outside the scope of the traditional services and programs available to disabled people. Joshua Committee members have to be prepared to help identify and create alternatives to access generic services. With a move away from traditional services, funding to provide what the disabled person has chosen may not be readily available. Committee members can help the individual, through group support, by lobbying for purchasing power to be vested in the individual, and by trying to reallocate acquired funding in ways that give the disabled person more control over what specific services to purchase, or even who as a personal care attendant to hire (or fire). However, committee members do not work alone but hand-in-hand with a service broker to obtain funding.

The organization, procedures, activities, and the interventions of Joshua Committee members on behalf of the disabled individual are not *ad hoc*. On the contrary; there are a number of functions that the committee must carry out if it is to be an effective support structure, and not simply a social or drop-in club at the beck and call of a disabled person. Joshua committees typically develop individual program plans (IPPs, Hicks 1985: 7–9). These are priorized systems, or "processes" of ends and means whereby individuals are helped to identify their own behavioral and psychosocial capabilities and weaknesses, set specific goals and objectives, develop possible action strategies and, most importantly, track, monitor and reflect on their progress and achievements.

Joshua committees guide disabled individuals through the empowerment process in adherence to the principles of independent living. These committees try to accomplish this by establishing and maintaining open and very flexible lines of communication between the disabled person and themselves, and service providers as well as funders. This ensures an awareness of the goals of the disabled person by all concerned, and makes possible the transfer and equal exchange of relevant information on which sound decisions can be made. This arrangement is clearly in contrast to the typical professional-client dyad.

Second, the committees work at coordinating the services that are required and utilized by the disabled person. A single service agency cannot provide all of the necessary supports required by individuals, and so the services of several agencies have to be contracted. Again in contrast to the professionalized helping model, however, it is the disabled person who decides what the needed services are going to be and who is to provide them. The purpose of coordination is to establish effective and efficient delivery of services, and to provide integrity to an overall "ecological" support strategy for an individual's program plan.

Third, all professional interventions (ecological, clinical and behavioral) are filtered and systematized. They are evaluated by the disabled person and his committee as to their necessity and relevance in meeting his or her community living objectives (i.e., employment, residence, personal relationships and money management). Only then are outside interventions put together in ways that ensure maximum consistency in overall approach (and positive) impact on the needs of the individual. Consistency of approaches facilitates evaluation and monitoring by JC members, involved IL centre staff and by the individual, making it easier to track and assess the progress of the person's growing independence or, alternatively, the lack of it.

Significantly, the focus is not only on personal abilities or deficits, but on the supports needed by the person in his or her chosen environment. This shift in focus is important because it enables a person to explore alternative environments, arrangements and support systems, rather than being "fitted" or programmed into a particular one. Unsatisfactory or no longer needed supports and services are dropped and replaced as required. A characteristic of the individual program plan is that it is a continuous self-correcting and learning process.

Finally, Joshua Committee members and the disabled persons with whom they work seek greater self-accountability. The committee is responsible to the disabled person in enabling his or her access to services and programs that are tailored to specific abilities and needs. In contrast, service providers may be accountable to both their respective departments, agencies or funding sources and to the disabled person and his or her committee. The effect of such a traditional arrangement is that the disabled individual is neither responsible nor accountable to anyone. The idea of accountability to the individual, an agency or a funding source has simply meant justification for continued financial support of whole programs and services whose objectives have seldom reflected the capability or potential of the individual disabled person.

One goal of independent living is to make the disabled individual accountable to service and program providers and funding sources, as well as to make *them* accountable to the disabled person. In the past, the thinking has been that services and programs must be monitored by third parties (i.e., not by disabled people). The implication is that disabled people may misuse funds and purchase poor quality services, or they may be exploited by unscrupulous service providers. It is implied that people on subsidies should be controlled, and that they do not have the freedom to choose or determine how or how much money should be spent. Self-accountability means that the individual has complete freedom of choice and dignity of risk in determining the quality of goods and services purchased and the money spent.

Service and Agency Brokerage:
Individual Empowerment and Personal Accountability

The Calgary Association for Independent Living has been innovative in developing the supported independence (SI) model—both as part of the service development function of independent living centres and as a systems approach to individual and collective empowerment. The Joshua Committee as a natural support network is clearly a necessary component, or dimension, of the SI model. The Joshua Committee is also a necessary and integral part of yet another innovation in consumer planning and control, namely brokerage.

The idea of brokerage is grounded in the recognition that if disabled individuals are to empower themselves to live as full participants in their communities and in society, some critically important links missing from present social service systems must be put into place. Brokerage and the SI model emerged from an understanding of how systems do not operate in ways that make them accountable to the people served, and from an awareness of how systems tend to impede the people served from effectively exercising influence in decision-making processes. Brokerage and personal support networks might be considered innovations that encourage the changing or eventual replacement of existing structures and relationships. They serve disabled individuals in ways that are consistent with a new understanding of the rights of disabled people. Brokerage is a means of bridging existing services, and it is in the bridging process that new services might be encouraged to develop to meet new needs.

As described by CAIL's brokers, independent service brokerage operates much like stock brokerage; consumers use a broker to gain access to and manage a portfolio of services that are designed to meet their individual needs. A portfolio might include tutors, schooling, attendants, funding, housing, therapies and prosthetics. Service brokerage is a technical and mediating support service; it is the technical arm of an autonomous planning mechanism that is community-based and consumer-controlled (Community Living Society n.d., MacLean 1985, MacLean and Marlett 1987b). Brokers assist those who are unable to manage their own services by contracting and negotiating for, and making available personal management support, information and training, skill development consultation, and individuals interested in becoming partners in support networks. Brokers act with, or on behalf of, disabled consumers in negotiating ongoing service agreements that facilitate consumer control and independent living. The broker typically works with the disabled consumer, in conjunction with his or her Joshua Committee (if one is used), in seeking funds needed for community living.

As individual funding becomes more available, brokers help disabled individuals select support personnel or service agencies from the Association's Service Registry (the Disability Information Brokerage System [DIBS line], which is a computer listing of over 2000 service resources ranging from agencies, personal assistance volunteers, wheelchair repair, to motor van converters). Brokers also assist in drawing up contracts between consumers and service providers, and they establish payment procedures. Combining elements of advocacy, support, information and referral (i.e., the core functions of IL centres), brokerage clearly is compatible with independent living principles. A brokerage advisory committee comprised of CAIL and community representatives ensures the smooth operation of the brokerage process, including the further development of the process through recruitment, training and supervision of new brokers.

There are several brokerage models that disabled consumers and IL centre personnel have developed. In the independent service brokerage model, developed by CAIL, the broker works only for the consumer/client, not for agencies, the government or government funding sources. CAIL brokers prepare service brokerage contracts for services and funding (MacLean et al. 1988, Marlett 1988) based on the needs identified by disabled consumers, their natural support networks, or their legal guardians if they are dependent adults. Once the needed services are defined, brokers search for the availability of what is required and prepare cost estimates. Funding estimates are based as much on available generic services as possible, and costs as well as the terms of the service provision are more readily and easily negotiated than would be the case with traditional service structures.

When funding is secured, it is allocated directly to individuals and their supports through the broker; the consumers and their networks are placed in a unique empowering position of securing, allocating and being directly accountable for government dollars. Brokers subsequently maintain contact with both consumers and service providers in order to help monitor the effectiveness of the service package, and to assist in changing the package whenever necessary. In addition to direct work with consumers, brokers also educate existing services about the needs of disabled people and the importance of direct consumer control and personal accountability.

Another type of brokerage is agency brokerage, developed by the Vancouver Community Living Society (a group of parents whose children and older dependents were residents of Woodlands, a provincial institution for the mentally handicapped) (Community Living Society, n.d.). In this situation, the broker is a member of the Society yet works as the technical arm of the referring agency, in this case the provincial institution. In fact, it is the institution/agency that appoints a broker to work with particular individuals and their families. The broker develops general service plans in cooperation with each disabled person's family and the agency, and acquires block funding on behalf of the agency that subsequently is dispersed to the individuals through the agency.

However, the agency rather than the disabled individual (or the family) is accountable to the government for the expenditures for the services that are acquired and contracted. The institution/agency ultimately decides which ones will be utilized, though in the majority of cases it will go with what the broker suggests and what the families want. In turn, the broker is accountable to the disabled individual in providing access to the best possible services and alternatives, and he or she must ensure that services are actually delivered as contracted.

In contrast to the independent service broker, the agency broker's prime responsibility and motivation is not the acquisition of funding but the development of service plans and the matching of available community resources with individual needs. The agency broker's concern does not necessarily have to be with costs, but with stimulating service providers to enhance their existing services and resources. The broker's task is still to assess the disabled individual's ongoing levels of well-being and growth, monitor the effectiveness of the general service plan or service package, and come up with better alternative strategies and plans. The broker's responsibility is to maximize the disabled individual's capacity for self-determination and independent living.

The reason some institutions and agencies use brokers is that their staff have neither the mandate nor the time to gain knowledge about the full range of existing community resource systems, to identify gaps between needs and services, or to help stimulate the development of missing resources and services. In the independent service and agency models the broker is a technical expert who is expected to have full knowledge of available generic and nongeneric services, but who is also committed to the philosophy of the independent living/disabled consumer movement.

The Basis for Brokerage: The Role and the Process*

Disabled individuals share common experiences in dealing with the govermental and voluntary/private service sectors, and they also experience considerable difficulty, at some point in their lives, in gaining access to even such basic services as community housing, employment, integrated educational settings, in-home supports, life-skills training and technical aides. These services may simply be nonexistent, of unacceptable quality, or they may not be responsive to the particular

---

* Much of the discussion in this section draws from Marlett and MacLean 1988, MacLean 1985, MacLean et al. 1987b, 1988, Marlett 1988, and Salisbury 1987.

needs of disabled individuals. Perhaps an even more fundamental problem is that complete and accurate information about the location, cost, accessibility and quality of existing service and program options is not easily available. Until recently, there did not exist a means by which disabled individuals could obtain services directly or directly access needed resources, much less negotiate for them themselves.

This situation has persisted because no one institution, agency or organization within the patchwork of social services has been equipped to assist a disabled person and his or her personal support network to develop ongoing programs for integrated community living. Fragmented planning has meant that often disabled persons are "bounced" from one service to another, from professional to professional, while their needs continue to go unmet. The traditional service sector is not mandated to assist individuals in planning their integration into the community. Not only is it not equipped for the task, but it lacks the comprehensive outlook, the ability to coordinate with other systems and the flexibility that is required by disabled people to satisfy their needs over time.

Identifying and putting into place the particular services, professionals and other resources that a disabled person might need at any given time obviously requires considerable knowledge, skill, energy, personal resources and a sense of competence—things that disabled individuals often have the least of but need to develop the most. Joshua Committee members or independent living centre staff help individuals identify their needs, are instrumental in formulating program plans and help coordinate existing services and resources. But they are limited in their ability, expertise and resources to "pound the pavement," to directly negotiate service or program contracts, or to initiate changes in existing service structures.

What has been needed was a means by which links could be forged between disabled persons, the resources and services available in the community and funding sources. For these links and arrangements to be empowering, the disabled person had to have the opportunity to be autonomous from service providers and funders, in a position to decide what he or she needed, and be responsible and accountable for services used and money spent. Since empowerment and self-determination entails learning how to gather information and how to make decisions, the "means" has to be enabling, not controlling or constraining. The personal support system and the broker are in the delicate position of working towards, initially, full sharing of control, and later, the gradual transfer of control to the consumer.

The personal support system and the broker are autonomous in the sense that they can neither be tied to nor controlled by a direct service system or a funding body. Without autonomy, they would be no more effective than an investment brokerage service that is offered by a firm directly owned and controlled by a corporation or company. Agency brokers are urged to maintain some distance from the service system to which they are attached in order to avoid the possibility of favoring their own agency when referring disabled consumers.

Together, an individual's personal support network and his or her broker constitutes what is called "the fixed point of responsibility," a central identifiable body to which the disabled individual can turn for information, advice, continuity of care and assistance. This fixed point also serves to legitimize the demands of the consumer, since by definition disabled persons are assumed to be unable to know what they want, cannot articulate demands, or do not have the skills to deal with the "outside world." The fixed point is a way of providing the disabled person with a power base that is understood or recognized by government and the traditional service sector. A key assumption underlying the idea of a fixed point is that it will continue to act in its capacity over time, and that brokerage services consequently will remain available to the individual on an as-needed basis. This continuity enables the disabled person to have access to an identifiable body as personal and/or service requirements change. This provides the person with the assurance that he or she can regularly gain access to the opportunities society provides to all nondisabled citizens.

Brokerage systems have unique features that make them especially useful to disabled individuals in the empowerment process. By definition brokerage is a mediating process that enables the broker to network across all system and organizational boundaries in the community, with and on behalf of an individual or group being served. Using a range of technical and professional skills, brokers mediate between disabled individuals requiring services, the people and agencies offering those services, and the structures enabling payment for the services. This flexibility ensures that the needs of individuals, rather than the needs of systems, remain the most important issue. Network involvement in the monitoring of services makes it possible for the broker to keep up-to-date about matters affecting the lives of those using brokerage; this is a prerequisite for making appropriate responses to changing needs. Brokerage is the technical arm of the fixed point of responsibility that literally extends the disabled person's ability to interact with others in society.

Independent service brokerage is flexible and controlled by the consumer. The broker's involvement is engaged only at the discretion of the disabled person and/or his or her personal network. In the case of agency brokerage, the broker's salary is paid by the organization using the broker; in this instance salaries are built into the core funding that is allocated to an individual's fixed point of responsibility. Independent service brokers currently survive on short-term and "soft" (discontinuous) funding, but this is not a viable long-term solution. One solution has been "fee for service," but since the disabled client is by definition unable to pay, the question is who pays. If the funder, usually governments, pays the broker's fee, the broker becomes responsible to the funder and not to the consumer. Though desirable for funders, this arrangement could undermine the essential relationship between the consumer and the broker.

How the broker is paid is an important aspect of brokerage. A funding arrangement must operate to ensure that brokers are responsive and accountable to the people they serve, and that checks-and-balances against professional control are included. How brokers are paid also is tied to the issue of how disabled consumers are funded. The more individualized, personalized or direct the funding to disabled persons, the greater their accountability to funders and the greater the relative objectivity of brokers.

The broker's relationship and involvement with the disabled consumer is clearly a paid one in which he or she provides a technical, professional support service. Accordingly, brokers operate on a general rather than a specific level of the service continuum. They are not directly involved in individual advocacy or in individual program plan (IPP) development and coordination. Brokers are involved in the development of general service plans. The broker allows matters at the "hands on" level to take their course; brokers should be proactive and reactive, never controlling. The brokerage idea is based on the traditional if overlooked principle that the proper role of the human service professional is that of an "auxiliary" of the disabled person who seeks to arrive at informed decisions while pursuing appropriate goods and services.

Brokers help interpret and explain to disabled persons and their networks the complex and sometimes confusing aspects of various community systems. The broker does not dictate to people what course of action should be taken in any specific situation. Instead, acting as an auxiliary support the broker enables individuals to see the range of options and to arrive at their own decisions. As mediators or interpreters, brokers also provide ongoing technical assistance to agencies and organizations by translating disabled persons' personal needs and goals into language that is understood. As a personal agent and technical resource, the broker is in a unique position to help mediate misunderstandings or disagreements between the disabled individual, his or her personal network, involved professionals, and the various service systems.

As one who facilitates planning and decision-making, the broker tries to maximize the self-determination and independence of the person he or she serves. The active partnership between the broker and the personal support network of the disabled consumer helps the broker do the job effectively. The broker draws from the information passed on by the network as it monitors services around the individual using brokerage. The broker reflects on the network's insights into the individual's personal situation, and it is this partnership that reinforces the empowerment of the individual. This relationship ensures that the individual remains the central focal point of demand in relation to services in the community, while making his or her own contributions to effective brokerage as well.

Service and agency brokerage are a means of putting a range of technical resources at the disposal of the disabled consumer. Properly conducted, the brokerage process should enable the disabled person to develop and act on his or her "vision" for a self-determining life in the community and in society. It is the disabled person who is allocated dollars, who is supported by a personal network made up of family and friends, and who augments his or her capabilities by using the technical and professional supports of a service broker. The individual, empowered by his or her personal network and by the broker, controls the planning and decision-making process while at the same time brings about a needed measure of service monitoring and evaluation.

A skilled generalist who operates within the broader social and system context, the broker possesses a variety of technical and interpersonal skills, and knowledge of the empowerment process in order to get the "best deal" possible for the disabled person, and to enable the person, through an active learning process, to re-contextualize himself or herself in community and everyday life. The brokerage process can act as a catalyst that stimulates innovative responses, by others in the community, to a disabled individual's diverse and often challenging needs.

Service and agency brokerage appears flexible because it is designed to be interdependent with the other components or means of delivering services of the independent living model. This interdependency of brokerage's operation could prevent it from developing into a large and inflexible bureaucratic structure. Without a healthy degree of openness to citizen input and consumer control, systems tend to expand, sometimes giving rise to powerful vested interests that also tend to consolidate power over those served (Gritzer and Arluke 1985). By contrast, brokerage, as envisioned by disabled consumers, presupposes individual input and control. It also presupposes the free operation of a number of checks and balances at work among the different yet related components of the independent living model, for example, IL centre staff, IL centre brokerage advisory team, peer support groups and natural support networks.

Checks and balances, usually excluded from larger structures, ensure that brokerage remains sensitive to the needs of those involved in the process, and that the brokerage system does not become an entity unto itself. Broker accountability, as disabled consumers and others are saying, remains a crucial aspect of the process. Yet there is the ever-present and not unfounded concern that brokers may act in unprofessional and unscrupulous ways to take advantage of the vulnerability of disabled persons by forcing solutions on the consumer by providing service packages that are more convenient to the broker than to the consumer, or by manipulating information that results in even greater dependency rather than empowerment. Brokerage may be as much a double-edged sword as any of the other strategies for community-building.

The Community as "Expert"

The concepts and philosophies of supported independence and independent living have become topical bywords for describing strategies of problem prevention, amelioration and community building, a lay basis for health and social service community efforts. Basic to this orientation is the view that social programs involving initiatives from professionals and experts, formal agency bureaucrats and hierarchical planning have either failed to produce significant success outcomes, or have only added to the weight of disabled citizen and consumer alienation from the health professions, government and the public.

From the "community as expert" perspective, many new initiatives have been created for which funding and other types of support have been sought and made available to establish "partnerships" between informal and formal solutions that address many of the problems of re-integrating and re-contextualizing disabled persons back into general community life. Independent living centres, personal support networks, Joshua committees and brokerage models are the new "organizing principles" or mediating-alternative structures. Where once patient, client or target population goals existed, one now finds community support strategies defined by significantly increased citizen participation acting in concert with natural helpers who are able to supplement or even to supplant experts.

A dichotomy of formal versus grassroots expertise has arisen in which the proper boundary or balance between the two, with brokers as go-betweens, is still in the process of being worked out and defined. As empowered disabled consumers discover more about the positive functions and consequences of parallel or alternative "enabling" systems in helping them cope with a variety of medical, social and life concerns, the importance of ensuring that public and private agencies offering services are not destroying or discouraging these enabling systems becomes clear.

The independent living/disabled consumer movement and the

empowerment strategies which it has generated symbolizes reaction to the overprofessionalization and the exceedingly high costs of services and institutional care. The following premises underlie the supported independence and independent living approaches.

1. There are limits to "social policy intervention" styles; i.e., the use of government, professionals and formal procedures is considered a finite strategy.
2. Grassroots involvement is a key to maximizing community action and local or individual empowerment; these actions can be conducted independently or in some reciprocal relationship (network) with specialized and formalized self-help groups, human service agencies and other community-based structures.
3. Recognizing that local individual and community skills and resources contribute to problem-coping, and that many of the social bonds at the local level have been weakened, the need for empowering individuals, families and social networks should be acknowledged; these would then come to see themselves as significant entities fully capable of contributing to their own well-being.

The first premise is grounded in the notion that communities, regardless of size or composition, have different agendas and value systems, and that in a pluralistic society it is not reasonable to design social, including medical and therapeutic, interventions that are based on models which are not grounded in differential consumer needs and interests. Without this grounding, policy formulations usually miss the mark of their intentions by considerable margins. There is a variety of opinion among disabled consumers of just what constitutes a problem or a solution for a particular disabled person; hence, standardized and predetermined formulae concerning ideal solutions are consciously avoided. The importance and usefulness of locality, variability and strategy flexibility are emphasized instead. Moreover, the right to reject proffered expertise and traditional service delivery mechanisms is also consciously exercised, and so serves to stimulate the empowerment process.

The second premise recognizes the vast potential of utilizing natural helpers and volunteers with respect to individual support and care. IL centre staff, Joshua Committee members and other consumer organizations involve, to a very significant extent, local community volunteers. The implementation and effectiveness of many independent living centre and agency programs appears to rest on an appropriate pattern of referral and linkages with informal helping networks that necessarily include fellow disabled persons. These linkages or networks are a very efficient means for moving, distributing or circulating needed goods and services.

The third premise concerns the emergent socio-psychological properties and utility of small social networks. The very acts of communicating needs and concerns, and sharing information and expertise—whether involving peers as well as professional helpers—encompasses the potential for common purpose and a shared sense of justice. There is a great deal of overlap and interplay between the situations and problems of disabled indviduals, and those of the larger community of which they are part. Innovative service delivery programs or mechanisms can instill a sense of self-confidence among many kinds of users that can stimulate newer and even further-reaching demands for services. The value of the consciousness-raising functions of many of the independent living solutions or innovations for community-building should be acknowledged.

In the community-building process, the basis of community depends not only on primary groups, natural or mediating support systems, or on helping networks alone such as what disabled people have created. It depends on the dynamic linkages between these and existing groups, institutions and community structures. The community-building process should be considered synonymous with the conscious "de-colonization" of the "life world," and the bridging, or re-integration, of the life world and the market/state system. The innovations for empowerment and independent living are considered the means by which disabled people individually and collectively can acquire and then exercise their reflexive monitoring skills, and restructure or reconstitute their motivations and interests in conscious ways. This relearning and restructuring is central to the normalization process, and to self-determination. This is what supported independence and independent living as the means and outcome of empowerment is all about.

Institutionalization, segregation and the categorization of people by ability, social class, ethnic origin or race, gender and age have all contributed to the weakening of social integration and community cohesion in general terms. This weakening has been a major source of social alienation and isolation that has resulted, unfortunately, in a burgeoning public agency and/or government "problem-solving" load, and in the tendency for professionals to "take over" and impose limited services using highly standardized and uniform definitions of problems and administrative procedures for assessing needs and allocating resources. In typical circular fashion, overspecialization, professionalization, standardization and even well-intentioned public policies further erode the social environmental basis of community, and exacerbate dependency, asymmetrical relations and alienation.

In the final analysis, the goal of independent and integrated community living that disabled persons envision—returning the person to the community and re-establishing personhood—depends ultimately and necessarily for its success on a balanced and integrated working partnership between informal or natural support systems and specialized formal systems. Disabled consumers point out that consumer organizations, independent living centres, Joshua committees and other types of social innovations have to be seen as means to certain ends, rather than as ends in themselves. Allan Simpson (1980: 30) stated quite explicitly that,

> The consumer group is not an island unto itself. It must not fall into the trap of becoming a social circle as an alternative to community integration. Rather, reaching out, it must be a sharing part of the community, always bridging gaps to enhance consumer involvement and recognition.

Simpson seems confident, as might other disabled consumers, that consumer involvement will extend beyond these mediating or alternative structures to direct participation in the political process itself.

> Growth through the consumer movement should equip many leaders with the skills to run for political office, and to offer their unique understanding of human needs, of the democratic decision-making process, and the integrity and honesty of a proven politician. Only when individual consumer involvement is established by legislation will the consumer movement have reached its pinnacle and become part of the establishment (Simpson 1980: 36).

It is the institutionalization of discourse, the expansion of the public realm via public policy formulation and legislation (Kallen 1989: 219, Chart 3, and passim) that will further enable the community-building process. In true dialectic fashion, the movement and the community influences and changes each other, and continues to do so.

IV
Towards Equal Citizenship

7

Emancipatory Politics
Equality Rights and
Reasonable Accommodation

P articipation in the independent living/disabled consumer movement, in consumer organizations and experience with different enabling structures has equipped many disabled individuals with the skills needed to participate in the democratic decision-making process at the individual, group, community, national and international levels. Action-oriented disabled individuals note the importance of establishing more independent living centres and lead the way with policy initiatives concerning integrated transportation systems, meaningful employment alternatives, dignified security income, minimum wage protection and integrated housing with appropriate forms of attendant or personal care support systems.

Further community participation necessarily calls for the involvement of disabled consumers in the political process. The 1990s offer a significant opportunity for the independent living/disabled consumer movement to establish its principles of self-determination and independent living, and for turning these concepts and principles into practical realities for the entire community. Employment, health, tax reform, transportation, housing, education and family needs are clearly pan-community concerns—not just the concerns of a few. That society is rapidly moving from a public-service and professional monopoly in the human and social services to a greater private-public mix requires that all citizens be critically aware of how their needs are going to be met. The trend towards the privatization of social services means that issues such as funding, responsibility, accountability and coordination of research will be important issues in the future.

Politically active disabled consumers no longer are concerned just with the immediate needs of only disabled people, but have over the past decade acquired a more global, holistic and integrated outlook, one that now takes into account community economic development as well as long-term social and health planning. One might speculate that the empowerment process has become as outward-directed as it once perhaps was inward-directed. An integrated and holistic outlook is the heart-and-soul of the community-building process. As Dobell and Mansbridge (1986: 28) explain,

> Social policy-making suffers, it is argued, when its major focus is seen to be exclusively the needy, the poor and the powerless. Instead, social policy should address the total community, and its objective should be the prosperity and well-being of all citizens. NGOs.... will achieve greater policy influence to the degree that they succeed in achieving identification with an informed citizenry.

Part of "getting in on" this process has involved coming to the realization that disabled citizens have a right to represent themselves in the community and to participate in the decisions that directly concern and affect them as individuals. Both political participation, self-representation and an integrated outlook are unquestionably part of self-determination. Disabled citizens do not want legislators and policy makers to identify their needs for them in the same way that traditional providers of care have done in the past.

Equality rights and the Canadian Charter of Rights and Freedoms are the basis for a variety of anti-discrimination legislation and policy developments whose intent is to enable disabled citizens to participate more fully in Canadian social and political life. The independent living/disabled consumer movement formulates a theory of equality that disabled citizens collectively insist give substance not only to the rights and freedoms contained in the Charter, but that enable their own empowering and community-building efforts as well.

The movement has tried to incorporate various concepts and approaches such as substantive equality and the notion of reasonable accommodation into a broader empowering theory of equality. The idea behind substantive equality and reasonable accommodation is to ensure as accessible a social environment as is physically and technically possible, in which disabled citizens can have the confidence to participate despite their physical or mental impairments. In the context of community-building, the notion of "unity in diversity" is important, since disabled citizens are equal to other citizens without having to be the same as them. This requires that their differences in fact be recognized and accommodated.

Federal Government Initiatives

The extent to which the independent living/disabled consumer movement has been successful in developing its particular approaches to equality rights and in reaching out to the general community might perhaps be reflected by government policy initiatives in response. In 1982 Canada's participation in the United Nation's Decade of Disabled Persons was confirmed. Since 1985, the federal government created a permanent Secretariat (Status of Disabled Persons Secretariat, which is part of the Secretary of State) to support federal initiatives that would influence positively the quality of life of disabled persons. The purpose of the Secretariat was to perform a "watchdog" function over federal departments and agencies, and to raise the consciousness of the public as well as government officials to how disabled citizens could be assisted in their quest for full citizenship. The Secretariat was to act as a catalyst in efforts to translate policies into reality.

In 1990, the Standing Committee on Human Rights and the Status of Disabled Persons recommended to the federal government that it should develop a national action strategy on the economic well-being of disabled persons. The response was the National Strategy for the Economic Integration of Persons with Disabilities, an initiative that allocates $158 million for distribution through ten federal departments and agencies (including Transport, Indian and Northern Affairs, Labour, Public Works, Employment and Immigration) over five years. In 1990 and 1991, the Coalition of Provincial Organizations of the Handicapped and the Canadian Disability Rights Council suggested to the federal government that it should introduce an omnibus bill that would amend such existing legislation such as the Canada Elections Act, the National Transportation Act and the Income Tax Act. These amendments would serve to increase disabled people's access to and participation in the greater society. While an omnibus bill was never introduced, the federal government has made some positive changes to access to polling booths, bus and air travel, and tax credits. In other areas, progress has been negligible.

Originally inspired by the efforts of the Special Parliamentary Committee on the Disabled and Handicapped (a standing committee whose members had worked closely with consumer organizations across Canada, and which had been renamed the Standing Committee on Human Rights and the Status of Disabled Persons in 1989), the federal government announced a set of organizing principles whose purpose was to guide all future policy and planning initiatives, including the National Strategy. The principles are *participation*, *access* and *awareness*. They were enunciated in recognition that, first, disabled persons should have the same opportunity to participate fully in all of the educational, employment, consumer, recreational and community activities that characterizes everyday society, and second, that the entire community was to be responsible for the necessary changes. The Chief Commissioner of the Canadian Human Rights Commission stated in his 1991 *Annual Report* that "nineteen ninety-two will be the acid test" of the government's resolve to move on the many recommendations of its own agencies and committees (p. 25). In his 1992 *Annual Report*, the Chief Commissioner stated that despite some government action, "the achievements of the last ten years have been thinly spread, often grudging, and won at a high cost to those individuals who laboured for their introduction" (p. 38).

Participation

By 1988 the federal government, in keeping with the Charter of Rights and Freedoms (especially section 15, the equality rights section) and at the behest of organized disabled citizens, took important steps towards realizing these policy principles. One of the first steps was to increase funding for the Disabled Persons Participation Program to $3.2 million per year, a five-fold increase over previous years. This program provides much-needed funding support for disabled consumer organizations, including advocacy organizations and, to a limited extent, independent living centres. The Canadian Labor Code was also amended to prohibit the discriminatory practice of paying disabled persons less than the minimum wage. By broadening the definition of disability for income tax purposes to include people with intellectual and psychiatric disabilities, the value of the income tax deduction was increased. This had the effect of enabling some 250,000 disabled consumers to qualify for the deduction, an increase in total numbers from previous years. From 1989 to 1992 the number of disability-related tax adjustments and credits was greatly increased (Canadian Human Rights Commission *Annual Report* 1992: 38).

The most comprehensive and far-reaching policy initiative undertaken in 1986 was Employment Equity legislation and the Federal Contractors Program (Employment and Immigration Canada 1986a, 1986b). The purpose of Employment Equity legislation (Bill C-62) was to promote the employment of disabled persons in the federally-regulated private sector and Crown Corporations. The latter were required to submit annual action plans for the approval by the Treasury Board which would be comprised of the identification of employment barriers, the establishment of three-year numerical targets by major occupation groups, and to increase the total number of disabled citizens hired.

By 1987 these requirements for Crown Corporations had been extended to cover all departments within the federal public service as a whole. Similarly, the Federal Contractors Program was established to create further employment opportunities in private sector firms seeking to do business with the federal government (Employment and Immigration Canada 1987c). Those companies seeking contracts with the government for goods and services valued at $200,000 or more would be required to sign a certificate committing themselves to implementing employment equity programs, subject to verification of this commitment by the government.

Despite the progress, it has not been rapid enough, especially in federal employment equity. The Disabled People for Employment Equity, a coalition only peripherally associated with COPOH, filed a complaint with the Canadian Human Rights Commission in November 1988 against nine major companies, including Canada Post, the CBC, Bell Canada and the five major banks. The coalition claimed that these nine companies hired only 94 disabled individuals out of 13,000 people that were hired in total (*Edmonton Journal*, November 18, 1988, page A5). A House of Commons committee reported that existing employment equity law lacks bite, and it recommended stringent fines and even enforcement by the Canadian Human Rights Commission (*Globe and Mail*, May 15, 1992). The CHRC's Chief Commissioner called the results "disquieting" (Canadian Human Rights Commission *Annual Report* 1991: 52), and in 1993 the Commissioner concluded that employment equity measures "have largely failed" (1992: 38).

Along with these policy initiatives in the area of participation, many federal government departments have begun to formulate their own policies and programs, or are beginning to modify their services. The National Transportation Agency has been working on accessibility standards for many years in regulations that address the requirements of disabled persons using air, rail, marine, road and other modes of transportation that come under federal jurisdiction. In 1992 the Agency published regulations pertaining to equality of service and better accessibility. From 1988 to 1990 the departments of Health and Welfare and the Secretary of State cooperated on the development of guidelines for the funding of independent living centres across Canada. This represented a "first" in moving towards a much-needed coordinated national approach in the implementation of independent living philosophies and programs.

Veterans Affairs and Canada Mortgage and Housing developed proposals for the provision of accessible housing for elderly and disabled veterans and others who qualify to reduce premature and inappropriate institutionalization. Canada Employment Centres through its "Revitalization Project 20–9" have been providing technological aids such as infra-red communication equipment, image enlargers, audio cassette players and recorders, as well as reader assistance for disabled persons using Employment and Immigration's self-help services. Employment and Immigration Canada continues to develop policies to ensure easier and more comprehensive telecommunication access to its services.

Access

One of the main program and policy initiatives concerning access was the expansion of the Court Challenges Program (Standing Committee on Human Rights and the Status of Disabled Persons 1989). Administered by the Canadian Council on Social Development, the purpose of the program was to cover all challenges to existing federal laws that were considered to conflict with the equality provisions of the Charter of Rights and Freedoms. In 1992 the federal government cancelled the Program as part of its austerity measures (Canadian Human Rights Commission *Annual Report* 1992: 33–34) and reinstated it in the winter of 1994 after much public pressure. The Justice Department produces and distributes law information packages that provide disabled citizens with information about the justice system.

Related to developments in the legal sphere, amendments to the Canada Election Act were introduced to remove restrictions on the right of mentally disabled persons to vote; existing restrictions were struck down by the courts in 1989. Interestingly, in early 1992 the Royal Commission on Electoral Reform recommended the use of competency tests to determine whether the institutionalized mentally handicapped could vote; at the end of the year the Commission withdrew its recommendation. Bill C-79, tabled in mid-1988 and becoming law in late 1989, ensured that physically disabled persons have improved access to polling stations; a Federal Court of Appeal decision in 1990 ruled in favor of the complainant, the Canadian Paraplegic Association, on this matter (*Canadian Paraplegic Association v. Elections Canada*). This decision resulted in the amendment of the Elections Act in 1992, allowing for level access to offices of all Returning Officers, advance polls and polling stations, and provinding for explanatory videos and information in braille and other formats.

With the creation of the Status of Disabled Persons Secretariat to help federal departments and agencies improve access by disabled persons to social and economic opportunities, formal consultation mechanisms have also been adopted by Treasury Board, Statistics Canada, Health and Welfare Canada, and other government departments. Treasury Board maintains ongoing consultations with an advisory committee of disabled persons on all matters related to the employment of disabled persons within the federal public service. Statistics

Canada consulted extensively with COPOH and its provincial affiliates in carrying out its Health and Activity Limitation Surveys. Health and Welfare Canada consulted with organizations of disabled consumers, their representatives and hired consultants to identify new directions for the 1988–89 federal-provincial-territorial review of the Canada Assistance Plan (CAP) and the Vocational Rehabilitation of Disabled Persons Act (VRDP). VRDP, supported by the CAP, is considered by the consumer movement to be the single most important piece of legislation affecting education and employment of disabled citizens.

The government also financed, at a cost of $720,000 over two and one-half years, the creation of the Disability Information System of Canada (DISC) at the University of Calgary's Walter Dinsdale Centre. This system was established for disabled persons to provide to other disabled persons first-hand access to current information. In late 1985 the Treasury Board issued a directive that all federal facilities be upgraded to ensure physical accessibility to the level of the Barrier Free Design Standard (BFDS) developed by Public Works Canada at an estimated cost of $110 million over ten years. In order to continually improve on existing BFDS guidelines, Public Works funded the Canadian Standards Association (CSA) to develop new technical standards on barrier-free design; the CSA consults regularly with disabled persons and consumer organizations.

Awareness

According to disabled consumer organizations, public education and awareness are quintessential to creating a climate in which positive social and economic change can occur. In advocating their own integration into the mainstream community life, disabled persons are creating an awareness of the need for concerted social action. The consumer movement has been successful in getting the federal government involved in taking initiatives with private sector umbrella organizations such as the Canadian Chamber of Commerce and the Canadian Manufacturers Association, to increase employer awareness of issues, especially reasonable accommodation in the workplace.

The government also was persuaded to provide technical and limited financial support for an annual National Access Awareness Week that began in 1988. In 1986, the federal government commissioned a comprehensive census of disabled persons in Canada at a cost of $6.4 million over three years. The goal was to help consumer organizations raise awareness about the scope and nature of their concerns. These data, argue disabled citizens, should aid policy planning processes in the public and private sectors.

Developments at other levels include: A push for the more positive portrayal of disabled citizens in government publications (Treasury Board), new provisions for disabled students under the Canada Student Loans Program, the development of an extensive data base on disabled people in different countries (External Affairs), the development of an information package to sensitize employees who deal with the public (RCMP), and the distribution of information on hazardous products to disabled consumers (Consumer and Corporate Affairs). These public sector initiatives represent the outcome of empowerment efforts by disabled people.

The Struggle for Charter Protection

The patriation of Canada's constitution on April 17, 1982 not only marked Canada's final assertion of independence from Britain, but it heralded a new era which provides constitutional protection for the rights and freedoms of all Canadians. The Canadian Charter of Rights and Freedoms which forms Part I of the Constitution Act (1982) prescribes the political, legal and egalitarian rights regarded by Canadians to be essential to Canadian society. Section 52 of the Act declares the Constitution to be the supreme law of Canada. All the laws of Canada must conform with the principles and standards articulated by the Constitution. Those laws which do not comply with constitutional standards can be struck down by the courts as being unconstitutional.

One of the most significant sections of the Charter of Rights and Freedoms that has received the most attention and debate as to its impact is section 15, the equality rights section. The potential social and political impact of section 15 caused Parliament to impose a three-year moratorium on the operation of this section to enable Parliament and the provinces to conduct a legal audit to ensure that various federal and provincial laws did not contravene the equality guarantees. Section 15(1)(2) of the Charter finally came into force on

April 17, 1985. It was the conviction of many groups and individuals, including disabled consumers, that the legal review carried out by governments between 1982 and 1985 accomplished very little and produced legislative changes that amounted to mere cosmetic and tokenistic gestures. Many equality issues, those pertaining to disability as well as those pertaining to other characteristics, subsequently have ended up or will end up in the courts for resolution.

The Charter of Rights and its equality rights section are products of a great deal of drafting and redrafting. The end result reflects considerable input from many interest groups and citizens. Prior to the final Constitutional accord assented to by the Prime Minister and the provincial First Ministers, the Special Joint Committee of the Senate and the House of Commons on the Constitution of Canada (also known as the Hays-Joyal Committee) convened hearings in 1980 and 1981, and invited interest groups to provide the committee with their views on rights and freedoms the Charter should protect. The committee considered about 1,000 written and oral submissions in all [Minutes and Proceedings of Evidence, 1st Sess., 32nd Parliament, 1980–81].

Initially the Joint Committee did not support the inclusion of persons with disabilities in section 15(1). The omission of disabled persons was deliberate. It was assumed that the needs of disabled citizens were adequately addressed by existing federal and provincial human rights legislation. As well, it was feared by some that the inclusion of disability in section 15(1) would force public sector expenditures of large sums of money to accommodate the rights of disabled persons. Curiously, in retrospect, disability was the only ground which caused the committee to consider dollar cost as a factor in its deliberations of extending constitutional protection to a designated, or enumerated, group.

According to Lepofsky and Bickenbach (1985), strong arguments for a handicap amendment actually came from three forums. First, the arguments were part of a more general public debate over patriation and were put forth in various public forums, in the media and in letters and petitions aimed at legislators. The second forum was the Special Commitee of the House of Commons on the Disabled and the Handicapped, an all-party committee struck in 1980 to inquire into the status and needs of the country's disabled persons. The committee heard from about 400 witnesses during hearings held through the summer of 1980 about the need for expanded legal protection against disability-based discrimination. Again, the arguments were strongly and consistently in favor of constitutional rather than legislative provisions to this effect.

Third, the case for stronger and more comprehensive rights of disabled people was articulated formally in briefs and presentations to the Special Joint Committee. Three principal advocates for the amendment appeared before the committee: The Coalition of Provincial Organizations of the Handicapped, the Canadian Association for the Mentally Retarded (CAMR), and the Canadian National Institute for the Blind (CNIB). Organizations such as the Canadian Labor Congress, the Royal Canadian Legion, the Canadian Human Rights Commission and even the Canadian Jewish Congress joined in support of COPOH, CAMR and the CNIB for the expansion of section 15(1)(2) entitlements (Minutes and Proceedings of Evidence, Vols. 10, 11; Lepofsky and Bickenbach 1985: passim).

Disabled citizens protested loudly and pressured politicians to reverse the committee's decision not to introduce the handicap amendment. COPOH appeared before the Special Joint Committee and argued strenuously that the inclusion of disability rights in the Charter would not only afford greater legal protection for the rights of persons with disabilities, but also would symbolize Canada's commitment to disabled persons as first class citizens (Minutes and Proceedings of Evidence, Vol. 12: 26–44; Lepofsky and Bickenbach 1985: passim). These arguments also were advanced when Canada, together with other nations, prepared to proclaim 1981 the International Year of The Disabled Person.

During the hearings in 1980 the Special Joint Committee was confronted by the fact that physically and mentally disabled persons in Canada constitute a significant and numerically large disadvantaged minority, that disabled persons are regularly victimized by intentional and unintentional acts of discrimination, and that overt and more subtle forms of discrimination constitute a major barrier to full participation in mainstream Canadian life.

In testimony before the committee the Chief Commissioner of the

Canadian Human Rights Commission (Gordon Fairweather, Minutes and Proceedings of Evidence, Vol. 5: 17; Lepofsky and Bickenbach 1985: passim) stated that over 20 percent of all complaints to the Commission dealt with alleged employment discrimination against disabled persons. Fairweather noted that an unemployment rate of almost 80 percent afflicted disabled persons. The Special Committee was presented with evidence that showed that discrimination on the basis of disability was reinforced by existing provincial legislation regarding group homes and sheltered workshops, coupled with municipal zoning bylaws that had the effect of segregating disabled people. There was also evidence of exceptions to minimum wage legislation that permitted the paying of even lower wages for a disabled person's labor. The Special Committee learned that blind persons could not serve on juries, that certain disabled persons were not entitled to welfare benefits, that disabled children were segregated from mainstream education institutions, and even that the federal Immigration Act discriminated against immigration applicants.

The pressure upon the government to accept and enshrine constitutional guarantees for disabled people was, in the words of disabled consumer advocates, overwhelming and unequivocal (Minutes and Proceedings of Evidence, Vol. 12: 30, statement by COPOH). Equality rights for the disabled were deemed no less important than they were for other minority groups enumerated in section 15(1). In January 1981, Jean Chretien, then federal Minister of Justice, responded to the demands and the evidence of the disabled community, and that of others, by announcing that section 15(1) would be extended to include the equality rights of persons who are mentally or physically disabled. This was to be the last minority category enumerated under the section. Moreover, the phrase "mental or physical disability" was inserted in section 15(2)'s list of designated minority groups for the purpose of affirmative action programs.

The final adoption of the handicap amendment was clearly a significant step (Kallen 1989: 16). By this act, Canada was the only country in the world that had specifically, and formally, accorded constitutional protection to rights of disabled persons. Canada has more than fulfilled its international obligations with respect to the rights of disabled persons (e.g., the 1975 United Nations Declaration of the Rights of Disabled Persons; see also Kallen 1989: 5–12).

Section 15(1) of the Charter of Rights reads as follows:

> Every individual is equal before and under the law and has the right to the equal protection and equal benefit of the law without discrimination and, in particular, without discrimination based on race, national or ethnic origin, colour, religion, sex, age, or mental or physical disability.

Under section 15(1), the term equality consists of four clauses, each of which represents a particular aspect of equality. "Equality before the law" refers to the application and administration of the law. That is, the law must apply equally to all persons; no one stands above the law. In general, equality before the law is concerned with how the law is carried out and not with what the law actually says or does. This type of equality is sometimes referred to as procedural equality. By contrast, "equality under the law" deals specifically with the content of laws and how they treat people. Laws which single out or classify on unreasonable, arbitrary and unfair grounds could be characterized as constituting an inequality under the law. For example, a particular law that prohibits blue-eyed persons from becoming doctors may be considered a clear denial of equality under the law.

For disabled citizens, "equal protection" and "equal benefit" of the law are the clauses which offer the greatest potential in extending the scope of section 15(1). These clauses can be used to not only advance equal opportunity but equality of results as well; this means that people must not only be treated equally, but that additional steps must be taken to ensure that people benefit equally. For example, an educational institution that makes its premises accessible to students with disabilities in order that they may enroll in the courses of their choice, provides those students with an equal opportunity to participate. That same educational institution, however, that provides additional services such as sign language interpreters, alternate media and technical aids, also provides equality of results by ensuring that disabled students can benefit to the same extent as their nondisabled counterparts.

It is thought that the "equal protection" and "equal benefit" clauses of section 15(1) have the potential of placing an onus on governments to accommodate the unique needs of disadvantaged persons. This concept receives further support from section 15(2) which endorses the development of affirmative action programs that have as their object the amelioration of conditions of disadvantaged individuals and groups.

The specific ramifications of the equality rights provisions have yet to be fully unravelled (see Smith et al. 1986). Complicating matters has been the Meech Lake Accord (1987) as well as the Charlottetown Accord (1992), unsuccessful proposed amendments to Canada's Constitution.

There was concern that the proposed amendments would have had negative impacts on the rights of specific ethnic and nonethnic minorities. It was suggested by women's groups, the disabled and by other nonethnic minorities originally enumerated under section 15 of the Charter that their rights would be weakened considerably by both the Meech Lake and Charlottetown Accord's focus on the rights of Canada's "founding majorities," and by the specific lack of reference to certain other groups. Also, it was argued that both Accords would have even further entrenched a hierarchy or "pecking order" of minority inequalities that the Charter of Rights had initially created (Gadacz 1988, Kallen 1988, 1989: 181–86, Cairns 1988, Canadian Disability Rights Council 1992: 3, 6, Advocacy Resource Centre for the Handicapped 1992: 2, COPOH 1992a, 1992b). Representatives of ethnic and nonethnic minorities were hopeful that had either of the two Accords become part of the Constitution it would have included a provision ensuring that all statutes, including the Constitution, would be interpreted in light of the Canadian Charter of Rights.

The Charlottetown Accord, especially the Canada Clause, drew the ire of disabled citizens. The original proposal for a Canada Clause included a commitment to the equality of men and women without regard to physical or mental disability, as well as a commitment to the rights of citizens as set forth in the Canadian Charter of Rights and Freedoms. This clause certainly would have addressed the Meech Lake problem for persons with disabilities. In the final legal text of the Charlottetown Accord, however, citizens with disabilities were dropped from reference in the Canada Clause while reference to gender and racial equality remained. In addition, the clause as set out in the legal text provided a *general* commitment to human rights, but did not specifically declare the Canadian Charter to be supreme law. The clause stated that courts and governments were to interpret the Constitution, including the Charter of Rights, in a manner consistent with its terms.

According to legal opinion (Advocacy Resource Centre for the Handicapped 1992), the omission of a reference to disabled people would have had the effect of giving people with disabilities a lower level of equality protection, if any at all, and a legal as well as symbolic downgrading of their place in Canada. The omission in the Canada Clause could have mandated constitutionally an adjustment of public priorities to the serious and widespread detriment of disabled citizens. What especially angered disabled citizens was that the wording of the clause, in its failure to reaffirm the rights of disabled citizens while at the same time setting out the fundamental characteristics of Canada (racial and ethnic equality, individual and collective human rights, equality of female and male persons, language duality, aboriginal rights, the distinctiveness of Quebec), made it seem like the equality rights of people with disabilities were not considered a fundamental characteristic of Canada. Believing that the Charter rights of disabled citizens were being undermined, COPOH issued a press release six days before the national referendum, urging a "no" vote. The Charlottetown Accord was rejected by Canadians on October 26, 1992.

Equality and the Disabled Consumer Movement

Yvonne Peters (1987b), legal counsel with the Canadian Disability Rights Counsel, suggests that a distinction should be made between formal and substantive equality. Representative organizations of the independent living/disabled consumer movement such as COPOH and its affiliates have believed it essential that a theory of equality be developed that reflects the movement's vision of full participation and equality of persons with disabilities. Disabled citizens have asserted that the task of constructing a framework for equality should not be done by lawyers, judges and even politicians, but that disabled people must participate.

A coherent theory of equality is said to be founded on certain assumptions, values and principles. Equality as a concept does not evolve in a vacuum; it is a product of definite moral and political ideals, and values. Awareness of the various political, social, moral and philosophical forces that influence the development of such a concept is important. Gold (1983: 132, op. cited in Peters 1987b) has stated that

> A particular conception of equality cannot be said to be right or wrong. The most that one can say is that it does or does not fit with a particular political or moral theory. As such, it is not surprising that equality is a political ideal around which revolves the most profound ideological controversies.

Peters suggests that a civil libertarian may view equality as the right to be left alone to pursue his or her goals without state interference. Alternatively, a feminist view of equality may adhere to the principle that to be equal is to be nonsubordinated to male dominance. A communitarian perspective on equality, notes Peters, may hinge on providing benefits that enhance the collective well-being of all members of a community.

The courts, including the Supreme Court of Canada, have rejected a narrow and technical interpretation of equality rights in favor of a purposive approach (Smith 1986: 356–60). The courts have eschewed a restricted view of the language employed by the Charter in favor of a more liberal approach that supposedly breathes life and meaning into the different sections by considering the value of a particular right or freedom that is protected. A "purpose and effect test" is applied to determine the validity of a law that is contrary to the spirit of the Charter.

To illustrate this point, consider the case of *R. v. Big M Drug Mart* [1985 1 S.C.R. 295]. The Supreme Court declared that the federal Lord's Day Act was invalid and had no force or effect, because it infringed on the religious freedoms guaranteed by the Charter. Had the court determined that the law in question possessed a secular purpose, the court would have then considered the effect of the law on those persons alleging the breach. According to the Big M Drug Mart decision, a law may be rendered unconstitutional not only because of a discriminatory purpose, but also because of a discriminatory effect (Pentney 1988: 22, n. 26b).

The independent living/disabled consumer movement has attempted to distinguish between *formal* and *substantive* equality in order to argue that both should be within the ambit of legislative and judiciary interpretation—at least according to section 15(1) of the Charter. The notion of formal equality concerns the similar or identical treatment of individuals regardless of their differences. Using gender to illustrate her point, Peters argues that under a theory of formal equality the desire to create a gender neutral and nonsexist world would focus on abolishing the differences between males and females. While there are many differences that could be eliminated because of their sexist and oppressive nature, treating women exactly the same as men would only have the effect of excluding such important issues as rape, prostitution and wife abuse that are of unique concern to women from equality considerations. Clearly, the focus should not be on gender or disability differences, but on the differences that gender or disability makes or creates. Applying a theory of formal equality would not address historical patterns of political and socioeconomic inequalities that are part of women's or any supposedly disadvantaged group's experience.

A similar result is produced were a theory of formal equality to be adopted in dealing with disabled people's rights. To treat disabled persons precisely in the same manner as nondisabled persons would completely disregard the various structural and systemic discriminatory barriers that exist in the community and in society that are of deep concern to the disabled consumer movement. The case of *Huck v. Canadian Odeon Theatres Ltd.* [1981 2 C.H.R.R. D/521, also Re: Saskatchewan Human Rights Commission and Canadian Odeon Theatres 1985 18 D.L.R. (4th) 93] serves to illustrate this point. Michael Huck was treated exactly like all other patrons wishing to see a movie in an Odeon theatre. However, because he used a wheelchair he was forced to view the movie from in front of the first row of theatre seats. Although Odeon Theatres treated Huck identically to other patrons, identical treatment created a negative effect because he is different in one respect from a nondisabled person or from other patrons.

The Saskatchewan Court of Appeal agreed with this analysis and ruled that identical treatment does not result necessarily in equal treatment. Measures such as reasonable accommodation and programs such as affirmative action, including employment equity, would probably find little favor under a formal approach to equality. In a society that welcomes gender, cultural, social, religious and other "differences" between people, such a formal approach to equality would seriously undermine the goals of liberal pluralism. From the perspective of disabled people there would certainly be little to gain from supporting a formal approach to equality. In its analysis of the Canada Clause of the Charlottetown Accord, the Canadian Disability Rights Council (1992: 6) suggested that the wording of the clause seemed to advance a formal theory of equality, since no mention was made of the historically experienced social, political and legal disadvantages of women and racial minorities. The CDRC and other organizations maintained that "true equality may require that people be treated differently to reflect their differing needs and circumstances" (Advocacy Resource Centre for the Handicapped 1992: 2).

Indeed, the "equal protection" and "equal benefit" clauses of section 15(1) and the affirmative action provisions of section 15(2), together with the "purpose and effect" test that the courts have applied, suggest that another dimension of equality exists and should be recognized. From the perspective of disabled citizens, applying neutral standards will not eliminate inequality and oppression. A theory of equality must recognize that there really are differences between people and that not everyone is the same. Equality does not mean "sameness." Factors such as powerlessness, exclusion and disadvantage are the direct consequence of the subordination of certain groups and the domination of others, and the application of neutral standards implies "sameness" or conformity to specific values and ideals.

Most human rights statutes in Canada now recognize that discrimination can be both intentional as well as have an adverse effect on people. This distinction has enabled individuals who have been affected adversely by a procedure, program, policy or law because of their "differences" to seek legal redress for the harm that was suffered. One can argue that one of the purposes of the equality rights section of the Charter is not only to ensure that people are treated in a "like manner," but also to recognize the inequalities created by disadvantage or adverse effect.

Disabled citizens perhaps would argue that the notion or idea of substantive equality does not imply a double standard. Clearly, one of the goals of disabled people is to be integrated into the community. This involves taking the same risks and, at the same time, assuming the same responsibilities as other citizens. A substantive approach to equality does not negate this goal, according to them. Rather, this approach provides a means by which to assert such demands as reasonable accommodation, affirmative action programs, special tax deductions and significantly greater access to the physically constructed environment.

A theory of substantive equality legitimizes the goal of ensuring equality of results; both formal and substantive equality have a place in section 15 of the Charter of Rights and Freedoms. Equality "before" and "under" the law implies a form of procedural equality. This means that the law must apply to and must treat everyone fairly. The guarantee of procedural equality is based on the notion of formal equality, that is, everyone has the right to expect that the law will be applied to all persons in an equal manner. To bring a challenge under the Charter, an individual must indicate that the law as it applies to him or her is discriminatory on grounds of arbitrariness, unfairness and unreasonableness.

By contrast, substantive equality would come into effect where a claim is made that a particular law perpetuates a certain socio-economic disadvantage. In a situation such as this, section 15(1) of the Charter sets out grounds which are also found in most provincial human rights statutes that may serve as a guide in identifying those groups in society who experience adverse effect discrimination. Other grounds such as political beliefs, citizenship, marital status and sexual orientation also have been cited as possible bases for substantive equality claims.

The disabled community recognizes that it is not enough to make a claim for substantive equality on the basis of one of these grounds or on any another enumerated in the Charter. But disabled citizens do argue that members of groups that have been victimized by discrimination and that suffer disadvantage and powerlessness should receive the protection of a substantive approach to equality under the Charter of Rights.

To advance a claim for substantive equality under section 15 one must first show that one is a member of one of the enumerated groups that are recognized by the Charter and specifically protected by it. Second, an individual must be able to demonstrate that he or she has suffered disadvantage worthy of a substantive equality remedy. Essential to community-building, a comprehensive theory of equality requires both formal and substantive approaches. As members of Canadian society we are all entitled to formal equality, while at the same time citizens who can show that they are being disadvantaged should also be entitled to substantive equality that takes into account some of the inherent social, cultural and physical individual differences between them.

Discrimination and the Law: A Basis for the Concept of Reasonable Accommodation

Lepofsky and Bickenbach (1985: 328) have pointed out that equality rights expressly for disabled people is a recent development which does not have its roots in the common law. According to these authors there is no general common law principle affirming the entitlement of disabled people to equality of rights under law. During the past ten years disabled Canadians have therefore made major strides in attaining equality by securing legal recognition of their community and citizenship rights in human rights legislation. Through considerable efforts, disabled citizens have succeeded finally in acquiring legal protection of their human rights at both provincial/territorial and federal levels. During the 1980s the federal government, along with several of the provinces, amended human rights legislation to ensure that such protection also extended to persons with mental disabilities.

The inclusion of persons with disabilities in human rights statutes means that, in theory, discrimination on the basis of disability is prohibited in areas as employment, housing accommodation, and access to goods, services and facilities. In the Charter of Rights and Freedoms, the equality rights section has filled a gap in Canadian human rights law. Applied specifically to disabled people, it is "a genuinely *new* and unprecedented right in Canada" (Lepofsky and Bickenbach 1985: 331–32).

Disabled persons have obtained statutory and constitutional protection of their rights over the past two decades represents an unequivocal accomplishment. Statutory rights to equality under the law without discrimination on the basis of physical disability were mostly nonexistent before the 1970s. As disabled citizens have come to discover, a great deal now depends on how existing power structures, including the governments and the courts, will interpret and apply these legislative protections and constitutional guarantees. Disabled persons must actively continue their efforts to press for the particular kind of equality they believe will help eliminate their often shared experiences of stigma, oppression and exclusion from mainstream community life. Identifying discriminatory barriers to integrated community living that exist and proposing methods of eliminating discrimination is an obvious place to begin.

Disabled citizens identify and confront several types of exclusionary and discriminatory barriers (Baker 1985: passim, Lepofsky and Bickenbach 1985: 324–26). Social bias discrimination denies a particular benefit to an individual solely because of ignorance, discomfort or hostility aimed at the group or category to which the individual supposedly belongs or with which he or she is identified. These attitudes have been responsible for the development of segregated services and for preventing full participation and integration into the community. Social bias also may manifest itself through stereotyping or stigmatization. Poverty, low levels of attained education and lack of self-worth—the consequences of discrimination—are factors that perpetuate the notion that disabled persons are helpless, incapable and dependent, and by implication, inferior to able-bodied persons. The barriers provoked by social bias have nothing to do with a disabled individual's ability and/or competence. A negative attitude about a particular trait connected with an individual or category of individual constitutes the basis of exclusion.

Standards as applied in law or elsewhere, appearing neutral, also can operate to exclude certain classes or categories of individuals. A "neutral standard" barrier establishes a general rule or condition that has, unintentionally, a negative impact on a disabled person's access to equal opportunity. Unlike some social bias barriers, neutral standard barriers are not intentionally aimed specifically at excluding persons, but they impede a person's access to equal opportunity. Examples might include standard telephones which are not compatible with hearing aid equipment; a request about a potential employee possessing a driver's license which cannot be obtained by visually impaired persons; a requirement that a potential employee pass a medical physical examination which obtains information pertaining to an individual's physical health which is not relevant to the job in question.

A third barrier, "failure to accommodate," arises when two factors are present: first, except for an individual's impairment, the individual possesses the qualifications necessary to perform the job in question; second, that efforts were not made to actively accommodate the individual's limitations created by his or her impairment. For example, a deaf university student would without question benefit from classroom participation, and no neutral standard otherwise would bar the student. However, the institution's or the student's inability or failure to provide interpreter services, combined with the student's communication impairment, would serve to prevent the student's full participation.

Disabled citizens cite "insurmountable impairment" barriers as those caused by an individual's disability that cannot be rectified to permit full participation in a program, service or employment situation (Baker 1985, passim). Absent drastic alterations, no degree of accommodation could reasonably provide the benefits of programs and services to the impaired person. Accommodation is virtually impossible since the impairment, whatever it might be, removes an essential capacity for benefitting from what the program, service or employment possibility might offer. In this situation, alternative programs, services and accommodating structures as an altogether different dimension to accommodation would be sought.

To these four barriers might be added an important fifth, namely "neglect" of differences. Disabled citizens find that exclusionary barriers exist primarily because "society" ignores or neglects differences between people. Society is composed of people exhibiting a wide variety of differences, which include linguistic, cultural and religious differences, as well as educational, physical and biological differences. Programs, services, policies and laws that treat people as if they were identical serve to maintain the domination and interests of a small group by further exacerbating discriminatory barriers. In reality, differences may not be perceived, they may be ignored on purpose, or it may be felt that, for utilitarian reasons, they need not even be addressed. This is how "differences" between people have often been dealt with in law and in public policy.

A discriminatory barrier identified by Kallen (1989: 75–77) that is not at all an obvious one is "discrimination of silence," or discriminatory acts of omission. Discrimination of silence is when "majority members—those with the legitimate power to do something—choose to say nothing and do nothing about discrimination against minorities." Majority members such as academic researchers, social scientists, educators, law enforcers, policy makers and others continue to violate the rights of minorities by discouraging research on particular topics and by insisting that stigmatized minorities are either deviants or categorically different from others in society. Whether those "in power" do nothing, cover up or continue to justify differences between people because they are afraid of stigma by association, face-to-face encounters or of exposing the invalidation myths on which policies are founded, their (in)actions continue to violate fundamental principles of human rights (Kallen 1989: 75).

To inject meaning into the goal of eliminating the various types of discrimination encountered by persons with disabilities, clearly, the concept of "reasonable accommodation" must be recognized and developed. Reasonable accommodation refers to measures that are designed to enable a disabled person to overcome barriers resulting from either his or her disability, or from the environment. Reasonable accommodation an equalizing force that ensures that a disabled person is no more burdened than his or her nondisabled peers when participating in normal community living. However, because reasonable accommodation allegedly is associated with large expenditures of public money as well as "inconvenience" to society in general, the idea has been negatively perceived.

Intentional and Unintentional Discrimination

To understand how the concept of reasonable accommodation can be useful in reducing or eliminating the effects and consequences of the discriminatory behaviors, the term "discrimination" must be defined. It has been only in the last twenty years or so that the scope and impact of discrimination on disadvantaged groups has received concerted attention. The last two decades have seen the introduction of human rights legislation and the establishment of human rights commissions to administer and enforce the legislation (Tarnopolsky and

Pentney 1985: Chapters 2, 3, 14, and 15). At the same time, the existence of human rights legislation precipitated the need to develop theories of discrimination to assist in the interpretation of such legislation. An evolution of an understanding of discrimination has developed that has probed the social, economic and political forces underlying such practices, behaviors and policies.

Discriminatory behavior can be divided into two general categories, or types: Intentional (direct) and unintentional (indirect) (Kallen 1989: 71). Initially, human rights legislation focused on prohibiting intentional forms of discrimination because it was obvious and relatively easier to identify. In the past, Canadian courts have given human rights legislation a very narrow interpretation. Frequently, direct discrimination is motivated by ill will, malice or prejudice, which is harboured by an individual against other individuals or groups (Tarnopolsky and Pentney 1985: 4.29). This form of discrimination occurs when an individual consciously and deliberately restricts or denies opportunities to certain persons who happen to possess a certain characteristic. The chief element that must be proven in a complaint of intentional discrimination is that the perpetrator intended to discriminate. Most human rights commissions seem to have developed a fair track record for handling complaints of this type (Canadian Human Rights Commission *Annual Reports* 1987–93).* However, remedies for this type of complaint usually only benefit the individual complainant, and do little to resolve broader, subtler and

---

* Edward Hore, writing in *Saturday Night* magazine (September 1989, p. 25–28), has all but condemned the commissions for the inordinate length of time it takes them to resolve cases (despite huge budgets), for the large costs that are incurred (usually by respondents), for inadequate investigations of often invalid complaints and for their political connections. Hore suggests that commissions should do nothing more than recommend cases to Crown prosecutors who would decide whether a case should go to court or not, and developing legal aid for those who need it. Hore's point may be a good one, in light of the need to often go beyond the individual case to address institutional and systemic discrimination. Research by Frideres and Reeves (1989) confirmed that the Canadian Human Rights Commission is very limited in its abilities and powers to investigate human rights complaints and to resolve them in cases of unintentional or indirect discrimination. Frideres and Reeves suggest that the Commission is designed to combat violations of formalized, institutionalized behavior.

more insidious forms of discrimination that are a great deal more pervasive in society.

As human rights law developed, it became clear that focusing on intentional, or direct, discriminatory practices and behaviors did little to remove the barriers to equality of opportunity. Policies, practices and procedures constituted barriers, either in and of themselves, or when carried out. Unintentional, or indirect, discrimination is referred to as adverse effect, institutional or systemic discrimination (Tarnopolsky and Pentney 1985: 4.34 ff, Hughes 1985: 228, Kallen 1989: 72–73, 80–100). An individual's intent and motivation is no longer the sole factor in determining whether discrimination has occurred. Rather, it is the harmful effect that a particular program, policy or practice may have on a group of individuals that becomes important. A policy or practice that appears neutral can be determined to have created a negative impact on a certain category of persons. The recognition of the harmful effects caused by unintentional discrimination requires that social institutions and systems be monitored and evaluated.

One of the earliest cases to address the effects of unintentional discrimination was rendered in 1971 by the United States Supreme Court in *Griggs v. Duke Power Company Ltd.* [401 U.S. 424 1971]. The Duke Power Company had an employment policy of hiring both black and white employees. However, to be considered for or to obtain a promotion employees were required to possess a grade twelve certificate and pass an aptitude test. Griggs alleged that such requirements were not employment related and that due to socio-economic factors, such requirements had the net effect of eliminating a disproportionately higher number of black individuals than other people. The U.S. Supreme Court agreed with Griggs, and held that practices or procedures which were neutral in their face, and which do not constitute a business necessity, cannot be maintained if they perpetuate discrimination against a category or class of persons.

Importantly, the Griggs analysis has been adopted in a number of Canadian cases (Tarnopolsky and Pentney 1985: Chapter 4; see the essays in Smith et al. 1986). Of particular note are two cases decided by the Supreme Court of Canada in 1985 (Pentney 1988: 14–17, 21–32, Hughes 1985: 228–29). The case of *O'Malley v. Simpson-Sears* [1985 2 S.C.R. 536] as well as *Bhinder v. Canadian National Railways*

[1985 2 S.C.R. 561] endorsed the practice of interpreting existing human rights statutes to include prohibitions of unintentional forms of discrimination. At issue in O'Malley was whether a complainant had to prove that there was an intention to discriminate before an allegation of discrimination could be substantiated.

O'Malley, a Seventh Day Adventist, was reduced from full-time to part-time work because her employer, Simpson-Sears, required her to work Saturdays. The company restricted her hours because she could not work Saturdays, which they deemed an essential requirement for a full-time position. The court subsequently rejected the notion that the Ontario human rights code only prohibited intentional discrimination, and it adopted the view that the code also protected persons from unintentional or "adverse effect" forms of discrimination. The requirement to work Saturdays in order to secure full-time work was found to be a form of adverse effect discrimination in that the requirement affected a person differently from others by imposing a particular obligation or penalty. The judgement discussed the duty of an employer to provide some form of reasonable accommodation for those employees adversely affected by an employment policy.

The reasoning articulated in the O'Malley decision was adopted by the Supreme Court of Canada in the Bhinder case, but with an entirely different outcome. Bhinder was decided under the Canadian Human Rights Act, and involved a man of the Sikh religion who worked in a CN coach yard. Canadian National's hard hat policy, making the wearing of a safety helmet mandatory for employees working in the coach yard, came into direct conflict with a fundamental precept of Bhinder's religion, namely that a Sikh male must always wear a turban, over which nothing could be worn. Bhinder would not compromise his religious beliefs by wearing a hard hat, and so was forced to terminate his employment with CN.

The main issue considered by the courts was not the employer's attitude toward Sikhs, but the effect of the hard hat rule on a class of persons because of their religious beliefs. While the court acknowledged that adverse effect discrimination was prohibited by the Act, Canadian National's rule was upheld on the ground that it was a *bona fide* occupational requirement (BFOR) as described by the Act. While the O'Malley case was decided under the Ontario Human Rights Act and the Bhinder case under the Canadian Human Rights Act which encompasses federal jurisdiction, the Supreme Court issued a clear message declaring that both intentional and unintentional forms of discrimination are prohibited by both provincial and federal human rights statutes.

Defences to Allegations of Discrimination

Intentional and unintentional forms of discrimination have taken their toll in preventing the participation of persons with disabilities in their communities and in society. Discrimination creates social and economic barriers that alienate and oppress persons with disabilities. An alleged act of discrimination even under human rights legislation may not necessarily entitle the complainant to a remedy.

Provincial and federal human rights statutes contain an "exception clause" usually pertaining to employment that permits the contravention of anti-discrimination provisions set out in the legislation. This clause refers to the "reasonable occupational qualification" (ROQ), or more commonly, the "*bona fide* occupational qualification" or requirement (BFOQ/R) clauses in a statute. Qualifications may be on the basis of age, gender, marital status and perhaps physical and mental disability (Tarnopolsky and Pentney 1985: 4.46–4.50, 9.22–9.27, Pentney 1988: 17–20). Their purpose is to provide employers with a defence to charges of discrimination where the employer can demonstrate that the "offending" practice or policy is necessary to the performance of a task or job.

The BFOQ clauses suggest that employers are allowed to intentionally discriminate on otherwise prohibited grounds. The BFOQ clauses in provincial human rights statutes often directly mention specific limiting characteristics, such as age, gender, marital status, and physical ability. The BFOQ clause found in the federal Canadian Human Rights Act, however, takes a slightly different approach. Employment practices exempted under the Act are not connected to a specific characteristic at all; rather, the Act merely states that any limitation or specification expressed by the employer must be a *bona fide* occupational requirement.

Despite differences between federal and provincial human rights legislation, employers are obliged to meet certain requirements before being able to claim a BFOQ (or BFOR) defense. *Ontario Human Rights Commission v. Borough of Etobicoke* [1982 1 S.C.R. 202], decided by the Supreme Court of Canada in 1982 (Tarnopolsky and Pentney 1985: 9.26, Hughes 1985: 231–32), is often cited. The case involved a firefighter who was mandatorily retired at age 60, which was in violation of the Ontario Human Rights Code. The respondent argued that firefighting was a demanding and rigorous occupation, which qualified age as a BFOQ. The Court said that to meet a BFOQ defense, the employer is obliged to show, first, that the requirement or limitation is based on an honest and genuinely held belief and, second, that this particular employment requirement is related in an objective sense to the performance of the job. In this instance, the employer had to provide factual evidence demonstrating or proving that persons over the age of 60 cannot fight fires effectively.

According to Supreme Court decisions and human rights tribunals rulings, however, it is not advisable to prohibit discrimination against certain classes or categories of persons in all instances. There might be some situations in which a distinction based on a characteristic *is* justifiable to ensure satisfactory job performance. For example, an employer of taxi drivers might reasonably deny employment to persons who are blind, even though that would, obviously, constitute discrimination on the basis of physical disability. In *Tymchyshyn v. Canadian Pacific Ltd.* (Canadian Human Rights Commission *Annual Report* 1992: 86) the issue was whether the company's blanket policy prohibiting insulin-dependent diabetics from working with machinery could be a legitimate BFOR, and that the policy was necessary to eliminate a genuine risk. But in order to justify discrimination against an entire category of persons (for example, blind persons), the reasoning has been that the employer must show that practically any person who can be identified as a member of that category, possesses a characteristic that prevents him or her from performing the necessary or essential duties of the job in a satisfactory way.

Stereotypical assumptions are not condoned. An employer cannot assume that a woman will not be able to perform strenuous manual labor even if, arguably, men on average have greater capacity for physical work. It is still necessary to show, as in the Etobicoke case, that there is a "problem" with all members of a class. Impressionistic evidence is not sufficient to establish a case. Onus of proof is on the employer and the evidence, if sufficient, must establish that few if any members of a particular category can meet the requirements of the job.

Disabled citizens argue that implicit in establishing an occupational requirement is the requirement that employers make a reasonable effort to accommodate an individual who would otherwise be subject to discrimination. Most provincial human rights legislation, even that amended or revised since the Charter of Rights became law and including the Canadian Human Rights Act, do not possess specific enough provisions prescribing a duty to provide reasonable accommodation. Reasonable accommodation would be a type of affirmative action because the concept requires positive action on the part of an employer to make reasonable accommodation to a known physical or mental limitation of an otherwise qualified employee.

Before an employment requirement can be deemed to be reasonably necessary, an employer must first show that providing reasonable accommodation is impossible or impractical. An employer could easily show that the exclusion of blind persons from positions as taxi drivers as being reasonably necessary in that the provision of some form of accommodation is impossible. However, an employer who excludes all persons who use wheelchairs because the worksite can only be accessed by climbing stairs would probably not meet the "reasonably necessary" element because it might be possible to make structural renovations to the worksite. An employer must be able to show that a specific characteristic of an otherwise protected category of persons can be predicted to almost always lead to employment failure, and/or that accommodations for such persons would be unreasonable, or impractical in terms of material costs and safety. The Bhinder case shows that reasonable accommodation may not always be possible, and that discrimination may be justified in law in some instances.

The Supreme Court in O'Malley stated that where it is shown that a rule has caused discrimination the onus is on the employer to make a reasonable effort to accommodate the needs of employees, short of "undue hardship" in the operation of that business. Significantly, the judgement in the O'Malley decision also included a statement to the effect that "no right is absolute," and that "rights must be limited in the interest of preserving a social structure in which each right may receive protection without undue interference from others" (*op. cit.* McIntyre, J. in Peters 1987a: 18cf., Kallen 1989: 6).

An employee should expect an employer to accommodate his or her religious beliefs—or disability. At the same time, an employer should not be expected to provide accommodations that are unreasonable, that could result in a disruption of business or that involves undue expense. A balance must be struck between these two positions, and it is the notion of reasonable accommodation that might provide it (Tarnopolsky and Pentney 1985: 9.27–9.33, Ratushny 1986).

Reasonable Accommodation: Definitions and Legal Issues

Achieving equality for persons with disabilities so that they may live independently and be integrated into the community cannot be attained by simply ensuring that disabled persons are treated the same as nondisabled persons. This deceptively simple proposition received overwhelming support from the Saskatchewan Court of Appeal in the case of *Huck v. Canadian Odeon Theatres Ltd.* (Kallen 1989: 196–97). Michael Huck used a motorized wheelchair as his primary means of mobility. He went to the Odeon Theatre in Regina and was sold a ticket in the same manner as all other patrons. However, when he entered the viewing area he was told by theatre staff that he would either have to transfer from his wheelchair into a regular theatre seat, or park his wheelchair in front of the front row of theatre seats.

Huck complained to the Saskatchewan Human Rights Commission and alleged discrimination on the basis of physical disability, and on the grounds that the theatre's seating arrangement did not provide spaces that could accommodate a wheelchair. Odeon Theatres argued that they did not discriminate against Mr. Huck because he was not denied an opportunity to view the movie, and that the theatre had in fact granted him a privilege by permitting him to park his wheelchair in front of the front row of seats. The Saskatchewan Court of Appeal rejected the theatre's arguments by stating that a physically reliant person does not "acquire" an equal opportunity to utilize facilities or services which are of no use to him or her; identical treatment does not necessarily mean equal treatment or lack of discrimination.

The Court of Appeal stated that if Odeon Theatre's interpretation were correct, the owner of a public facility who offers washroom facilities to a disabled person that is of the same kind offered to the public generally, or offers any other service notwithstanding that it cannot be used by a wheelchair reliant person, will then be found to have discharged his or her obligation under the Human Rights Code. From that perspective, no changes would ever have to be made. The theatre's interpretation was found to be incorrect.

Achievement of equal opportunity depends on more than just equal treatment or equal sevices and programs for all. Reasonable accommodation may be regarded as an "equalizing device" which ensures that equal access translates into equal results. Transcribing printed text books into braille or audio cassettes simply enables a blind student and a sighted student to access the same material and to learn, or compete, on a more realistic and equal footing. Though an integral part of human rights law, the concept of reasonable accommodation is a relatively young one in Canadian human rights legislation, so that a concrete and legally useful definition of the concept is still developing (Tarnopolsky and Pentney 1985: 9.27–9.33, Hughes 1985: 239–40).

The phrase reasonable accommodation as it pertains to persons with disabilities first appeared in employment regulations issued pursuant to a section of the U.S. *Rehabilitation Act* of 1973. The concept of accommodation was gradually broadened into a generic term that came to encompass the removal of architectural, transportation and communication barriers. A 1983 report issued by the U.S. Commission on Civil Rights attempted to set out a working definition. The report stated that reasonable accommodation means "providing or modifying devices, services or facilities, or changing practices or procedures in order to match a particular person with a particular program or activity" (Peters 1987a: 24–27, Hughes 1985: 238).

This working definition was premised on two orienting principles. The first principle espouses that a disabled individual requesting a service or applying for an employment opportunity would otherwise be qualified were it not for a physical or mental limitation. The meaning of "otherwise qualified" was addressed in a number of U.S. cases. In one case, a hearing disabled nurse sought admission to a college degree nursing program in order to fulfill eligibility requirements for certification as a full registered nurse. In this instance, the court held in favor of the college who rejected her application on the grounds that the college could impose necessary or essential physical requirements for its nursing program. The court determined that the candidate could not safely participate in the nursing/clinical program without extensive modification of the program, and that the ability to hear was a necessary requirement; the court did not consider the student to be "otherwise qualified." Reminiscent of the Bhinder decision, the court also determined that some requirements and practices could legally exclude disabled persons if they were determined to be necessary and essential, or that modification to an existing program would be unreasonable, impractical or impossible.

In another U.S. case, an employer refused to absorb the costs of an assistant reader who was hired by some maintenance workers employed by the Department of Public Welfare; the reader was engaged to facilitate the paperwork that the job had come to entail. The employer argued that the blind workers were not "otherwise qualified" as they did not possess the ability to read printed material, and that the accommodation necessary (for example, paying the costs) was a hardship for the employer. The court held that with the assistance of a reader, the blind employees met the requirements of the position in all respects in the same way as sighted employees, and could be considered "otherwise qualified." The court went on to hold that the cost of providing a reader represented only a fraction of the Department's administrative budget, and that the department had failed to meet a defense of "hardship." Paying the costs of a reader would have been a reasonable accommodation to the needs of the blind workers.

The second orienting principle underpinning the U.S. Commission on Civil Rights' concept of reasonable accommodation is individualized assessment. Arguably, unlike other protected characteristics such as gender and race or ethnic origin, disability is not a homogenous or static characteristic. A variety of physical and mental conditions, impairments and limitations may be classified under the broad rubric of "disability." Within each classification are sub-classifications which encompass a wide range of abilities, skills and aspirations. It is impractical, perhaps even impossible, to devise a uniform formula for providing reasonable accommodation to persons with disabilities.

Disabled citizens argue that the accommodation that an individual requires will depend largely on the degree and nature of his or her disability, on his or her coping strategies, and on the essential requirement of the job or program in question. One approach might be to determine under what circumstances reasonable accommodation is not possible from the point of view of the employer or service provider. Following these two orienting principles, disabled citizens in the United States and in Canada have argued that, for the concept of reasonable accommodation to be embodied in policy and put into practice, the following are crucial questions necessary to operationalize the concept:

1. What are the requirements of the program or employment opportunity? Can the essential requirements be distinguished from the arbitrary or unreasonable requirements?
2. What are the skills and abilities of the disabled individual? Is the disabled person otherwise qualified, but for a physical or mental limitation?
3. Is it possible to alter or modify requirements to accommodate the limitations caused by an individual's disability?
4. Is the accommodation necessary, feasible, or does it fundamentally alter the nature of a program or employment opportunity, or is it financially burdensome?

The Canadian Human Rights Commission has developed guidelines that prescribe the relationship between the Canadian Human Rights Act (section 14(a), concerning the BFOQ/R clauses) and employment practices. Implicit in the guidelines is the duty of an employer to provide accommodation when he or she offers an employment opportunity to a person with a disability. The guidelines identify criteria which may assist in determining when reasonable accommodation is impractical. The following guidelines illustrate this criteria.

> Where an employer finds that he or she cannot make reasonable accommodation in order to offer an employment opportunity to a handicapped person, and before he or she [denies] such employment opportunity based on a *bona fide* occupational requirement, the employer shall support his or her findings based on evidence that:

(a) No method of accommodation exists that would permit the handicapped person to perform the job in a safe and satisfactory manner;
(b) To make an accommodation would impose an undue hardship involving either financial cost or business inconvenience to the employer; or,
(c) To make an accommodation would create a predictable safety hazard for the employees or the general public. (CHRA, section 14(a) cited in Hughes 1985: 240, and in Peters 1987a: 28)

Though these guidelines are binding upon the Commission and upon any tribunal that hears or reviews a complaint under the Canadian Human Rights Act, they are not binding on the courts in all circumstances. According to disabled citizens this fact, together with the Supreme Court's ruling in the Bhinder case that a BFOQ/R does not always include a duty to accommodate, may diminish the effectiveness of the federal guidelines.

Implementing Reasonable Accommodation

The idea of reasonable accommodation has come to be embodied in different ways in the law and public policy. Largely as a result of significant efforts by the disabled consumer movement through lobbying efforts, appearances before parliamentary committees and the consultation process, the federal government finally introduced employment equity legislation in the summer of 1986, beginning with the Abella Commission's (1984) recommendations. The aim of this legislation was to ensure that designated groups, including the disabled, could achieve a degree of representation within the workforce.

Employment equity has been defined to include special measures including the accommodation of differences. One of the tools for enforcing commitment made in the legislation is the powers contained in the Canadian Human Rights Act (Greschner 1988). However, because the Bhinder decision essentially rejected the requirement to accommodate in all cases, disabled consumers doubt that the Human Rights Commission has the ability to carry out its purported enforcement mandate. Nevertheless, Employment and Immigration

Canada prepared a Guide for Employers which defines the terms "special measures" and "reasonable accommodation"; they provide some insight as to how these terms will be applied at the federal level (Employment and Immigration Canada 1986a, 1986b, 1987a, 1987b). Employment equity includes not only the removal of barriers, but also the implementation of special measures and the application of the concept of reasonable accommodation. Special measures such as targetted recruitment or special training initiatives are aimed primarily at correcting, over a specific period of time, employment "imbalances" that are a consequence of past discrimination.

These special measures are intended to hasten the achievement of fair representation in the work force of qualified women, Native people, visible minorities and persons with disabilities (Canadian Human Rights Commission *Annual Report* 1990: 41–48, 1991: 49–56, 1992: 37–39, 1993: 34–35). In most jurisdictions employers must base special measures on a thorough work force analysis. Employers also are advised to consult with the relevant federal or provincial human rights agency prior to carrying out the program, so that they can be in a position to assure employees and managers that a particular special measure is an appropriate and necessary strategy (see Kallen 1989: 208–10).

According to Employment and Immigration Canada's definition, reasonable accommodation requires that adjustments to employment policies and practices be made so that no individual is denied benefits, is forced to compete at a disadvantage for employment opportunities, or is blocked from carrying out the essential components of his or her job because of race, color, gender or disability. Human rights tribunals have placed employers under a duty to be flexibile in meeting the needs of employees; it is no longer acceptable for employers to assume that all employees will "fit in" regardless of their special needs, or that they cannot be accommodated without exception.

Reasonable accommodation can involve measures as redesigning job duties, adjusting work schedules, providing technical, financial, and human support services, and upgrading facilities (Rioux 1985: 628–34, Peters 1987a: 33–34). More specifically, there are some six possible types of accommodation that can be introduced in the workplace and the work setting:

Environmental: These may include improved lighting, adequate or improved ventilation, reduction of temperature fluctuations and changes, lowered noise levels, etc.

Physical: Here, the use of adjustable tables, relocation of switches, use of interchangeable light or sound signals (for the deaf or visually impaired), might be considered.

Minor Worksite: This would encompass process flow modifications, rearrangement of equipment or machines, and some organizational restructuring.

Job Structuring: This form of accommodation may involve task modification, task elimination (entirely or in part), task reassignments, or recombinations of tasks. The latter may assist in providing additional employment opportunities at lower skill levels, additional promotional lines, job enrichment, or situations designed to meet the specific needs of disabled employees or qualified disabled applicants.

Support Services: Examples of this type of accommodation may include the use of readers, sign language interpreters, part-time helpers, and personal care attendants.

Rearrangement of Work Schedules: In some instances it may be necessary to rearrange hours of work to meet certain needs. Such rearrangement may include flexible hours, compressed work weeks, job or time sharing, or part-time work hours.

COPOH has suggested that reasonable accommodation of other types can sometimes benefit employees of all kinds. The provision of allowances for child care expenses when employees take company-sponsored courses not only removes a barrier that blocks many women, but assists any employee faced with sole parenting responsibilities. Even tax exemptions, deductions and credits for low-income earners, or those with expenses that the majority in society would not have, are an accommodation that make available cash that can then be put back into the economy.

Policies promoting reasonable accommodation frequently are incorporated into comprehensive affirmative action plans. Nevertheless, reasonable accommodation and affirmative action are two distinct measures. Affirmative action plans usually are implemented as a remedial measure to redress patterns of past discrimination against disadvantaged groups. The aim of the program involves altering the composition of certain "sectors" of society such as employment and education by means of a quota system, goals, timetables or other preferential treatment that serves to achieve the desired rate of participation by members of a class or category that has been injured by discrimination (Tarnopolsky and Pentney 1985: 4.80–4.81, Pentney 1988: 37–41).

By contrast, reasonable accommodation is not geared towards achieving a particular rate of participation by disabled individuals. The objective of reasonable accommodation is to ensure that capable individuals are not denied employment or education opportunities because of physical barriers or because they cannot meet nonessential program or job requirements. The duty to accommodate has become an integral component of nondiscrimination law, whereas affirmative action is one strategy for overcoming a history of discrimination against certain categories of people.

Disabled citizens further distinguish between reasonable accommodation and accessibility. The latter refers to changes that employers can undertake to make the personnel process, the work site and other auxilliary services available to persons with disabilities. Removing environmental barriers in areas such as physical access, transportation and communication benefits disabled people so that they can take advantage of educational or employment opportunities with the assistance of reasonable accommodation. Accommodation, by contrast, refers to modifications which allow disabled employees to perform the essential duties of the job for which they were hired.

Although the distinction between accessibility and accommodation can be blurred, the elimination of environmental barriers for greater physical accessibility generally entails a comprehensive strategy involving building codes and equipment standards designed to assist disabled persons as a group.

Reasonable Accommodation: The Political Response

Throughout the 1980s disabled consumer organizations put the pressure on the federal government and the Canadian Human Rights Commission to amend the Canadian Human Rights Act to include language that explicitly declares that employers and service providers have a duty to provide reasonable accommodation. In early 1986 Gordon Fairweather, then Chief Commissioner of the Canadian Human Rights Commission, submitted a letter to John Crosbie, then Minister of Justice, that outlined the view of the Commission regarding the Bhinder case (cited in Peters 1987a). The Commission recognized that the Bhinder case was decided after the 1982 amendments to the Act but the Commission advised that there was still a risk that the new language would not be considered a significant change, and that the courts may still not recognize accommodation. According to Fairweather's letter, the Commission's position stressed that amendments are crucial to make it absolutely certain that "to refuse to make reasonable accommodation for special needs or obligations related to a prohibited ground of discrimination" would be a discriminatory practice.

In the spring of 1986 the federal government undertook a review of the Canadian Human Rights Act and invited human rights experts and interested individuals and groups to submit their views on needed changes to the Act. In June 1986, the Coalition of Provincial Organizations of the Handicapped submitted its brief to the federal Department of Justice; the brief dealt with many issues, but chief among them was an appeal to amend the Act to include a duty to make reasonable accommodation. In a report entitled "Toward Equality" (The Response to the Report of the Parliamentary Committee on Equality Rights, 1986) the federal government dealt with the issue of reasonable accommodation as put forward in the Committee's recommendation.

> We recommend that the Canadian Human Rights Act be amended so that employers are obliged to make "reasonable accommodation," that is, such special provisions as would not cause undue hardship to the employer in response to the needs peculiar to those

classes of employees that are protected from discrimination by the terms of the Act.

The government's response subsequently agreed in principle that the suggested amendments were necessary, but it indicated that further considerations were necessary to determine the best way for amending the Act to include the required changes. Since the release of the government's statement COPOH made countless inquiries to the Department of Justice. Although assurances were given in 1990 (Canadian Human Rights Commission *Annual Report* 1991) that amendments were forthcoming and that the courts and human rights tribunals would put the onus on employers to accommodate their employees, specific changes to the Act were not made until 1992. A Supreme Court decision did interpret the Act the way COPOH and others would like. In *Alberta Human Rights Commission v. Central Alberta Dairy Pool* (1990), the majority opinion noted that "where a rule has an adverse discriminatory effect, the appropriate response is to uphold the rule in its general application and consider whether the employer could have accommodated the employee adversely affected without undue hardship" (Canadian Human Rights Commission *Annual Report* 1990: 25). At the end of 1992, the federal government amended the Human Rights Act by listing "operational effectiveness" as a criteria for determining whether a given accommodation would cause undue hardship. The Canadian Human Rights Commission (*Annual Report* 1992: 32), however, suggested that this amounted to a watering-down of the principle of reasonable accommodation, and it urged the federal government to recommit itself.

Disability-related decisions and rulings of the early 1990s by the Supreme Court of Canada and human rights tribunals have tended to make it clear to employers and service providers that they have a duty to take steps to accommodate individual needs and circumstances and must prove that a specific and an alleged illness, physical or mental condition or disability that would prevent an individual from performing their jobs cannot be accommodated or would prevent that person from doing his or her job (Canadian Human Rights Commission *Annual Report* 1990: 60–63, 1991: 71–75, 1992: 85–87). Nowhere does this have the greatest impact than in cases of HIV infection or AIDS, and in age-related cases (*Annual Report* 1990: 37–40, 56–57; 1991: 44–48, 65–66, 1992: 41, 87).

Disabled consumers are opposed to the highly controversial issue of mandatory drug testing in employment. The fear is that drug testing will unfairly discriminate against otherwise qualified job applicants or employees, not least because of the limitations of what test results can show as indicators of impairment, including genetic impairment. Employers, particularly in the United States and Europe, have introduced testing as a job requirement. In Canada, the Toronto-Dominion Bank and the Canadian Armed Forces instituted a screening policy for all would-be employees and recruits; the Canadian Civil Liberties Association launched a complaint with the Canadian Human Rights Commission to challenge that policy. The Commission is firmly against testing for employment reasons and in early 1992 attempted conciliation (*Annual Report* 1991: 29–30). The Toronto Dominion Bank and the Armed Forces continue with this policy, despite opposition and evidence from the Addiction Research Foundation and the Canadian Medical Association that suggests drug testing measures little and is a poor predictor of safe or competent performance (Canadian Human Rights Commission *Annual Report* 1992: 39–40, 1993: 35–36).

The independent living/disabled consumer movement in Canada considers the concept of reasonable accommodation of more than passing importance in giving life and substance to the hard-won statutory recognition and constitutional guarantees afforded the rights of disabled people. The concept serves as a catalyst for ensuring that disabled persons can really enjoy equality of opportunity. Disabled consumer organizations have determined that disabled persons often are barred from obtaining employment, not necessarily because they are not qualified or incapable, but because they encounter barriers within the system that could be reduced or eliminated altogether. The suggestion has been made by them, and others, that legislation which does not specifically enforce reasonable accommodation, such as the Canadian Human Rights Act and various provincial statutes, renders the rights of disabled citizens such as those given to them under the Canadian Charter of Rights and Freedoms to be empty, hollow promises and platitudes.

COPOH and its provincial affiliates have been active in developing a comprehensive strategy designed to expand and advance the concept of reasonable accommodation. Disabled citizens have advocated that the term reasonable accommodation should be given a broad *social* interpretation and should include, but not be limited to, adjustments or modifications made to the environment, the work site, the job structure and the work schedule. It should include providing technical aids, mechanical or other devices and personal support services that increase or supplement an individual's capability of participating in community life. Accommodation is a means of assisting "otherwise qualified" individuals to meet stated job requirements, where it is recognized that the right to employment is essential to integrated community living.

Disabled consumers suggest that to avoid the inevitable limitations imposed by confining or restrictive language, the duty to accommodate should be assessed on a case-by-case basis. Assessment should take into account factors such as the various forms of relevant accommodation available, the degree of benefit extended to the disabled person by the accommodation, and the size and financial position of the company, employer or service provider. Unlike affirmative action and accessibility, which are strategies and means by which benefits can be granted to disabled people as a whole, disabled persons argue that the implementation of reasonable accommodation should be tailored to meet the unique needs of the individual disabled person. Individual abilities, coping mechanisms and individual aspirations should be taken into account.

Disabled consumer advocates can suggest many legislative and policy changes. All human rights legislation should contain explicit language prescribing a duty to make reasonable accommodation for the benefit of those persons protected by the legislation. The onus should be placed on the employer or community service provider to demonstrate that requested accommodations might be unreasonable or would produce an undue hardship. Advocates further argue that an interpretation of the Charter's equality rights section 15(1)(2) should include reasonable accommodation as a key concept (Smith 1986: 373–75). Guidelines or regulations governing the development and implementation of affirmative action (section 15(2)) and employment equity programs should also require participating organizations to develop policy statements and practices that incorporate the concept of accommodation.

COPOH has believed that it would not be unreasonable to provide tax incentives to employers who provide accommodation in excess of a predetermined amount of money. Finally, COPOH suggested that a data base could be established that would help disabled consumers and employers facilitate the selection and implementation of forms of accommodation according to different contexts by compiling information. Information could be obtained on the organizational structures of public and private sector organizations and businesses, labor relations policies, job and task descriptions, and of the availability, cost and quality of technical aids, devices and personal support services.

Accommodating Our Citizens: Community Obligations

There has been a gradual improvement in the provision of goods and services to disabled people in society in recent years. Nevertheless, many unnecessary barriers remain that inhibit disabled persons from participating as fully as possible in their communities and in their society. This situation was demonstrated effectively in the "historic" 1981 *Obstacles* report of the Special Parliamentary Committee on the Disabled and Handicapped. This particular document identified a significant number of key obstacles to integrated community living, and made some practical suggestions that would overcome them. A wide range of recommendations contained in the report called for legislative, fiscal and administrative action by the federal government in almost every significant sphere of community life, including employment, transportation, housing, education and recreation. The Parliamentary Committee's reports have dealt with the importance of prevention of disabilities, research and development, and most significantly, the changing of attitudes.

Complete equality of accessibility to goods and services is simply not possible in current reality. As a result, the independent living/disabled consumer movement has worked to develop the concept of reasonable accommodation as the basis for anti-discrimination law, for the reason that, as Ratushny (1986: 257) states, the concept is perceived as serving a realistic middle ground "between doing nothing and doing everything." The concept of reasonable accommodation is not only an acknowledged fundamental element in the guarantee of nondiscrimination for disabled persons (Tarnopolsky and Pentney 1985: 9.27), but is a means of letting the wider community know what the needs of disabled citizens are.

The concept refers to a legal duty or responsibility to take positive action to accommodate the unique needs of disabled people in the workplace, and in the provision of services, facilities or dwelling places in the wider community. It can also be used as a defence to an allegation of unintentional, or adverse effect discrimination, if reasonable attempts to satisfy this responsibility can be demonstrated. According to Pentney (1988: 21) the combined effect of the O'Malley, Bhinder and other cases has been to establish the following two propositions in Canadian human rights law:

(a) adverse effect discrimination and the duty to accommodate short of undue hardship are applicable to the various Canadian human rights codes;
(b) the scope of adverse effect discrimination as well as the duty to accommodate is limited by factors that are inherent in the concepts (i.e., business rationality, undue hardship), and also by external factors (i.e., the BFOQ defense).

The first proposition should increase the protection offered by anti-discrimination laws and make them easier to administer. Complainants and human rights commissions will examine the impact of policies and practices rather than gathering circumstantial evidence relating to the individual complaint. The "adverse effect" approach to discrimination is useful in enlarging the remedial scope of human rights law in quantitative and qualitative ways. A rule, policy, procedure or practice that can be proven to have an adverse effect on an individual because of an assumed group-based characteristic will usually affect others who are "similarly situated." The remedy sought in an adverse effect case will benefit the single complainant as well as others who share the relevant characteristic (Kallen 1989: 202).

At the community level, the focus in an adverse effect case is on the ongoing and continuous effect of a policy or practice that is part of an employment, education or service provision system. If that impact is adverse to the interests of individuals because of a group-based characteristic, the remedy logically should be directed to changing some community structures. It is for this reason that the O'Malley and other decisions mark a turning point in anti-discrimination law. The concept of reasonable accommodation also is incorporated into human rights law in the O'Malley decision. The duty to accommodate is an integral and vital part of "equality" as that ideal is defined by many disadvantaged groups, including disabled citizens.

The second proposition refers to the impact of a required accommodation on the employer's or service provider's business or enterprise. The question of whether a measure of reasonable accommodation will impose an "undue hardship" on an employer cannot be resolved by focussing only on the claimed expense or inconvenience involved. There has to be a consideration of a "balancing" of rights in the interest of preserving a community structure in which the rights of both employer/public and employee/citizen receive protection. A claimed hardship that will be caused by an accommodative change must be measured in light of the benefits gained by the complainant as well as others who might benefit in order to determine whether the change really constitutes a burden.

Undoubtedly, anti-discrimination law has been made rather complex because of these developments. The full legal implications for an adverse effect approach to discrimination, for those who administer it and those who benefit by it, are not likely to be known for many years. The most dramatic immediate impact of the case decisions probably will be in respect of access to community services and facilities because most human rights codes have not incorporated specific defenses that are equivalent to the BFOQ in employment. Besides, few of the cases directly concern disability; the cases have involved questions of religion (O'Malley and Bhinder) and age (Etobicoke). Only Huck is outstanding in directly addressing the issues of adverse effect and reasonable accommodation with respect to disability.

From the perspective of COPOH, those disabled consumers COPOH represents and perhaps others, reasonable accommodation means taking such steps as are considered reasonable to not preclude individuals with disabilities from participating fully in every aspect of community life, particularly in employment, with resultant benefits going to both the disabled person and to the community as a whole. Important factors of individual and public safety, developing technology and economic considerations also must be considered in determining the extent and degree to which disabled persons can be accommodated.

The development of the reasonable accommodation concept as disabled citizens have tried to develop and advocate it, is in large measure a direct result of their concern with the operationalization and enforcement of section 15(1)(2) of the Charter of Rights. Ratushny (1986: 257) suggests in the end the courts are likely to fall back on the general criterion of "reasonableness" in defining the boundaries of corresponding rights and duties imposed by the equality rights provision. Because the courts may not be the most appropriate forum for balancing such factors, disabled citizens advocate defining reasonable accommodation on a case-by-case basis, stressing flexibility and sensitivity to particular situations. COPOH has made the argument that statutory amendment of the Canadian Human Rights Act and other human rights legislation is a necessary *a priori* step in developing a framework of standards in such areas as transportation, communications, housing, education and in employment.

Various federal government departments already are active in regulation-making pertaining to accessibility standards in private housing, public facilities and transportation. While these developments may not be wholly satisfactory, disabled citizens stress the need to continually shape equality in the context of individual and public needs, evolving technology, changing consumer and labor market conditions—without loosing sight of the fundamental notions of basic human dignity and without compromising the principles of independent and integrated community living.

One of the most significant developments in the area of affirmative action in the implementation of Charter equality rights has been the enactment of the federal Employment Equity Act (1986). Employment equity derives from an understanding of the O'Malley and Bhinder decisions, namely that of adverse effect, unintended or systemic discrimination. The purpose of the Act is to reinforce that equality means more than treating persons in the same way, and equality requires special measures and the accommodation of differences. The Act imposes an obligation on employers to not only identify but to eliminate employment practices that have discriminatory effects by putting into place positive policies and practices that accommodate persons in designated groups.

The Employment Equity Act illustrates the importance of the purposive approach in the interpretation of human rights law (notwithstanding its apparent failure in the eyes of the Canadian Human Rights Commission), and combines formal and substantive approaches to equality rights—at least in the area of employment. There is recognition of the validity of affirmative action as one solution to overcome adverse effect discrimination (Black 1985). The Federal Contractor's Program, which came into effect in September 1986, is an initiative that complements the Employment Equity Act. Its purpose was to try to extend federal law into both provincial jurisdictions and the private sector.

Human rights legislation in Canada aims at the elimination of actions based largely on stereotypes. Individualized assessments are required, rather than decisions based on stereotypes about groups. The leading cases decided during the 1980s make it clear that identical treatment is not necessarily equal treatment if that treatment fails to account for relevant differences. A BFOQ or an undue hardship defense of alleged adverse effect discrimination requires an individualized assessment. In most situations it will be necessary to look at the needs of specific individuals. The idea of individualized assessment is crucial for understanding the thrust of the independent living/disabled consumer movement's advocacy of the notion of reasonable accommodation in the context of community integration.

Disabled citizens do not seem to be arguing for equality rights based on membership in an identifiable minority category alone. Kallen (1982, 1989: 46) has argued that a contentionist social reform movement such as that represented by the independent living/disabled consumer movement will pursue individual as well as categorical rights claims:

> Individual-rights claims represent demands for recognition and protection of the individual human rights of minority members. Such claims may seek specified changes in constitutional and/or statutory law. Categorical-rights claims represent demands for collective redress against the adverse impact of systemic discrimination upon the minority as an entity. Such claims may seek the implementation of affirmative action programs designed to remedy

group inequities. Categorical claims do not rest on assumptions about cultural distinctiveness or alternative lifestyles; thus, they can justifiably be put forward by representatives of minorities with and without a viable cultural base.

As well, a minority category such as the disabled,

> ... represents a conceptual or statistical classification of a population based on one or more criteria ... that may or may not give rise to a sense of collective consciousness or to minority organization. Minority categories are more likely than minority groups to be represented empirically by dispersed, fragmented population aggregates whose members' only common attribute is the stigmatizing label imposed upon them by majority authorities (Kallen 1989: 43).

Kallen (1989: 46) makes a distinction between minority categories and categorical claims, and minority groups and collective rights claims. She defines the latter as based on a distinctive ethnoculture or subculture. In Kallen's framework, members of an ethnoculture or subculture constitute a minority group which possesses an institutional infrastructure that enables it to maintain and transmit the cultural values, cultural orientation and lifestyle of its members from generation to generation. Perhaps unlike a minority category a minority collectivity is more likely to have a collective consciousness and an organizational basis for movement activities.

While the disabled might remain a vaguely-defined or difficult-to-define statistical entity and a dispersed or fragmented population, there is no question that over the past decade there has emerged a collective consciousness, an institutional infrastructure as well as a broad organizational basis for movement activity. For many, there also might be value and lifestyle differences that set them apart both from other disabled individuals and from the nondisabled that possibly no degree of integration into mainstream life could reduce or mitigate. While there is no single culture of disability, there has developed an experienced sense of collective or common identity based on a cross-disability orientation. In addition, the structures developed by disabled people can parallel mainstream social organizations and serve as alternatives to them. These enabling structures transmit a sense of identity, knowledge and the movement's philosophy and principles to successive "generations" of disabled individuals.

The disabled consumer movement shares some important features of both contentionist and revitalization movements, in that disabled people's rights claims are collective at the same time as they are categorical and individual, and in that its empowering structures offer alternatives to the value orientation and organizational forms of majority cultural and institutional norms and forms as much as they parallel them. Indeed, the idea of community-building that is at the heart of the disabled consumer movement is always one that works for the transformation of the existing social order and *its* conformity to, or legitimation of, "minority" values and lifestyles. What is contention in community-building if it is not an attempt to *revitalize* the existing social order and community structures, and what is integration if it is also not the mutual legitimation of value and lifestyle differences? For disabled citizens, integration means not only participation in the social, economic and political life of the community, but also the community's full acceptance of disabled people.

Disabled citizens have argued that in attempting to remove barriers to integrated community living that include adverse effect policies and so forth, reasonable accommodation should not be defined in a way that sets up a separate category of the disabled. It is not appropriate for accessibility standards to require programs, services or facilities which are "separate but equal" *unless* separation is the only reasonable way of providing them: According to the independent living model's principle of integration, "specialized services if necessary, but not necessarily specialized services." Otherwise, attempts to accommodate would only create additional barriers to the full participation of disabled people in community life. It is also recognized that certain individual rights are of no consequence unless enjoyed in community with others.

The rights afforded to individuals should benefit and protect collectivities or categories as wholes. The movement's focus and insistence on individualized assessments, on the unique needs of individual disabled persons, and on a case-by-case approach with respect to reasonable accommodation might serve to distinguish the disabled consumer's approach to equality rights and the Charter from that of other nonethnic and/or ethnic groups enumerated in section 15. By contrast, women, ethno-cultural minorities, religious minorities and others seem to be asking to be treated equally as members of groups or collectivities.

Disability—unlike skin color, ethnic origin, gender and perhaps sexual orientation—is neither a homogeneous condition nor one that is temporally "fixed." Rather, disability is socially and culturally defined, is based on perception and social environment, is a function of available intervening technology, and is experienced individually. Because of this, disabled consumers seem reluctant to characterize themselves as a group except in the most general way and then only in relation to the common experience of stigma and disenfranchisement. It is also because of this that they consciously and cautiously distinguish reasonable accommodation from affirmative action and employment equity.

Reasonable accommodation is part of the community-building process that focuses on the unique needs of individuals. Affirmative action and employment equity are comprehensive policy strategies aimed at categories of individuals that end up including some and excluding others. Significant human and equality rights case law developments notwithstanding, disabled citizens are cautious about the "similarly situated" phrase that sometimes is used in adverse effect discrimination cases. The argument is that laws and public policies must never be applied in such a way that differences, or similarities, between citizens determine how those laws and policies are applied.

A ruling or policy of "similarly situated" may end up treating existing conditions as given, and to use them to determine whether individuals are similarly situated or not. Stereotypes, social designations, labels and categories that human rights legislation has tried to eliminate from legal or policy decision-making, may instead be perpetuated. Individualized assessment as the focus of reasonable accommodation and reasonable accommodation as a practical interpretation of equality in community life are important means by which full participation and integration into community life can be achieved.

8

Personhood and Consumerism as Part of the Community-Building Process

A "new minority" group has made its presence felt in our society. Certainly not insignificant in numbers, its members represent one in about every seven Canadian citizens. They are the disabled who, historically, have been relegated to the position of second-class citizenship. Until very recently they remained hidden from view in institutions or special housing, sequestered from the able-bodied public and the larger community. This was accepted by most as proper and legitimate for persons whose damaged bodies or minds and spoiled identities serve as a vivid reminder to the rest of us of the fragility of the human physical state. In a society that demands uniformity and "sameness" and that worships physical health and beauty, the physically and mentally disabled have been regarded and treated as virtual outcasts from mainstream social and community life.

Oppression and discrimination is experienced by disabled people, individually and collectively. Their various attempts, through the independent living/disabled consumer movement, to recontextualize and reintegrate themselves into society and into community life are described throughout this book. Another purpose of this study was to examine the relevant social issues of the 1980s, 1990s and beyond, that have emerged in such disciplines as social anthropology, sociology, rehabilitation medicine and human rights law. The pressing issues of personal and collective self-determination, social movement and empowerment, social reproduction and community-building are an essential part of the process of social and cultural change.

These issues are well within the social science endeavor: The striving to recontextualize the disabled person, to deconstruct and demedicalize his or her disability as a "condition," to reintegrate, in Habermas's words, the system and disabled people's life worlds, and to reaffirm the value of his or her's full community partnership and citizenship. These are shown to be interrelated issues. What they have in common is the conscious and purposive renewal or building of something called community. The task of a critical and progressive social science is to tie these issues together, and to examine the processes by which they are connected and the manner in which they are related to change in our culture and society.

The disintegration and decontextualization of the disabled person is not fundamentally different from what is experienced by certain language, religious, ethno-cultural, gender, age and other power(less) minorities. The pursuit of community and personhood clearly involves the process of overcoming all sorts of externally (structurally) imposed and internally (motivationally) reinforced language, cultural, color, gender and age handicaps—not solely physical or mental ones. Handicaps are recognized as essentially socio-cultural consequences, that is, "translations" of perceived objective facts into meaningful and shared social designations and labels. Accordingly, society's normative institutions through which the translation process operates must be dismantled or rebuilt.

Social and cultural renewal and community-building involves mental and physical/structural activities. The empowerment process is an action process that strategically and consciously combines these mental and structural activities in order to change current attitudes by providing counter-images of ability, and to revise existing structures by changing, encouraging and initiating new practices, behaviors and interactions.

Taking the lead from Giddens's theory of action, changes in the ways people interact with one another will generate changes in social categories and structures, and perhaps transform them. Because the relationship between action and structure is necessarily a reciprocal one, engaging in new practices and interactions over time should transform the very social and community structures against which these empowerment efforts are directed.

Partially motivated by other disadvantaged minority groups who have organized, fought for and won new personal and collective freedoms, disabled citizens are no longer satisfied with their second-class, second-best status. They are no longer content to accept a community that has, by omission or commission, pushed them out of the employment market, out of public buildings and public transportation systems that are not accessible, out of educational systems that are not designed to accommodate them, and *into* a health care system that has depersonalized them.

From this new perspective, successful coping with impairment and disability necessitates more than merely learning to live with recurring pain, limited mental and/or physical functions and abilities, and frustration. It means learning skills and gaining new knowledge to pursue the lifestyles in which the disabled person himself or herself actively works to not only confront and challenge dominant societal attitudes, but also to develop and put into place new enabling structures that are founded on a vision of personal independence, community integration and uncompromised personhood (Giddens 1991: 226).

Personhood: A Prerequisite for Community Building

For many citizens it is not disability that should be the focus of attention, but the social and community structures and the social and work environments in which disabilities occur and which continue to produce and maintain disability. This "ecological" perspective is central to the disabled consumer independent living model. From this perspective, too, the concept of reasonable accommodation can be appreciated as a means by which disabled persons can gain more control over their environment, however limited it might be. The concept also can be appreciated as a means, or as a starting point, from which the organizing principles of social life can be reconceptualized and reconstituted.

The basis of the community-building process that disabled people are engaged in is self-determination, which is linked to the notion of personhood. Just as action is linked to structure by way of social movement, so is agency necessarily linked to action by a particular conception of what a "person" is. What a person "does" is going to be determined largely by what he or she thinks he or she can actually do; this in turn will be determined by what he or she has been taught or socialized into believing is expected or possible. The notion of person is normative, processual, and highly ideological. The notion is bound up with what is deemed significant about ourselves as capable and mutually recognized human beings (Giddens 1991: 214–17).

In the context of community life, different conceptions of personhood can be enabling as well as constraining. Within limits, we are "self-legislatively, self-defining creatures" (Rorty 1987). The process of self-definition involves a learning process that takes place within the context or limits of pre-existing social categories and structures. What a person "will do" may be determined by rejecting what he or she has been taught or has experienced, and by imagining different possibilities. Vision is an intrinsic part of rejecting any limits imposed upon the process of self-definition, and is realizable only in association and communication with others (Tinder 1980, Community Living Society, n.d.).

"Community" is both a means of questioning and rejecting pre-existing social categories and structures, as well as an outcome of self-actualization and self-fulfilment. It is essentially a vision of a context that further enables, as much as possible, the process of self-definition. It has been argued that participation in community life satisfies the deep human need and desire for self-determination and self-actualization (Plant 1974). Perhaps, following Freire, community-building is our ontological vocation. Community-building is an ongoing process of self-definition for the participants.

Tinder has taken this idea one step further. He suggests that community "is not in the nature of an order that is changeless and that members must simply accept or quit" (Tinder 1980: 80). Rather, community is defined as a *process* of participation, communication and inquiry through which personhood is discovered and continually created:

> The familiar idea that community consists in agreement of any kind, that it consists, for example, in common acceptance of a nar-

row and stifling set of customs inherited from the past.... grossly distorts human nature and obscures the ideal of community. It tends to reconcile human beings to social conditions under which *they are far less than they should be*.... Community can live only if people insist again and again, by speech and occasionally by violent resistance, that not any kind of unity that habit, circumstances, or a momentary elite can induce everyone to accept is a community. Only cooperation in the most serious of human concerns—*and this means above all in the exploration of being*—calls forth a community (Tinder 1980: 31, emphasis added).

Tinder states, "community is unsettled and must call upon the creative resources of its participants" (1980: 80). Human beings are essentially critical and questioning creatures, and so community is an ever-shifting context for their inquiries. Anything less than that would constrain and stifle the process of self-definition and self-determination. Tinder (1980: 34) makes the further insightful comment that,

Entering into community is not linking a completed self with others; rather, it is forming the self in association with others.... [A] human being, unlike an object of experience such as a stone, is not finished and wholly present in his empirical nature. He must be formed and discovered through the clarification of consciousness that takes place in inquiry or communication.

If human beings are not "finished" and continually are being formed, then by definition community and, indeed, society, is "inherently unfinished." Community, following Giddens, is "ever a process, never a product," or as Tinder (1980: 81) states, "it is not the product of the activity but is the activity itself." COPOH's Allan Simpson says essentially the same thing when he suggests that the means is perhaps more important than the solution or outcome, in reference to individual involvement in disabled consumer organizations. The relationship between individual self-realization and community is a close one. This is perhaps why disabled citizens see no inherent contradiction between independent living and community integration. Independent living is only possible in the context of relationships and communication, and is an ever-evolving and unending process.

Conflict exists; the so-called limits of self-definition can be manipulated or are imposed. Different conceptions of personhood, of community and of society can clash. According to Rorty (1987: 72), any particular conceptualization or definition of what constitutes a "person" and "community" might not function to provide a basis for resolving conflicts among competing interests and claims for rights and duties, because the concept embeds and expresses those conflicts. Personhood and community are best expressed as a duality. They are simultaneously the means and outcome of competing values and interests.

Disabled citizens' claims for equality before and under the law, equal protection of the law, equal benefit of the law without discrimination, as well as reasonable accommodation including employment equity and affirmative action programs, all presuppose certain conceptions of personhood and what a "person" is. Inherent in the claims is a vision of community. Significantly, issues of human rights, equality in law and even public sanction of specific programs and services geared towards an identified (or enumerated) category of individual are issues of how different groups in society view each other, whether their conceptions of "person" coincide or whether they differ, and which view dominates.

As Rorty (1987) has pointed out, societies and communities which "weigh" the conditions for personhood differently will be structured differently. It is the implicit conditions for personhood (the limits of community) that will be contested, and that subsequently determine the interactions and behaviors that constitute structure, and the nature of community life. Consider what constitutes a "person" (Rorty 1987: passim):

- persons are capable of critical reflective rationality;
- persons are autonomous agents, capable of self-defined and self-defining choices;
- persons are capable of forming and modifying their own beliefs, desires and actions;
- persons are capable of entering into mutually affective and effective relationships.

A great deal depends on the degree to which consensus in society over the truth of these presuppositions exists, and so whether they are accepted or denied (Giddens 1991: 215–16). Indeed, the various structures of domination experienced by disabled people and other minorities will probably reflect either the acceptance or denial of these presuppositions. The degree to which they are accepted will therefore determine whether and to what extent :

- persons are going to be treated as ends (subjects) or as means (objects);
- persons are connected to a range of social, political and material goods;
- persons may have or exercise specific rights and duties, or responsibilities and obligations, of participation in decision-making, representation and governance;
- persons may participate in public life, actively forming or at least modifying the social and political policies and institutions that shape their own lives. (Rorty 1987: passim)

Structurally, the idea of "person" ensures that we are taken seriously and respected as individuals. The notion also ensures that we have rights that allocate and limit the exercise of power, and that structural conditions exist that enable us to pursue our interests and goals of self-realization. Absent these presuppositions, rights and structural conditions, some persons will not be considered or treated as persons at all. That is, they will be treated as objects, will be disconnected from social, political and material goods, will be differentially denied responsibilities and obligations shared by others, and, by being denied the opportunity to choose or construct their own system of values, will have the least input into shaping the social and cultural policies and institutitions that in turn shape their own lives. Disabled people have until recently been the classic example of "nonpersons," though they have not been the only ones (Kallen's (1989) *Label Me Human*).

The imposition of handicap, whether physical, mental, linguistic, ethno-cultural, gender or age-based reflects the serious lack of agreement over and denial of some of the rather fundamental presuppositions of personhood. The disabled have long been thought incapable of reflective rationality, incapable of forming or articulating their own beliefs and desires, and were deemed dependent and unable to act with others in a common world. Evidence to the contrary has been down-played and even denied, and has instead been interpreted as deviance. In fact, the process of social and cultural disintegration and decontextualization is justified by these negative presuppositions, and is further reinforced by institutional structures, practices and conceptual machinery.

The medical/rehabilitation model is an example of this process. The model is evident in the way clinics, hospitals, special institutions, workshops, government departments and their programs and services are organized and delivered. The process of reintegration and recontextualization (community-building), from the point of view of the handicapped, involves asserting the positive aspects of the presuppositions that constitute personhood or showing that the negative aspects are illegitimate, by creating alternative, parallel or mediating structures that prove participatory competence, responsibility, autonomy and that demonstrate a capacity for self-determination.

New structures that enable disabled consumers to demonstrate competence and pursue self-determination become necessary. The particular model of community living and citizenship that disabled consumers have in mind is, however, not simply one of parallel structures or an alternative lifestyle. Rather, as part of the process of reconstructing and thus *revitalizing* society, the function of parallel/alternative structures (such as independent living centres, personal support networks, brokerage systems, and consumer organizations and coalitions) is to provide workable alternatives to those normative structures that are considered by their proponents to be founded and operating on "false assumptions."

As parallel and/or alternative structures to mainstream organizations that provide valuable services, the assumption is that disabled people (or others) are capable of being directed by their own conceptions of their own identities and by what is important to that identity, that they are indeed capable of acting with others, and that they are community-context sensitive. These structures may be temporary or permanent, depending on the continued need for them and on the extent to which normative structures begin to change.

As part of a vision of community and citizenship, the idea of "enabling structures" and all that they entail seems to underscore the point that persons, no matter how deformed, however constitutionally or socially deprived, are able to form a system of practices that define their own lives. They are equally the creators of their stories that are their lives, to paraphrase Rorty. Furthermore, this vision of a new citizenship is based on the understanding that persons are self-defining and self-legislating only as members of a "community" defined by shared practices. The different enabling structures created by disabled citizens bring people together; the case approach, the institution and the specialized services they deliver, by contrast, marginalizes and alienates them. Parallel and alternative structures such as the ones created by disabled people serve to unify; the normative structures of society seem instead to fragment.

Self-determination is not individualistic or atomistic, but rather communitarian. Individuals become "persons" to their fullest potential only in relation to others. From this perspective it is easy to see that today's emphasis on group, collective and even categorical rights is an expression of the desire to finally realize or achieve what has been a duality of social life all along: One's self-realization is possible only in the context of group life, while at the same time group life facilitates the development of the "person." It is in this new vision of community and citizenship, with its empowering and unifying structures, that the democratization of social life finally can be realized. Integration and participation, as expressions of an equal citizenship and a shared community, will have become a reality—not merely a reasonable accommodation.

Barriers to Community:
The Production and Maintenance of Disability

The dynamics of the struggle to build community have turned on three areas: the production and maintenance of disability, "official" definitions of disability, and the medical/rehabilitation process. Efforts to change perceptions, attitudes and lifestyles, and to create and put into place new enabling structures have, of necessity, included *a priori* critical evaluations of the sources of disability. One positive outcome of the independent living/disabled consumer movement is that there has been a deep questioning and a consciousness raising of how and why disability occurs, and "what" it is in our social system and cultural practices that keeps producing impairments and disability. There has been a growing awareness of the effects of personal lifestyles, kinds of employment or types of jobs, the quality of working life, the politics of health and welfare administration and the state of the physical environment on the overall physical and mental health of all citizens. In efforts to rebuild community, disabled consumer groups have urged greater research and development in the area of "disability production."

Clearly, eliminating stereotypes, destigmatization, and changing attitudes and labels is only one side of the coin. All the best intentions, positive attitudes, reasonable accommodations, human rights legislation and regulations geared towards the disabled either as individuals or as a category are of no real consequence if social, technical and other forces continue to produce disabled people. A partial list would have to include acquired occupational diseases and accidents, the psychosomatic and mental illnesses related to work and personal stress, the incapacitation caused by road and highway vehicle accidents, diseases of early childhood, the effects of environmental pollution and even the illnesses brought on by, or associated with, unemployment and poverty.

Occupational health and safety administration and welfare/income security legislation should be identified as two of the most significant *loci* for the production and maintenance of disability.

Reasons et al. (1981), Dickinson and Stobbe (1988), Bolaria (1991) and others have thoroughly documented the nature of the dangerous and often fatal hazards associated with different kinds of work and occupation types. Their research has exposed the politics and economics of industrial management, occupational health and safety administration and the related regulatory process in Canada which, according to them, have both directly contributed to the ideology of blaming the victim and the myth of the "dumb worker."

A second area of disability creation is in the area of production and work organization (Lowe and Krahn 1984: 303–26, Dickinson and Stobbe 1988: 433–35). The classic syndrome in late or advanced capitalist society is illustrated by speed-up on the assembly line and reduction of the work force, which is achieved by increased automation, the de-skilling of workers, and job/task breakdown. These are the characteristics of scientific management, or Taylorism, which according to Sass (1988: 14),

... produces the aggregates which make up the workforce—shift workers, women, injured workers, unemployed, etc.,—and causes the pitting of members of a family one against another: husband and wife, father and son, father and daughter; resulting from scheduling of work affecting non-work time. Thus shift work or scheduling of work has an enormous effect on marital breakdown, alcoholism, drug abuse, etc., showing up in work last, because all is sacrificed by the worker to maintain the employment relationship.

From Marx's first writings on alienation with respect to the psychic and economic costs suffered by workers, to recent work on the social epidemiology of hypertension and stress (recognized in law as a disabling impairment) (Pentney 1988: 70, Northcott 1991: 188–89), the findings are the same: People are not machines. When pushed to behave as though they are, they not only become increasingly prone to work-related accidents, but they begin to seek refuge in alcohol, become addicted to tranquilizers, suffer neurotic conflicts, and abuse their children and/or spouses. In turn, the social crises of inflation, recession and cutbacks in services provide a rationale for increasing the pressure "to produce," and a fiscal excuse for refusing to treat the physical, mental and spiritual wreckage that results (B. Russell 1991).

It is important to consider the lower visibility areas of disability production and maintenance (Bolaria and Wotherspoon 1991, Bolaria 1988b). Since the late 1970s welfare, disability pension and old age security payments have remained at unacceptable near-starvation levels while the cost of food, housing and energy has continued to increase at a phenomenal rate. The middle class has thus been set against the poor, for the middle class is expected to pay for any increases in supports to the poor, the disabled and the elderly. Due to an overall lack of funding, the consequence is the continuing chronic malnutrition of the poor and elderly, with its attendant consequences of chronic respiratory diseases, insufficiently fed pregnant mothers, malnourished newborns, rapidly deteriorating health, increased incidence of new disabilities and aggravation of existing chronic disabilities (McElroy and Townsend 1989: 197–200; Chapter 6).

The relationship between poverty and living on a fixed income, and higher rates of mental and physical disability is an established one. The continued production of disability through the maintenance of poverty by virtue of the welfare and social security system is less recognized (Piven and Cloward 1971, Gordon 1988). The administration of our welfare and disability income systems, not unlike occupational health and safety administration, is identified as a significant locus of the production and maintenance of disability, and requires substantial reconstruction. In fact, overall health care administration has been singled out as a major policy problem and economic concern, particularly in light of a drastically and rapidly changing demographic profile of our society.

The majority of early federal social assistance/welfare/income security legislation and programs (prior to the 1966 Canada Assistance Plan (CAP)) were aimed at the elderly and the disabled, for example, The Blind Persons Act (1937), the Allowances for Disabled Persons Act (1954), the Old Age Assistance and Security Acts (1952) and the Vocational Rehabilitation of Disabled Persons Act (VRDP) (1952). VRDP, to be fair, was different from other legislation; it was initially designed as a social service program emphasizing the vocational rehabilitation of physically and mentally disabled persons. The program's aim was to facilitate the entry of disabled individuals into the work force even though it seldom succeeded, and to that end it provided medical, social and vocational assessment, counselling, training, maintenance allowances, prostheses, tools, books and equipment (Day 1984). CAP was intended as an integrated, comprehensive and general assistance program (cost-shared between the federal and provincial governments) that would be useful to all citizens.

Unfortunately, both CAP and VRDP have been "tarred with the welfare brush," although this orientation is less pronounced in the VRDP than in the CAP. The welfare world is not one that fits well with the disabled consumer philosophy; in many instances disabled consumers have spoken out against the stigmatization of being on welfare. Many of the welfare-associated delivery systems treat disabled persons either paternalistically or as the "undeserving poor." Indeed, social services in Canada have been heavily influenced by the view that poverty is the result of "flawed character," that it is the individual's own fault. The traditional response to poverty has been to rehabilitate, or "fix," the person so that he or she can enter the labor force in order to earn his or her own income. This has led to the case services approach to social services, an approach in which systemic or structural problems are discounted or simply ignored. Case services are problem-oriented, and focus primarily on adjusting the individual to fit the existing environment; there is also an unduly heavy emphasis on employability.

VRDP and CAP were under review during the late 1980s. For their time VRDP and CAP were progressive pieces of legislation, in that they recognized that noninstitutionalized disabled people required resources in order to live within the community. Despite their serious limitations, they still remain the major legislation governing the provision of services to disabled people (Day 1984). By participating in the 1987–1990 review of VRDP and CAP, disabled citizens hoped to bring the fiscal arrangements affecting them into line with the current realities of their social situations.

In the years since the passage of VRDP and CAP, disabled people have altered their position within society; witness the development of consumerism and independent living as movements, deinstitutionalization and the emergence of IL centres. Since the Acts have been in existence, ideas about the role of persons with disabilities (conceptions of personhood) have changed, as have models of progressive social and other services affecting disabled people.

The fiscal arrangements that affect disabled people have not kept pace with the changes, nor are emerging community needs being met. This view is shared inside and outside the consumer movement. In particular, COPOH and other organizations have argued that the federal government lacks an appropriate legislative framework to share with the provinces the cost of services designed specifically to meet the *nonmedical* needs of disabled people. Disabled consumer advocates suggest that there needs to be a movement away from the current emphasis on case services towards what they call a public/social utility community service model. Examples of public/social community utilities would include libraries, museums, day care facilities, family planning services, walk-in medical clinics and friendship centres.

Unlike the focus on the individual person which is characteristic of the case services approach, the public/social utilities approach is directed toward improving the quality of community life, where the emphasis instead is on improving the environment in which the individual operates. Users of a public/social utility-type service do not have to prove illness or disability, poverty or any other kind of "problem." Users approach the service(s) as citizens, not as patients, clients or cases; services are used at the option of individuals (based on their needs and requirements), or on the basis of their status (age, disability). There is no diagnostic testing involved, such as needs, means or income testing. Disabled citizens argue that there must be greater support for public utility-type services for disabled people, and that this service delivery should be eligible for support from existing fiscal arrangements between the provincial and federal governments.

One of the outcomes of the review of VRDP and CAP was the public recognition of independent living centres as a legitimate and *bona fide* public and community service utility. IL centres work to improve the quality of life for disabled individuals by assisting them to take greater control of the management of their own lives. IL centres provide training, counselling, brokerage, personal support services and many other nonmedical services that can empower individuals to learn the management functions necessary to live independently in the community. Independent living does not only mean the performance of physical tasks, but refers to the control of the decisions that are associated with everyday life. The argument is that IL centres should receive funding because they deliver services which, by definition, are eligible for CAP funding.

Disabled citizens have stressed the importance of adequate funding, the development of new and innovative approaches to social assistance and service delivery mechanisms, and the creation of opportunities for meaningful vocational training. VRDP and CAP have been criticized for being too welfare-oriented and, by isolating services available under their respective programs from available generic services, for not sufficiently integrating disabled people. Disabled citizens argue that all disabled people must have adequate opportunities to develop their skills and talents in the community regardless of perceptions of their abilities, educability and employability.

Narrow perceptions about what constitutes gainful employment, occupations and education for disabled people—and what disabled people are capable of—must not restrict the choices for the available funding or fiscal arrangements. Comprehensive education and training provisions need to be buttressed by a variety of social assistance and income schemes. Disabled people should not be restricted to using certain types of services or receiving certains kinds of income assistance because the service or funding has traditionally been offered that way. Clearly, flexibility to meet emerging needs and solutions is required.

The issue of an adequate income is even more pressing than that of the availability of education and training programs and provisions. Like other citizens who derive their incomes from employment, assistance recipients such as disabled persons require funds that are adequate enough to secure resources needed for economic security, personal growth and inclusion in mainstream community life. Low levels of support are a disincentive mechanism that encourages dependence on the social assistance system. Many of the services and much of the funding provided under CAP and VRDP could be useful in assisting disabled individuals to develop independent living as well as employment skills; however, because CAP is essentially welfare legislation, only those on social assistance are eligible for those services and funding.

Disabled citizens rightly point out that they find themselves in a position of double jeopardy. On the one hand, because of existing barriers to full participation in economic life, it is virtually impossible for the majority of disabled persons to find fulfilling renumerative employment. On the other hand, low levels of social assistance that are designed to encourage re-entry into the work force actually works to prevent re-entry. In actual fact, disabled citizens argue that a situation of *triple* jeopardy exists: Currently, social assistance does not take into account the extra cost of disability in a realistic way. For example, the costs of personal care attendants, technical aids, transportation, and prescription drugs may not be covered entirely under a program, service or funding budget provision.

Systemic discrimination bars disabled persons from participating in the workforce in more than one way, and necessitates their dependence on social assistance. Social assistance rates are kept low in order to force people back into the workforce; the rates, low for disabled persons, are also expected to meet the extra costs of disability. It is this no-win situation that has continued to produce and maintain disability.

From the point of view of health and welfare administration, for disability to even exist, to the point where the injured and disabled worker, the unemployed disabled person, or the incapacitated elderly person can get help, his or her disability must be officially recognized (Stone 1984). While an individual's own subjective and psychological definition of disability is important in understanding his or her progress in the rehabilitation process, it is significant that others do the defining as well. These other definitions are clearly more fateful and more consequential, for they determine whether there is going to be help in the first place, and what type of help it is going to be.

Disability definition can be considered from many points of view. Medical definitions refers to the abstract degree of physical or mental health of the defined individual; capacity to function is the criterion used here. Pure medical definitions are rare. They are usually mixed, in real-world situations, with social and cultural role definitions, in which the capacity to perform a role is the criterion. Paralysis from the waist down will affect a university lecturer and a steel worker in different ways. It is the steel worker in this case who will probably need an entirely new occupation to become re-employed. Legal definitions of disability based on both medical and socio-cultural definitions determine whether an individual qualifies for entry into certain programs, or for funding that enables the individual to acquire vocational training and subsequent placement in a new job.

Social role definitions involve the conditions of the labor market, while legal definitions are the outcome of political struggles that determine whether laws, programs and funds are made available. When the labor market tightens, the medically disabled might enter the social role category of the unemployable. In economic hard times, it is less likely that even the state will maintain the status quo in terms of allowing legal definitions of disability to go unchallenged and unchanged. The tighter the budgets for programs, the stronger will be the pressure on policy makers to make legal definitions that require adequate and dependable state financing. In any case, the important issue of definition has come up time and again in the review process of VRDP and CAP.

The definition of disability used in VRDP is broad enough to include a wide spectrum of people with many kinds of disabilities (Day 1984). Alcohol and drug addiction programs can be funded through VRDP, though this has been challenged on the argument that alcohol and drug dependency is self-induced. Disabled citizens defend this type of program funding, however, reasoning that this dependency is not necessarily self-induced, and that the dependency is a disabling condition. Furthermore, they argue that it is dangerous to base program funding on such subjective criteria as who is "deserving" or who is not.

Under VRDP, the definition of a disabled person hinges on the concept of employability. For purposes of the Act, a disabled person is defined as someone who, because of physical or mental impairment, is incapable of pursuing regularly any substantially gainful occupation. The obvious operative concept in this definition is "gainful occupation." This concept, unfortunately, serves as a gatekeeper for entry into training programs; those individuals perceived as not being capable of eventually securing gainful occupation will not considered eligible for VRDP support. Under the Act, a "substantially gainful occupation" means the pursuit of the following: The practice of a profession, self-employment, home-making, farm work, sheltered workshop employment and home industries.

Disabled citizens have criticized the Act for including home-making and sheltered workshop employment in the same definition of gainful occupation. They argue that until home-makers receive unemployment insurance benefits and/or are part of a federal pension plan as other wage earners, this category would seem to encourage discrimination against disabled women who may wish to improve their education to get into another profession. Sheltered workshops have always been considered a form of exploitation by the independent living/disabled consumer movement, where support of these segregated environments is wholly opposed in any case.

Eligibility for VRDP support should not depend on narrow perceptions of ability, or what constitutes a gainful occupation. All citizens should have the opportunity to improve themselves and learn new skills; often training and exposure to new environments can open up doors for individuals and create possibilities hitherto unimagined. Furthermore, VRDP excludes individuals who are workers' compensation recipients, those who are already employed, and those who are not pursuing vocational objectives. Many disabled people become employed through affirmative action programs, and so are placed in primarily entry level positions that pay the minimum wage. Though working, they are doing so at subsistence levels, and should have the option to upgrade their qualifications. The effect of exclusion is to, again, maintain a preconceived socio-cultural definition of disability and to turn it into a self-fulfilling prophecy.

Similarly, the definition of vocational rehabilitation contained in

VRDP means any process of restoration, training and employment placement, including related services, the object of which is to enable a person to become capable of pursuing a substantially gainful occupation. Again, this definition, once applied, effectively rules out those individuals who wish to pursue work in the voluntary sector, those who wish to pursue an advanced university education at the graduate level, and even those who seek careers in music, fine arts and the performing arts.

Spokespersons of the independent living movement have argued repeatedly that more comprehensive education and training program provisions should be included in legislation such as VRDP, that these provisions need to be supported by adequate funding, and that the formulation and implementation of acts such as CAP and VRDP must, to be effective, be based on a new kind of citizenship and community living model. This new model of citizenship and community membership must be based on new conceptions of personhood.

Clearly, disabled citizens still have a struggle ahead of them: VRDP, the main legislation affecting disabled citizens, was originally administered by the Department of Labor, and later by the Department of Manpower. It was subsequently administered by Employment and Immigration Canada, but true to the medical/rehabilitation model of disability, shifted to Health and Welfare Canada in the mid-1970s. The effect of this shift, unfortunately, was to reinforce the misconception that disability issues were health and welfare issues. There were attempts to have a revised VRDP administered by Employment and Immigration Canada (Day 1984). Again, a social/structural problem was transformed into an individual/medical one. As a result of these changes, how can disabled people be viewed in any way other than as patients, clients, or worse, sick people?

The Promise of the Disabled Consumer Movement: Self-Determination as a Universal Right

The market assumptions and relations of the capitalist mode of production, while efficient and useful on one level, come with a cost—a human cost. The social context of disability, with reference to situations and contexts that produce disability or in which disability occurs, draws attention to the problematics of work and the production process, in relation to the ideals of self-determination and personhood.

What is occupational health and safety administration and welfare or income security legislation (including such legislation as the Vocational Rehabilitation of Disabled Persons Act and the Canada Assistance Plan) if not "the means" by which market assumptions and relations are maintained, albeit indirectly? VRDP and CAP reveal how close in fact are the connections between the idea of skills and labor as commodities, the emphasis on employability, and that of blaming the victim and the marginalization of the so-called nonproductive worker. Consider as evidence of these connections the definition process and the eligibility criteria set out by these Acts.

Legislation and administration of this type is not a defense or protection against the victimization of individuals or categories of individuals, but in a curious way actually promotes it. VRDP and CAP (only two of many other examples) unfortunately maintain a false opposition between two conceptions of the proper role of human beings in economic and political life—that of producer and consumer.

The opposition between producer and consumer also might be framed as the opposition between the needs of capitalist production relations and the needs of individuals. To take it one step further, there is an equally false opposition between two views of human capacities that legislation, especially VRDP and CAP, maintains: One views human beings as self-developers (as "bundles of capacities and powers"), and the other views humans as infinite consumers, or as "bundles of appetites seeking satisfaction" (Leiss 1988). VRDP and CAP treats these as opposites or as incompatible views, in the sense that they create and try to maintain a separation between an individual's capacity used in the work/production process, and the individual's ability to develop his or her capacities outside the production process.

In this view, individuals have no personal stake in the production process; they own neither the means of production and what they produce, nor do they have anything to say about the relations of the market or of production. Accordingly, people have no value apart from their ability and willingness to sell their labor. The fiction is maintained that production, market and work relations do not permeate all community relations, that they are somehow separate and distinct from other spheres of life, yet that at the same time they govern and determine the nature of all private and community relations.

These are false oppositions. There is, in the social context that produces and maintains mental and/or physical handicap, an implicit denial that work/production is really the reproduction of social relations in the satisfaction of personal and individual needs, and that market relations embody a reciprocal recognition of social identity and social role. Production and consumption are two aspects of the same thing; what is required to maintain market and production relations need not be at the exclusion of the pursuit and satisfaction of personal as well as community needs. In fact, it is market/production/work relations that provide the impetus and incentive for personal growth and development.

The issue of consumerism as articulated by disabled people is a type of integration of an acceptance as well as critique of market and production relations, and the development of personhood in the context of community. Consumerism is one of the means by which community relationships and identities can be reappropriated and reoriented, in which the consumer becomes the central or major factor in the production process itself. Consumption, in this sense, is "a significant domain of human creativity and satisfaction—as an expression of individuality, as a source of diverse and genuine satisfaction, and even as an end in itself" (Leiss 1988: 102). Consumerism is bound up with independent living, self-determination and self-actualization—or personhood. Yet, if personal and collective independence and self-determination is possible within the context of market and production relations and, indeed, if it depends on such relations, how then is it possible to address the negative consequences and impact of capitalist market and production relations on individuals?

Part of the answer might be found in the post-World War II development and growth of human rights consciousness, and in the parallel historical relationship between "rights" and "property" (Claude 1976, Macpherson 1978, Leiss 1988: 103–9, 135–37). With the spread of a developing capitalist market economy from the late seventeenth century onwards, an increasing emphasis on private property became the basis upon which the market economy and market relations were founded. However, not all individuals competed successfully in the open labor market, nor were all individuals able to accumulate property which was supposed to provide their security. The market assumption (the classical liberal ideal of autonomous individualism) that all were capable of participating equally in pursuing their interests and objectives as free individuals turned out to be a false one.

Those who accumulated property came to control the labor of others, and the rights of those who sold their labor as their only means to life was ultimately reduced to trying to secure the rights of access to the means of labor. The right not to be excluded from the means of production has since become critical in an intensified wage-labor system found in industrial capitalism. However, having rights of access even to the means of labor became problematic by virtue of changing market conditions. In keeping with the liberal ideal that every person is entitled to a fully human life and the opportunities to develop his or her potential, the right not to be excluded from the relations of production (equal employment rights) has transformed, since World War II, into the right to an income (welfare/social security rights). More recently, the right not to be excluded from the accumulated productive resources of society has been transformed into the right to share in the control of these resources or of production as shown by the development of rights of self-determination, equality rights and consumer rights.

According to Claude and Macpherson, the development of the idea of property has gone hand-in-hand with the development of rights. The development of the two concepts are rooted in each other. In property there has been a change (a) from public property and a right to revenue based on social status and moral contract, to (b) private property as a right *to exclude others* and a right to labor based on legal contract, to (c) the right to access the means of labor, that is, the right to be employed and *not to be excluded* from the accumulated productive resources of society. Interestingly, the right "not to be excluded" (from access to, or the use of something) is also the definition of public property.

There have been changes from (a) rights protecting individuals against the powers of the state (freedom of speech, religion and conscience, from arbitrary arrest, and the right to contract), to (b) rights as a means of participating in state affairs (the right to vote, freedom of assembly and of association), to (c) rights guaranteeing a person protection by way of intervention or obtaining benefits provided by the state (rights to medicare, social assistance, education, employment, income, an adequate standard of living, equality rights, anti-discrimination law). One conclusion that can be drawn is that historically, in the context of capitalist market and production relations, there has been a development towards rights "not to be excluded" from protection and/or benefits provided by the state. Leiss (1988: 104–5) observes from his analysis of Macpherson's work on property,

> The key change in the meaning of property in the twentieth century is a process of "broadening." The dominant earlier notion of the right of an individual or corporation to exclude others from the use of things is by no means abandoned, but competing notions have been added, especially the claim to a right of access for everyone to a minimum share of resources. This share is in effect an entitlement to a stream of revenue that is sufficient to sustain every person at a decent level of existence, whether this stream of revenue is generated by earning an income by paid employment or receiving various kinds of welfare benefits from the state. This is the idea of property as a universal right, a right "to the means of a fully human life," that is to say, (a) a right to a share in political power to control the uses of the a-massed capital and the natural resources of the society, and (b), beyond that, a right to a kind of society, a set of power relations throughout society, essential to a fully human life.

The conclusion is that political power becomes the most important type of property (Leiss 1988: 105) and that access to political power as a kind of "public property" must be guaranteed and protected by the state. This is a crucial development in the history of capitalist market relations and the growth of human rights consciousness. An implication of this conclusion, following Leiss's analysis of Macpherson, is that the state comes to assume many of the allocative functions that before were managed within the context of market relations. This in fact is what may already be occurring. In Canada, the allocative functions performed by the state (shared between the federal and provincial governments) includes such social programs as universal health care, transfer and equalization payments, family allowance, national pensions and welfare support, wages and income security, and child welfare. Interestingly, the Constitutional discussions of 1991–92 included proposals by provincial and federal New Democrats to include a "social charter" that, blended into the Charter of Rights and Freedoms, constitutionally would define, enforce and protect these programs. Social and economic rights are known as "second-tier rights," and are included in more than half the constitutions of the world, including the majority member countries of the Organization for Economic Cooperation and Development. A social charter enables citizens to challenge state actions to cut, limit or curtail elements of these programs or the programs themselves (*Globe and Mail*, September 25, 1991, January 13, 1992).

In what is a provocative analysis, Leiss (1988: Chapter 4) discusses the development and nature of a quasi-market society in the context of a critique of both capitalism and socialism, and in the context of an evaluation of OECD countries (including Canada) and major socialist nations. As a hybrid social formation emerging on a global scale (increasingly rapidly since the end of World War II), a quasi-market society is one in which fully-developed market relations exist side-by-side with a state apparatus that oversees the national economy and takes responsibility for major social programs through transfer payments.

What is significant here is that although the main features of quasi-market societies maintain the essential centrality of market and production relations in the lives of individuals (maintaining inequalities in the distribution of wealth and income to some degree), the negative consequences and impact of these relations and inequalities are alleviated by mechanisms of income redistribution, transfer payments and welfare or social assistance entitlements. One effect of this public sector involvement is that the extreme polarization of wealth and poverty that would occur under unregulated capitalism would be avoided. At the same time this commitment to market forces still provides the motivation and incentive for individuals to pursue their goals of self-determination and personhood in the contexts of both production as well as consumption. According to Leiss, the institutional make-up of a quasi-market society would promote "consumerism as the single most important zone of gratification in the lives of individuals." It is in this context of a movement towards a public property and a positive theory of market relations that the late 1980s review and critique of the Vocational Rehabilitation of Disabled Persons Act (VRDP), the

Canada Assistance Plan (CAP) and the idea of a Social Charter can be appreciated.

Thus, the advocacy of the public/social utilities approach that is directed towards improving the quality of social and cultural life, and the public recognition of independent living centres as legitimate public/community service utilities might be recognized for what it is: The claim for the universal and public right of self-determination for all people. What is self-determination and, indeed, community-building, if it is not the pursuit and fulfilment of consumer ideals and the creation of the very conditions by which the satisfaction of individual and community needs can be met?

> We may pick up again what is a very old idea, the idea that used to prevail before the market economy converted us all into consumers: the idea that life is for *doing* rather than just *getting*. You may ask, can the right to such a full and free life of action and enjoyment be made an individual property, i.e. a legally enforceable claim that society will enforce in favor of each individual? There is no intrinsic difficulty about this (C.B. Macpherson *op. cit.* in Leiss 1988: 106–7; original emphasis).

From the perspective of community, disabled citizens and, for that matter, all citizens would heartily agree with C.B. Macpherson: There should be no intrinsic difficulty about this.

Bibliography

Aaker, D. and G. Day
    1978   A Guide to Consumerism. In *Consumerism: Search for the Consumer Interest*, ed. by D. Aaker and G. Day, pps. 2–18. New York: The Free Press.

Abella, R.S.
    1984   *Equality in Employment: A Royal Commission Report*. Volume 1. Ottawa.
    1985   *Equality in Employment. Research Studies*. Volume 2. Ottawa.

Advocacy Resource Centre for the Handicapped
    1992   *Opinion, The Canada Clause of the Charlottetown Accord*. Unpublished, 9 pps. Toronto.

Ainlay, S., G. Becker and L. Coleman
    1986   *The Dilemma of Difference: A Multidisciplinary View of Stigma*. New York: Plenum Press.

Alberta Committee of Citizens With Disabilities (Edmonton)
[Selected Papers]
    n.d.   *Board of Directors Manual*.
    1972   *Research on the Life Styles of the Physically Disabled*. 62 pps., appendices.

280 Bibliography

1975 *Recommendations Relating to the Individual's Rights Protection Act and the Alberta Bill of Rights.* 56 pps., including appendices. Submitted to the Alberta MLA/Handicapped Joint Committee.
1979a *Presentation to the Alberta Human Rights Commission.* 56 pps., attachments.
1979b *Barriers to Employment and Persons with Physical Disabilities.* 26 pps., including appendices. Submitted to the Minister of Labour, Province of Alberta.
1980a *Basic Background Information on the Alberta Committee.* Approx. 80 pps., including letters, newspaper clippings, etc.
1980b *Vocational Integration: The Role of the Disabled Consumer in Their Vocational Rehabilitation.* 7 pps. Submitted to the Alberta Legislative Assembly.
1980c *Vocational Integration: The Role of the Disabled Consumer in Their Vocational Rehabilitation.* 23 pps. Submitted to the Alberta Human Rights Commission.
1980d *Educational Integration.* 30 pps. Submitted to the Alberta Teachers' Association's Task Force.
1980e *Job Adaptations and Persons with Physical Disabilities.* 12 pps. Submitted to the Canadian Human Rights Commission.
1980f *The Consumer Group in Alberta.* 6 pps. Submitted to the Special Committee on the Disabled and the Handicapped.
1981a *Barrier-Free Environment and Persons with Physical Disabilities.* 23 pps.
1981b *The Disabled Consumer Movement in Alberta.* 46 pps.
1981c *Technological Aids: A Review of A.A.D.L. and Related Programs.* 19 pps. Submitted to Members of the Legislative Assembly of Alberta.
1981d *Comprehensive Personal Relief and Support Services: A Needs Analysis Survey and Report.* 28 pps., attachments.
1982 *Historical Overview: Alberta Committee of Consumer Groups of Disabled Persons.* 16 pps.
1983a *Concerns of the Alberta Committee of Consumer Groups of Disabled Persons in Relation to the Human Rights Act.* 6 pps. Submitted to the Canadian Human Rights Commission.
1983b *Final Report of the Alberta Committee's Human Rights Information Officer.* 73 pps.
1983c *Outreach Report (Board Members in touch with the grassroots).* 27 pps., attachments.
1984a *Bona Fide Occupational Requirements: Response.* 4 pps. Submitted to the Canadian Human Rights Commission.
1984b *Presentation to the Committee on Tolerance and Understanding.* 9 pps.
1984c *Presentation to the Alberta Human Rights Commission.* 4 pps.
1985 *Affirmative Action: A Position Paper.* 25 pps.
1987a *Employment Equity Survey: Final Report.* 27 pps.

1987b   *Personal Support Options for Individuals with Physical Disabilities: Position Paper.* 12 pps.
1987c   *Community Living/Independent Living.* 25 pps., appendices.
1988   *Plan of Action 1988–89.* 4 pps.
1989   *"Linkages": A Proposal.* Submitted to Health Promotion Directorate (Government of Canada). 10 pps.
1990   *Response to: The Alberta Premier's Council on the Status of Persons With Disabilities Action Plan.* 30 pps.
1990   *Response to: The Rainbow Report: Our Vision for Health (Alberta Premier's Commission on Future Health Care for Albertans).* 28 pps.
1985–91 *Awareness is the Key* (Newsletter, Volumes 1–7).
1991–94 *Alberta Citizen* (Newsletter, Volumes 1–4).

Alberta, Health Economics and Statistics
  1991 *Dimensions of Disability in Alberta: Results of the Health and Activity Limitation Survey, 1986.* Edmonton.

Alberta, Human Rights Commission
  1987 *Annual Report, April 1986–March 1987.*

Alberta, Premier's Commission on Future Health Care for Albertans
  1989 *What You've Said.* Newsletter Special Edition.

Alberta, Premier's Council on the Status of Persons with Disabilities
  1987 *A Proposal for the Premier's Council on the Status of Persons with Disabilities.* The Steering Committee, in consultation with Humanité Services Planning Ltd., Edmonton.
  1989 *Towards a New Vision of Abilities in Alberta.*
  1990 *Integration.* Position Paper.
  1990–91 *Annual Report.*
  1990–94 *Status Report.* Quarterly Reports.

Alberta, Social Services
  1988 *Caring and Responsibility: A Statement of Social Policy for Alberta.*

Albrecht, G.
  1976 Socialization and the Disability Process. In *The Sociology of Physical Disability*, ed. by G. Albrecht, pps. 3–38. Pittsburgh: University of Pittsburgh Press.

Albrecht, G. and J. Levy
  1981 Constructing Disabilities as Social Problems. In *Cross-National Rehabilitation Policies: A Sociological Perspective*, ed. by G.L. Albrecht, pps. 11–32. Beverly Hills: Sage Publications Limited.

Apter, D.
  1971 *Choice and the Politics of Allocation.* New Haven: Yale University Press.

Aronowitz, S.
  1992 *The Politics of Identity: Class, Culture, Social Movements.* New York: Routledge.

Aronson, D.
  1970 Social Networks: Towards Structure or Process? *Canadian Review of Sociology and Anthropology* 7(4): 258–68.

Attendant Care Action Coalition
  1986 *Options for Independent Living Assistance.* Brief submitted to Minister of Community and Social Services, Edmonton.

Baker, D.
  1985 *Equality for Disabled People.* Advocacy Resource Centre for the Handicapped (ARCH), Toronto.

Barth, F.
  1969 *Ethnic Groups and Boundaries.* Boston: Little, Brown and Company.

Bauman, Z.
  1987 *Legislators and Interpreters: On Modernity, Post-Modernity and Intellectuals.* Ithaca: Cornell University Press.

Becker, H.
  1963 *Outsiders: Studies in the Sociology of Deviance.* New York: The Free Press.

Bell, D.
  1973 *The Coming of the Post-Industrial Society.* New York: Basic Books.

Benditt, T.
  1975 The Concept of Interest in Political Theory. *Political Theory* 3: 245–58.

Berger, P. and T. Luckmann
  1967 *The Social Construction of Reality.* New York: Doubleday.

Berger, P. and R. Neuhaus
  1977 *To Empower People: The Role of Mediating Structures in Public Policy.*

Washington, DC: American Enterprise Institute for Public Policy Research.

Black, W.W.
    1985   *Employment Equity: A Systemic Approach*. Ottawa: Human Rights Research and Education Centre, University of Ottawa.

Black, W. and L. Smith
    1989   The Equality Rights. In *The Canadian Charter of Rights and Freedoms* (2nd. ed.), ed. by F. Ratushny, pps. 557–651. Toronto: Carswell.

Blau, P.
    1964   *Exchange and Power in Social Life*. New York: Wiley.

Boissevain, J.
    1968   The Place of Non-Groups in the Social Sciences. *Man* 3: 542–56.
    1974   *Friends of Friends: Networks, Manipulators and Coalitions*. Oxford: Basil Blackwell.

Bolaria, B.S.
    1988a The Politics and Ideology of Self-Care and Lifestyle. In *Sociology of Health Care in Canada*, ed. by B.S. Bolaria and H. Dickinson, pps. 537–49. Toronto: Harcourt Brace Jovanovich.
    1988b The Health Effects of Powerlessness. In *Sociology of Health Care in Canada*, ed. by B.S. Bolaria and H. Dickinson, pps. 439–59. Toronto: Harcourt Brace Jovanovich.
    1991   Environment, Work, and Illness. In *Social Issues and Contradictions in Canadian Society*, ed. by B.S. Bolaria, pps. 222–46. Toronto: Harcourt Brace Jovanovich.

Bolaria, B.S. and T. Wotherspoon
    1991   Income Inequality, Poverty, and Hunger. In *Social Issues and Contradictions in Canadian Society*, ed. by B.S. Bolaria, pps. 464–80. Toronto: Harcourt Brace Jovanovich.

Bott, E.
    1957   *Family and Social Network*. London: Tavistock.

Bourdieu, P.
    1977   *Outline of a Theory of Practice*. Cambridge: Cambridge University Press.

Boyte, H.C. and F. Riessman
  1986 *The New Populism: The Politics of Empowerment*. Philadelphia: Temple University Press.

Bright, C. and S. Harding
  1984 *Statemaking and Social Movements: Essays in History and Theory*. Ann Arbor: University of Michigan Press.

Brown, J.
  1977 *A Hit-and-Miss Affair: Policies for Disabled People in Canada*. Ottawa: Canadian Council on Social Development.

Brown, R.I.
  1988 *Quality of Life for Handicapped People*. London: Croom Helm.

Brown, R.I., M. Bayer and P. Brown
  1992 *Empowerment and Developmental Handicaps: Choices and Quality of Life*. London: Chapman and Hall.

Brown, R.I., M. Bayer and C. MacFarlane
  1989 *Rehabilitation Programs: The Performance and Quality of Life of Adults with Developmental Handicaps*. Toronto: Lugus Publications.

Cairns, A.C.
  1988 Citizens (Outsiders) and Governments (Insiders) in Constitution-Making: The Case of Meech Lake. *Canadian Public Policy* 14, Special Supplement: 121–45.

Canada, Health and Welfare
  1988 *Canada's Health Promotion Survey: Technical Report*. Ottawa: Minister of Supply and Services.

Canada, Secretary of State
  1981–87 *Obstacles*. Reports by: Special Committee on the Disabled and the Handicapped; Standing Committee on the Disabled and Handicapped; Status of Disabled Persons Secretariat.
  1988a *Independence, That's Living!* National Access Awareness Week (May 29–June 4).
  1988b *National Access Awareness Week: "How To" for Provincial and Community Organizations*.
  1989–92 *National Access Awareness Week: Integrating Disabled People*. "Profiles of Canadians with Disabilities."

Canadian Disability Rights Council
    1992   *Opinion, Exclusion of People with Disabilities from the Canada Clause, Charlottetown Accord.* Winnipeg. Unpublished, 6 pps.

Canadian Human Rights Commission
    1987–93   *Annual Reports.* Ottawa: Minister of Supply and Services.
    1988   *Operational Procedures for Ensuring Compliance with Employment Equity.* Ottawa.

Canadian Rehabilitation Council for the Disabled
    1987   *CRCD Rehabilitation Classification Scheme.* Toronto.

Carroll, W.K.
    1992   *Organizing Dissent: Contemporary Social Movements in Theory and Practice.* Toronto: Garamond Press.

Caws, P.
    1974   Operational, Representational and Explanatory Models. *American Anthropologist* 76: 1–10.

Citizens Task Force for Physically Disabled Persons
    1987   *Report of the Citizens Task Force.* Edmonton.

Claude, R.P.
    1976   The Classical Model of Human Rights Development. *Comparative Human Rights*, ed. by R.P. Claude, pps. 1–50. Baltimore: John Hopkins University Press.

Coalition of Provincial Organizations of the Handicapped (Winnipeg) [Selected Papers]
    n.d.   *History of COPOH.* 12 pps.
    1985a   *Independent Living: Made in Canada.* 17 pps.
    1985b   *Conference Report, 6th Open National Conference.* 88 pps. Montreal.
    1985c   *Policy Manual.* 58 pps.
    1985d   *Board Manual.* 170 pps., updates and revisions.
    1985e   *Disabled Women's Issues: Discussion Paper.* 41 pps.
    1986–91   *Annual Reports.*
    1987a   *COPOH's Response to the Special Joint Committee on the 1987 Constitutional Accord.* 9 pps.
    1987b   *COPOH's Preliminary Position on Fiscal Arrangements Affecting Disabled Canadians.* 25 pps.
    1987c   *"Natives Speak Out": Discussions Papers.* 51 pps.
    1987d   *Defining the Parameters of Independent Living.* 113 pps.

1987e   *Proceedings of a Workshop on Disabled Women's Issues.* 48 pps.
1987f   *Tax Reform and the Disabled Person.* A Response to Income Tax Reform 1987. Submitted to the Minister of Finance. 6 pps.
1988a   *Defining Equality.* Papers and Workshop. 62 pps.
1988b–93 *COMPASS.* Quarterly journal.
1989a   *A COPOH Evaluation of the Decade of Disabled Persons: A Conference Report.* 93 pps.
1989b   *Human Rights: Can't Get No Satisfaction.* 127 pps., appendices and attachments.
1992a   *Disabled Canadians Dropped From Canada Clause.* Press Release, September 8, 1992. 1 pp.
1992b   *Disabled Canadians Given No Option But To Vote No.* Press Release, October 20, 1992. 1 pp.
1994   *Abilities.* Quarterly magazine.

Coe, R.
    1976   Some Notes on Rehabilitation and Models for Interdisciplinary Collaboration. In *The Sociology of Physical Disability and Rehabilitation*, ed. by G. Albrecht, pps. 247–56. Pittsburgh: University of Pittsburgh Press.

Cohen, Abner
    1974   *Two-Dimensional Man: An Essay on the Anthropology of Power and Symbolism in Complex Society.* London: Routledge and Kegan Paul.

Cohen, A.P.
    1975   *The Management of Myths: The Politics of Legitimation in a Newfoundland Community.* ISER Publication 14. St. John's: Memorial University of Newfoundland.

Cohen, J.
    1982   Between Crisis Management and Social Movements: The Place of Institutional Reform. *Telos* 52: 21–40.
    1983   Rethinking Social Movements. *Berkeley Journal of Sociology* 28: 97–113.
    1985   Strategy or Identity: New Theoretical Paradigms and Contemporary Social Movements. *Social Research* 52(4): 663–716.

Comaroff, J.
    1985   *Body of Power, Spirit of Resistance: The Culture and History of a South African People.* Chicago: University of Chicago Press.

Community Living Society
    n.d.   *Brokerage.* Vancouver. 15 pps.

Conrad, P.
　1992　Medicalization and Social Control. *Annual Review of Sociology* 18: 209–32.

Conrad, P. and J. Schneider
　1980　*Deviance and Medicalization: From Badness to Sickness.* St. Louis: C.U. Mosby and Company.

Conrad, P. and R. Kern
　1986　*The Sociology of Health and Illness: Critical Perspectives.* New York: St. Martin's Press.

Cordell, A.
　1985　*The Uneasy Eighties: The Transition to an Information Society.* Science Council of Canada, Background Study 53. Ottawa.

Coser, L.
　1956　*The Functions of Social Conflict.* New York: The Free Press.

Coxon, M.
　1981　*Independent Living Centres.* Calgary. 24 pps., appendices.

Crewe, N. and I. Zola
　1983　*Independent Living for Physically Disabled People: Developing, Implementing and Evaluating Self-Help Rehabilitation Programs.* San Francisco: Jossey-Bass.

Cunningham, F., S. Findlay, et al.
　1988　*Social Movements/Social Change: The Politics and Practice of Organizing.* Toronto: Between the Lines Press.

D'Amico, R. and A.J. Layon
　1988　AIDS and the Politics of Morbidity. *Telos* No. 76: 115–29.

Day, H.
　1984　*Vocational Rehabilitation in Canada: Extent and Nature.* Ottawa: VRDP/Health and Welfare Canada.

DeJong, G.
　1983　Defining and Implementing the Independent Living Concept. In *Independent Living for Physically Disabled People*, ed. by N. Crewe and I. Zola, pps. 4–27. San Francisco: Jossey-Bass.

DeJong, G. and T. Wenker
1983   Attendant Care. In *Independent Living for Physically Disabled People*, ed. by N. Crewe and I. Zola, pps. 157–70. San Francisco: Jossey-Bass.

Department of Justice (Canada)
1985   *Equality Issues in Federal Law: A Discussion Paper*. Ottawa.

Derksen, J.
1980   *The Disabled Consumer Movement: Policy Implications for Rehabilitation Service Provision*. COPOH, Winnipeg. 22 pps.
1983   *The Independent Living Movement and the Self-Help Process*. Paper presented to Disabled Peoples' International, Bangkok, Thailand (April). 12 pps.

Dickinson, H. and M. Stobbe
1988   Occupational Health and Safety in Canada. *Sociology of Health Care in Canada*, ed. by B.S. Bolaria and H. Dickinson, pps. 426–38. Toronto: Harcourt Brace Jovanovich

Disabled People's International
1980   *Charter*. Brochure.

Dobell, A.R. and S. Mansbridge
1986   *The Social Policy Process in Canada*. The Institute for Research on Public Policy. Montreal.

Douglas, M.
1970   *Natural Symbols: Explorations in Cosmology*. New York: Vintage Books.

Driedger, D.
1986   Speaking for Ourselves: A History of COPOH on Its 10th Anniversary. *Caliper* (December): 8–13.
1989   *The Last Civil Rights Movement: Disabled Peoples' International*. London: Hurst & Company.

Eder, C.
1982   A New Social Movement? *Telos* 52: 5–20.
1985   The "New Social Movements": Moral Crusades, Political Pressure Groups, or Social Movements? *Social Research* 52(4): 869–90.

Edmonton Social Services (Housing and Social Planning Branch)
1987   *Edmonton's Physically Disabled Citizens: Their Needs and Services (Survey of Service Providers)*.

Eisenberg, M., C. Griggins, R. Duval
    1982   *Disabled People as Second-Class Citizens*. New York: Springer Publishing Company.

Employment and Immigration Canada
    1986a   *Employment Equity Act and Reporting Requirements*. Regulations, Schedules, Technical Papers.
    1986b   *Employment Equity System Review*. Employment Equity Consulting Service.
    1987a   *Employer's Handbook: Reporting on Employment Equity*.
    1987b   *Employment Equity: A Guide for Employers*.
    1987c   *Federal Contractors Program: Questions and Answers*.
    1988–92   *Employment Equity Act: Annual Reports to Parliament*.

Enns, H.
    1983   *Independent Living: A COPOH Perspective*. Winnipeg. 12 pps.

Fine, M. and A. Asch
    1988   *Women with Disabilities: Essays in Psychology, Culture and Politics*. Philadelphia: Temple University Press.

Flathman, R.
    1966   *The Public Interest*. New York: Wiley and Sons.

Foss, D. and R. Larkin
    1986   *Beyond Revolution: A New Theory of Social Movements*. Massachusetts: Bergin and Garvey Publishers.

Foucault, M.
    1965   *Madness and Civilization: A History of Insanity in the Age of Reason*. New York: Vintage Books.
    1973   *The Birth of the Clinic: An Archaeology of Medical Perception*. London: Tavistock.
    1977   *Discipline and Punish: The Birth of the Prison*. New York: Vintage Books.
    1980   *Power/Knowledge: Selected Interviews and Other Writings, 1972–1977*. New York: Pantheon Books.

Frank, A.W.
    1990   Bringing Bodies Back In: A Decade in Review. *Theory, Culture and Society* 7(1): 131–62
    1991   *At the Will of the Body: Reflections on Illness*. Boston: Houghton Mifflin Company.

Frankel, B.G.
　1988　Patient-Physician Relationships: Changing Modes of Interaction. In *Sociology of Health Care in Canada*, ed. by B.S. Bolaria and H. Dickinson, pps. 104–14. Toronto: Harcourt Brace Jovanovich.

Freeman, J.
　1983　*Social Movements of the Sixties and Seventies*. New York: Longman.

Freire, P.
　1984　*Pedagogy of the Oppressed*. New York: Continuum Press.

Frideres, J. and W. Reeves
　1989　The Ability to Implement Human Rights Legislation in Canada. *Canadian Review of Sociology and Anthropology* 26(2): 311–32.

Fried, M.
　1967　*The Evolution of Political Society*. New York: Random House.

Frieden, L.
　1983　Understanding Alternative Program Models. In *Independent Living for Physically Disabled People*, ed. by N. Crewe and I. Zola, pps. 62–72. San Francisco: Jossey-Bass.

Fuchs, V.
　1968　*The Service Economy*. New York: Columbia University Press.

Furrie, A.
　1990　*A Profile of the Disabled in Canada*. Catalogue No. 98–126. Ottawa: Statistics Canada.

Gadacz, R.
　1987　Agency, Unlimited. *Canadian Journal of Political and Social Theory* 11(3): 158–63.
　1988　Charter Politics. *Policy Options/Politiques* 9(5): 19–20.

Gamson, W.
　1968　*Power and Discontent*. Homewood (Illinois): Dorsey Press.
　1975　*The Strategy of Social Protest*. Homewood (Illinois): Dorsey Press.

Gartner, A.
　1987　*Images of the Disabled, Disabling Images*. New York: Praeger.

Gartner, A. and F. Riessman
    1974   *The Service Society and the Consumer Vanguard*. New York: Harper and Row.

Gaventa, J.
    1980   *Power and Powerlessness*. Urbana: University of Illinois Press.

Gerhardt, U.
    1989   *Ideas About Illness: An Intellectual and Political History of Medical Sociology*. London: Macmillan.

Giddens, A.
    1976   *New Rules of Sociological Method*. London: Hutchinson.
    1977   *Studies in Social and Political Theory*. New York: Basic Books.
    1979   *Central Problems in Social Theory*. Berkeley: University of California Press.
    1982   *Profiles and Critiques in Social Theory*. Berkeley: University of California Press.
    1984   *The Constitution of Society: Outline of the Theory of Structuration*. Berkeley: University of California Press.
    1985   *The Nation-State and Violence*. Berkeley: University of California Press.
    1986   Action, Subjectivity, and the Constitution of Meaning. *Social Research* 53(3): 529–45.
    1987a   Structuralism, Post-Structuralism and the Production of Culture. In *Social Theory Today*, ed. by A. Giddens and J. Turner, pps. 195–223. Stanford: Stanford University Press.
    1987b   *Social Theory and Modern Sociology*. Cambridge: Polity Press.
    1990   *The Consequences of Modernity*. Stanford: Stanford University Press.
    1991   *Modernity and Self-Identity: Self and Society in the Late Modern Age*. Cambridge: Polity Press.

Gleidman, J. and W. Roth
    1980   *The Unexpected Minority*. New York: Harcourt Brace Jovanovich.

Goffman, E.
    1961   *Asylums*. New York: Doubleday.
    1963   *Stigma: Notes on the Management of Spoiled Identity*. Englewood Cliffs: Prentice-Hall.

Gold, M.
    1983   A Principled Approach to Equality Rights: A Preliminary Inquiry. In *The New Constitution and the Charter of Rights*, ed. by E. Belobaba and E. Gertner, pps. 131–61. Toronto: Butterworths.

Goldiamond, I.
   1976   Coping and Adaptive Behaviors of the Disabled. In *The Sociology of Physical Disability and Rehabilitation*, ed. by G. Albrecht, pps. 97–138. Pittsburgh: University of Pittsburgh Press.

Gordon, L.
   1988   What Does Welfare Regulate? *Social Research* 55(4): 609–30.

Gove, W.
   1976   Societal Reaction Theory and Disability. In *The Sociology of Physical Disability and Rehabilitation*, ed. by G. Albrecht, pps. 57–71. Pittsburgh: University of Pittsburgh Press.

Government of Canada
   1986   *Toward Equality*. The Response to the Report of the Parliamentary Committee on Equality Rights. Ottawa.
   1987   *Accepting the Challenge*. The Government's Response to the Standing Committee on the Status of Disabled Persons. Ottawa.

Gower, D.
   1988   *Labour Market Activity of Disabled Persons in Canada*. Statistics Canada. Labour and Household Surveys Analysis Division (Results from the Canadian Health and Disability Survey 1983–84), Report No. 1.

Greschner, D.
   1988   *Notes for Remarks* (Commissioner, Canadian Human Rights Commission). Conference of the Alberta Committee of Disabled Citizens. 11 pps. Calgary.

Gritzer, G., and A. Arluke
   1985   *The Making of Rehabilitation: A Political Economy of Medical Specialization, 1890–1980*. Berkeley: University of California Press.

Habermas, J.
   1975   *Legitimation Crisis*. Boston: Beacon Press.
   1979   *Communication and the Evolution of Society*. Boston: Beacon Press.
   1981   New Social Movements. *Telos* 49: 33–37.
   1984   *Reason and the Rationalization of Society (Volume 1 of Theory of Communicative Action)*. Trans. by T. McCarthy. Cambridge: Polity Press.
   1987   *The Philosophical Discourse of Modernity*. Cambridge: MIT Press.

Hammersley, M. and P. Atkinson
   1983   *Ethnography: Principles in Practice*. London: Tavistock Publications.

Harding, J.
    1988   Environmental Degradation and Rising Cancer Rates: Exploring the Links in Canada. In *Sociology of Health Care in Canada*, ed. by B.S. Bolaria and H. Dickinson, pps. 411–25. Toronto: Harcourt Brace Jovanovich.

Haug, M. and B. Lavin
    1983   *Consumerism in Medicine: Challenging Physician Authority*. Beverly Hills: Sage Publications Limited.

Heath, A.
    1976   *Rational Choice and Social Exchange*. Cambridge: Cambridge University Press.

Herpin, N.
    1981   Off the Record: The Consequences of Constructing Dossiers on Clients. In *Cross-National Rehabilitation Policies: A Sociological Perspective*, ed. by G.L. Albrecht, pps. 65–81. Beverly Hills: Sage Publications Limited.

Herrmann, R.
    1978   The Consumer Movement in Historical Perspective. *Consumerism*, ed. by D. Aaker and G. Day, pps. 27–37. New York: The Free Press.

Hicks, J.
    1985   *Joshua Committees: An Examination of the Use of IPP's in the Self-Help Model*. 10 pps., appendices. Calgary.

Hill, K.
    1983   *Helping You Helps Me: A Guide Book for Self-Help Groups*. Ottawa: Canadian Council on Social Development.

Holy, L. and M. Stuchlik
    1981   *The Structure of Folk Models*. London: Academic Press.

Honneth, A.
    1987   Critical Theory. In *Social Theory Today*, ed. by A. Giddens and J. Turner, pps. 347–82. Stanford: Stanford University Press.

Hughes, P.
    1985   Discrimination and Related Concepts: Definitions and Issues. In *Equality in Employment: A Royal Commission Report (Research Studies)* by R. Abella, pps. 219–43. Ottawa.

Hum, D.P.
   1983   *Federalism and the Poor: A Review of the Canada Assistance Plan.* Toronto, Ontario: Economic Council.

Illich, I.
   1976   *Medical Nemesis: The Expropriation of Health.* New York: Pantheon Books.
   1977   *Disabling Professions.* London: Calder and Boyars.

Jenkins, J.C.
   1983   Resource Mobilization Theory and the Study of Social Movements. *Annual Review of Sociology* 9: 527–53.

Joas, H.
   1990   The Democratization of Differentiation: On the Creativity of Collective Action. In *Rethinking Progress: Movements, Forces and Ideas at the End of the 20th Century*, ed. by J. Alexander and P. Sztompka, pps. 182–201. Boston: Unwin Hyman.

Jones, M. and D. Gardner
   1976   *Consumerism: A New Force in Society.* Lexington: D.C. Heath and Company.

Kallen, E.
   1982   *Ethnicity and Human Rights in Canada.* Toronto: Gage Publishing.
   1988   The Meech Lake Accord: Entrenching a Pecking Order of Minority Rights. *Canadian Public Policy* 14, Special Supplement: 107–20.
   1989   *Label Me Human: Minority Rights of Stigmatized Canadians.* Toronto: University of Toronto Press

Karp, I.
   1986   Agency and Social Theory: A Review of Anthony Giddens. *American Ethnologist* 13(1): 131–37.

Kinloch, G.
   1979   *The Sociology of Minority Group Relations.* Englewood Cliffs: Prentice-Hall.

Kleinfield, S.
   1979   *The Hidden Minority: A Profile of Handicapped Americans.* Boston: Little, Brown and Company.

Kleinman, A.
    1988   *Illness Narratives: Suffering, Healing, and the Human Condition.* New York: Basic Books.

Kornhauser, W.
    1959   *The Politics of Mass Society.* New York: The Free Press.

Krause, E.
    1976   The Political Sociology of Rehabilitation. In *The Sociology of Physical Disability and Rehabilitation*, ed. by G. Albrecht, pps. 201–21. Pittsburgh: University of Pittsburgh Press.

Lamoureux, H., R. Mayer, and J. Panet-Raymond
    1989   *Community Action: Organizing for Social Change.* Montreal: Black Rose Books.

Langton, S.
    1978   *Citizen Participation in America.* Lexington (MA): Lexington Books.

Lash, S.
    1990   *Sociology of Postmodernism.* London: Routledge.

Lauderdale, P.
    1980   *A Political Analysis of Deviance.* Minneapolis: University of Minnesota Press.

Leiss, W.
    1976   *The Limits to Satisfaction: An Essay on the Problem of Needs and Commodities.* Toronto: University of Toronto Press.
    1988   *C.B. Macpherson: Dilemmas of Liberalism and Socialism.* Montreal: New World Perspectives.

Lenski, G.
    1966   *Power and Privilege.* New York: McGraw-Hill.

Lepofsky, M.D. and J.E. Bickenbach
    1985   Equality Rights and the Physically Handicapped. In *Equality Rights and the Canadian Charter of Rights and Freedoms*, ed. by A. Bayefsky and M. Eberts, pps. 323–80. Toronto: Carswell.

Lieberman, M., L. Borman, et al.
    1979   *Self-Help Groups for Coping With Crisis: Origins, Members, Processes and Impact.* San Francisco: Jossey-Bass.

Lonsdale, S.
    1990   *Women and Disability: The Experience of Physical Disability Among Women*. London: Macmillan Education Limited.

Lord, J. and L. Osborne-Way
    1987   *Toward Independence and Community: A Qualitative Study of Independent Living Centres in Canada*. Ottawa: Disabled Participation Program.

Lowe, G. and H. Krahn
    1984   *Working Canadians: Readings in the Sociology of Work and Industry*. Toronto: Methuen.

Lyon, L.
    1987   *The Community in Urban Society*. Philadelphia: Temple University Press.

MacLean, H.
    1985   *Components of a Brokerage System*. Prepared for the Calgary Association for Independent Living, Calgary.

MacLean, H., et al.
    1987a   *Supported Independence: One More Step in the Evolution of Individualized Services*. Prepared for the Dignity of Risk Conference, Calgary.
    1987b   *Service Brokerage: Challenging the Past, A Chance for the Future*. Calgary.
    1988   *Brokerage Policy Paper: Funding Alternatives that Foster Empowerment*. Prepared for the Canadian Association of Independent Living Centres.

Macpherson, C.B.
    1978   *Property*. Toronto: University of Toronto Press.

Marcus, G.
    1986   Contemporary Problems of Ethnography in the Modern World System. In *Writing Culture: The Poetics and Politics of Ethnography*, ed. by J. Clifford and G. Marcus, pps. 165–93. Berkeley: University of California Press.

Marcus, G. and M. Fischer
    1986   *Anthropology as Cultural Critique*. Chicago: University of Chicago Press.

Marcuse, H.
1964 *One-Dimensional Man: Studies in the Ideology of Advanced Industrial Society*. Boston: Beacon Press.

Marlett, N. (editor)
1988 *Independent Service Brokerage: Achieving Consumer Control Through Direct Payment*. Walter Dinsdale Centre for the Empowerment of Canadians with Disabilities. 69 pps.

Marlett, N., R. Gall and A. Wight-Felske
1984 *Dialogue on Disability: A Canadian Perspective, Volume 1: The Service System*. Calgary: University of Calgary Press.

Marlett, N. and H. MacLean
1987 *A New Lifestyle for Persons with Severe Disabilities: Supported Independence*. Prepared for SHAPE Conference. 12 pps. Calgary.
1988 A New Life-Style for Persons with Severe Disabilities: Supported Independence. In *Alternative Futures for the Education of Students with Severe Disabilities*, ed. by D. Baine, D. Sobsey, et al., pps. 50–59. Edmonton: University of Alberta.

Maslow, A.
1970 *Motivation and Personality*. New York: Harper and Row.

Mayer, A.
1966 The Significance of Quasi-Groups in the Study of Complex Societies. In *The Social Anthropology of Complex Societies*, ed. by M. Banton, pps. 97–122. London: Tavistock.

McCarthy, T.
1978 *The Critical Theory of Jurgen Habermas*. Cambridge: MIT Press.

McCarthy, J. and M. Zald
1973 *The Trend of Social Movements in America: Professionalization and Resource Mobilization*. Morristown (NJ): General Learning Press.

McDaniel, S.
1986 *Canada's Aging Population*. Toronto: Butterworths.

McElroy, A. and P. Townsend
1989 *Medical Anthropology in Ecological Perspective*. Boulder: Westview Press.

Melucci, A.
    1981   Ten Hypotheses for an Analysis of New Movements. In *Contemporary Italian Sociology*, ed. by D. Pinto, pps. 173–94. Cambridge: Cambridge University Press.
    1985   The Symbolic Challenge of Contemporary Movements. *Social Research* 52(4): 789–816.
    1988   Social Movements and the Democratization of Everyday Life. *Civil Society and the State: New European Perspectives*, ed. by J. Keane, pps. 245–60. London: Verso.

Merleau-Ponty, M.
    1963   *Phenomenology of Perception*. London: Routledge and Kegan Paul.

Merton, R.
    1968   *Social Theory and Social Structure*. New York: The Free Press.

Mishler, E.G.
    1984   *The Discourse of Medicine: Dialectics of Medical Interviews*. Norwood (NJ): Ablex Publishing Corp.

Murphy, R.
    1987   *The Body Silent*. New York: Henry Holt.

Nagler, M.
    1993   *Perspectives on Disability: Text and Readings on Disability*. Palo Alto: Health Markets Research.

Navarro, V.
    1983   Work, Ideology and Science: The Case of Medicine. In *Health and Work under Capitalism*, ed. by V. Navarro and D. Berman, pps. 35–65. Farmingdale (NY): Baywood Publishing Company.

Northcott, H.
    1991   Health Status and Health Care in Canada: Contemporary Issues. In *Social Issues and Contradictions in Canadian Society*, ed. by B.S. Bolaria, pps. 178–95. Toronto: Harcourt Brace Jovanovich.

Ng, R., G. Walker, and J. Muller
    1990   *Community Organization and the Canadian State*. Toronto: Garamond Press.

Oberschall, A.
    1973   *Social Conflict and Social Movements*. Englewood Cliffs: Prentice-Hall.

Offe, C.
   1985   New Social Movements: Challenging the Boundaries of Institutional Politics. *Social Research* 52(4): 817–68.

Olson, M.
   1965   *The Logic of Collective Action.* Cambridge: Harvard University Press.

O'Neill, J.
   1985   *Five Bodies: The Human Shape of Modern Society.* Ithaca: Cornell University Press.

Ortner, S.
   1984   Theory in Anthropology Since the Sixties. *Comparative Studies in Society and History* 26(1): 126–66.

Parliamentary Committee on Equality Rights
   1985   *Equality For All.* Ottawa: Report of the Committee.

Parliamentary Forum on the Status of Disabled Persons
   1988   *3,300,000 Canadians.* Ottawa: Office of the Speaker.

Parsons, T.
   1937   *The Structure of Social Action.* New York: McGraw-Hill.
   1951   *Toward a General System of Action.* New York: Free Press.

Pentney, W.F.
   1988   *Discrimination and the Law: Including Equality Rights Under the Charter.* Fourth Cumulative Supplement (August 1988, 104 pps.). Don Mills: Richard De Boo.

Penz, G.
   1986   *Consumer Sovereignty and Human Interests.* Cambridge: Cambridge University Press.

Peters, Y.
   1987a   *Why Is Reasonable Accommodation Necessary?* Report submitted to COPOH. 37 pps. Winnipeg.
   1987b   *Equality Rights of Persons With Disabilities and the Canadian Charter of Rights and Freedoms.* Report submitted to COPOH. 16 pps. Winnipeg.

Piven, F. and R. Cloward
   1971   *Regulating the Poor.* New York: Random House.

1977   *Poor People's Movements.* New York: Vintage Books.

Plant, R.
1974   *Community and Ideology: An Essay in Applied Social Philosophy.* London: Routledge and Kegan Paul.

Powell, T.
1987   *Self-Help Organizations and Professional Practice.* Silver Spring (MD): National Association of Social Workers.

Pross, A.P.
1986   *Group Politics and Public Policy.* Toronto: Oxford University Press.

Rappaport, J., C. Swift and R. Hess
1984   *Studies in Empowerment: Steps Toward Understanding and Action.* New York: Haworth Press.

Ratushny, E.
1986   Implementing Equality Rights: Standards of Reasonable Accommodation with Legislative Force. *Righting the Balance: Canada's New Equality Rights*, ed. by L. Smith, et al., pps. 255–72. Saskatoon: The Canadian Human Rights Reporter.

Reasons, C.E., L. Lois, and C. Paterson
1981   *Assault on the Worker: Occupational Health and Safety in Canada.* Toronto: Butterworths.

Rioux, M.
1985   Labelled Disabled and Wanting to Work. *Equality in Employment: A Royal Commission Report (Research Studies)* by R. Abella, pps. 611–39. Ottawa.

Rogers, C.
1951   *Client-Centered Therapy: Its Current Practice, Implications and Theory.* Boston: Houghton-Mifflin.
1977   *On Personal Power.* New York: Dell Publishing.

Rorty, A.O.
1987   Persons as Rhetorical Categories. *Social Research* 54(1): 55–72.

Rose, S. and B. Black
1985   *Advocacy and Empowerment: Mental Health Care in the Community.* Boston: Routledge and Kegan Paul.

Russell, B.
    1991   The Welfare State and the Politics of Constraint. In *Social Issues and Contradictions in Canadian Society*, ed. by B.S. Bolaria, pps. 481–501. Toronto: Harcourt Brace Jovanovich.

Russell, S.
    1989   From Disability to Handicap: An Inevitable Response to Social Constraints? *Canadian Review of Sociology and Anthropology* 26(2): 276–93.

Safilios-Rothschild, C.
    1970   *The Sociology and Social Psychology of Disability and Rehabilitation*. New York: Random House.

Sagarin, E.
    1971   *The Other Minorities*. Toronto: Ginn and Company.

Sahlins, M.
    1976   *Culture and Practical Reason*. Chicago: University of Chicago Press.

Salisbury, B.
    1987   *Service Brokerage: Individual Empowerment and Social Service Accountability*. Downsview: G. Allan Roeher Institute.

Sarason, S.B.
    1974   *The Psychological Sense of Community*. San Francisco: Jossey-Bass.

Sass, R.
    1988   Working Towards Safety. *Policy Options* 9(9): 13–14.

Schalock, R.
    1990   *Quality of Life: Perspectives and Issues*. Washington: American Association on Mental Retardation.

Schilts, R.
    1987   *And the Band Played On: Politics, People and the AIDS Epidemic*. New York: St. Martin's Press.

Schon, D.
    1976   Consumerism in Perspective. In *Consumerism: A New Force in Society*, ed. by M. Jones and D. Gardner, pps. 1–19. Lexington: D.C. Heath and Company.

Schur, E.
　1979　*Interpreting Deviance: A Sociological Introduction.* New York: Harper and Row.
　1980　*The Politics of Deviance: Stigma Contests and the Uses of Power.* Englewood Cliffs: Prentice-Hall.

Schutz, A.
　1967　*The Phenomenology of the Social World.* Evanston: Northwestern University Press.

Scott, A.
　1990　*Ideology and the New Social Movements.* Boston: Unwin Hyman.

Scott, J.
　1990　*A Matter of Record: Documentary Sources in Social Research.* Cambridge: Polity Press.

Simpson, A.
　1980　*Consumer Groups: Their Organization and Function.* Paper presented to the World Congress on Rehabilitation. 36 pps. Winnipeg.

Smart, B.
　1992　*Modern Conditions, Postmodern Controversies.* London: Routledge.

Smelser, N.
　1959　*Social Change in the Industrial Revolution.* Chicago: University of Chicago Press.
　1962　*The Theory of Collective Behavior.* New York: The Free Press.

Smith, D.E.
　1974　The Social Construction of Documentary Reality. *Sociological Inquiry* 44(4): 257–68.
　1984　Textually Mediated Social Organization. *International Social Science Journal* 36: 59–75.

Smith, L.
　1986　A New Paradigm for Equality Rights. In *Righting the Balance: Canada's New Equality Rights*, ps. 351–407. Saskatoon: The Canadian Human Rights Reporter.

Smith, L., G. Cote-Harper, R. Elliot, and M. Seydegart
　1986　*Righting the Balance: Canada's New Equality Rights.* Saskatoon: The Canadian Human Rights Reporter.

Social Research
    1988   *In Time of Plague: The History and Social Consequences of Lethal Epidemic Disease.* Collected Essays. Volume 55, No. 3.

Solomon, B.
    1976   *Black Empowerment: Social Work in Oppressed Communities.* New York: Columbia University Press.

Sontag, S.
    1978   *Illness as Metaphor.* New York: Farrar, Straus and Giroux.

Standing Committee on Human Rights and the Status of Disabled Persons
    1989–92   *Minutes of Proceedings and Evidence.* House of Commons. Ottawa.
    1989   *Court Challenges Program.* First Report to the House of Commons.
    1990a   *A Consensus for Action: The Economic Integration of Disabled Persons.* Second Report to the House of Commons.
    1990b   *Human Rights Considerations and Coherence in Canada's Foreign Policy.* Third Report to the House of Commons.
    1990c   *Unanswered Questions: The Government's Response to a Consensus for Action.* Fourth Report to the House of Commons.
    1993   *Completing the Circle.* Report to the House of Commons.

Standing Committee on the Status of Disabled Persons
    1988   *No News is Bad News.* First Report to the House of Commons. Ottawa.

Statistics Canada
    1985   *Highlights from the Canadian Health and Disability Survey, 1983–1984.* Cat. 82–563.
    1986   *Report of the Canadian Health and Disability Survey, 1983–1984.* Cat. 82–555.
    1986–87   *Health and Activity Limitation Survey.* Includes HALS 1988 Update.
    1987   *A National Database on Disabled Persons: Making Disability Data Available to Users.*
    1990a   *Highlights, Disabled Persons in Canada.* Cat. 82–602.
    1990b   *Selected Socio-Economic Consequences of Disability for Women in Canada.* HALS Special Studies Series. Cat. 82–615.
    1990c   *Barriers Confronting Seniors with Disabilities in Canada.* HALS Special Studies Series. Cat. 82–615.
    1991   *Leisure and Lifestyles of Persons with Disabilities in Canada.* HALS Special Studies Series. Cat. 82–615.
    1992   *1991 Health and Activity Limitation Survey. The Daily,* October 13 1992. Cat. 11–001E.

1993 1991 Health and Activity Limitation Survey: Employment and Education. *The Daily*, July 27, 1993. Cat. 11–001E.
1994 Disability and Housing, 1991 Aboriginal Peoples Survey. *The Daily*, March 25, 1994. Cat. 11–001E.

Stevenson, H.M. and A. Williams
1988 Physicians and Medicare: Professional Ideology and Canadian Health Care Policy. In *Sociology of Health Care in Canada*, ed. by B.S. Bolaria and H. Dickinson, ps. 92–103. Toronto: Harcourt Brace Jovanovich.

Stone, D.
1984 *The Disabled State*. Philadelphia: Temple University Press

Stone, S. and J. Doucette
1988 Organizing the Marginalized: The DisAbled Women's Network. In *Social Movements/Social Change: The Politics and Practice of Organizing*, ed. by F. Cunningham, et al., ps. 81–97. Toronto: Between the Lines Press.

Stroman, D.
1982 *The Awakening Minorities: The Physically Handicapped*. Washington, DC: University Press of America.

Stubbins, J.
1988 The Politics of Disability. In *Attitudes Towards Persons with Disabilities*, ed. by H. E. Yuker, ps. 22–32. New York: Springer Publishing Company.

Sub-Committee on the Disabled and the Handicapped
1987 *Challenge: Putting Our House in Order*. Standing Committee on Communications and Culture, Initial Report. Ottawa.

Sussman, M.
1976 The Disabled and the Rehabilitation System. In *The Sociology of Physical Disability and Rehabilitation*, ed. by G. Albrecht, pps. 223–46. Pittsburgh: University of Pittsburgh Press.

Symington, D.
1983 *Integration: Are We Ready?* Paper presented to the First Canadian Congress of Rehabilitation. 20 pps., attachments.

Sztompka, P.
1990 Agency and Progress: The Idea of Progress and Changing Theo-

ries of Change. In *Rethinking Progress: Movements, Forces and Ideas at the End of the 20th Century*, ed. by J. Alexander and P. Sztompka, pps. 247–63. Boston: Unwin Hyman.

Tarnopolsky, W.S. and W.F. Pentney
    1985   *Discrimination and the Law: Including Equality Rights Under the Charter*. Don Mills: Richard De Boo.

Tate, D. and T. Lee
    1983   Learning from Methods Used in Other Countries. In *Independent Living for Physically Disabled People*, ed. by N. Crewe and I. Zola, pps. 88–112. San Francisco: Jossey-Bass.

Thompson, J.
    1984   *Studies in the Theory of Ideology*. Berkeley: University of California Press.

Tilly, C.
    1978   *From Mobilization to Revolution*. Reading, MA: Addison-Wesley.
    1984   Social Movements and National Politics. In *Statemaking and Social Movements: Essays in History and Theory*, ed. by C. Bright and S. Harding, pps. 297–317.
    1985   Models and Realities of Popular Collective Action. *Social Research* 52(4): 717–47.

Tinder, G.
    1980   *Community: Reflections on a Tragic Ideal*. Baton Rouge: Louisiana State University Press.

Touraine, A.
    1977a   *The Self-Production of Society*. Chicago: University of Chicago Press.
    1977b   Crisis or Transformation? *Beyond the Crisis*, ed. by N. Birnbaum, pps. 17–45. New York: Oxford University Press.
    1981   *The Voice and the Eye: An Analysis of Social Movements*. Cambridge: Cambridge University Press.
    1985   An Introduction to the Study of Social Movements. *Social Research* 52(4): 749–87.
    1988   *Return of the Actor: Social Theory in Postindustrial Society*. Minneapolis: University of Minnesota Press.
    1992   Beyond Social Movements. *Theory, Culture and Society* 9(1): 125–45.

Treasury Board Secretariat
　　1988　*On Target: Progress in Employment Equity in the Federal Public Service 1985–1988.* Personnel Policy Branch, Communications Division.

Turner, B.S.
　　1984　*The Body and Society: Explorations in Social Theory.* Oxford: Basil Blackwell.
　　1992　*Regulating Bodies: Essays in Medical Sociology.* London: Routledge.

Turner, V.
　　1967　*The Forest of Symbols.* Ithaca: Cornell University Press.

Unger, R.M.
　　1987　*Social Theory: Its Situation and Its Task.* Cambridge: Cambridge University Press.

United Nations
　　1983　*United Nations Decade of Disabled Persons 1983–1992.* World Programme for Action Concerning Disabled Persons. Division for Economic and Social Information. New York.
　　1986a　*Manual on the Equalization of Opportunities for Disabled Persons.* Department of International Economic and Social Affairs. New York.
　　1986b　*Development of Statistics of Disabled Persons: Case Studies.* Department of International Economic and Social Affairs, Statistical Office, and the Centre for Social Development and Humanitarian Affairs.

Valenzuela, A.
　　1977　*Political Brokers in Chile: Local Government in a Centralized Polity.* Durham, NC: Duke University Press.

van Steenbergen, B.
　　1983　Cultural Renewal in Western Societies: The Role of Social Movements as Vanguard. In *Changing Lifestyles as Indicators of New and Cultural Values,* pps. 109–31. Zurich: Gottlieb Duttweiler Institute.

Varela, R.
　　1983　Changing Social Attitudes and Legislation. In *Independent Living for Physically Disabled People,* ed. by N. Crewe and I. Zola, pps. 28–48. San Francisco: Jossey-Bass.

Vash, C.
1981 *The Psychology of Disability*. New York: Springer Publishing Company.

Verba, S. and N. Nie
1972 *Participation in America: Political Democracy and Social Equality*. New York: Harper and Row.

Vickers, D. and O. Endicott
1985 Mental Disability and Equality Rights. In *Equality Rights and the Canadian Charter of Rights and Freedoms*, ed. by A. Bayefsky and M. Eberts, pps. 381–409. Toronto: Carswell.

Vincent, J.
1974 The Structuring of Ethnicity. *Human Organization* 33: 375–79.

Waitzkin, H.
1983 *The Second Sickness: Contradictions of Capitalist Health Care*. New York: Free Press.

Waitzkin, H. and B. Waterman
1974 *The Exploitation of Illness in Capitalist Society*. Indianapolis: Bobbs-Merrill.

Warren, D.
1981 *Helping Networks: How People Cope with Problems in the Urban Community*. Notre Dame (IN): University of Notre Dame Press.

Weinberg, N.
1988 Another Perspective: Attitudes of People with Disabilities. In *Attitudes Towards Persons with Disabilities*, ed. by H.E. Yuker, pps. 141–53. New York: Springer Publishing Company.

Wells, L.M.
1984 *The Integration of the Physically Disabled in Community Living*. Toronto: Faculty of Social Work, University of Toronto.

Weston, M. and B. Jeffery
1988 AIDS: The Politicizing of a Public Health Issue. In *Sociology of Health Care in Canada*, ed. by B.S. Bolaria and H. Dickinson, pps. 514–26. Toronto: Harcourt Brace Jovanovich.

Wolfensberger, W.
1973 *The Principle of Normalization in Human Services*. Downsview: National Institute on Mental Retardation.

1983   *Reflections on the Status of Citizen Advocacy.* Downsview: National Institute on Mental Retardation.

World Congress of Rehabilitation International
1980   *Report*, 54 pps. June 22–27, Winnipeg, Manitoba.

World Health Organization
1980   *International Classification of Impairments, Disabilities and Handicaps.* Geneva.

Zola, I.
1982   *Missing Pieces: A Chronicle of Living with a Disability.* Philadelphia: Temple University Press.
1983a Developing New Self-Images and Interdependence. In *Independent Living for Physically Disabled People*, ed. by N. Crewe and I. Zola, pps. 49–59. San Francisco: Jossey-Bass.
1983b Toward Independent Living: Goals and Dilemmas. In *Independent Living for Physically Disabled People*, ed. by N. Crewe and I. Zola, pps. 344–56. San Francisco: Jossey-Bass.

Zolo, D.
1990   Autopoiesis: Critique of a Postmodern Paradigm. *Telos* 86: 61–80.

Zukas, H.
1979   *CIL History.* 15 pps. Berkeley: Centre for Independent Living.

Index

able-bodiedness, 69–70, 138
access, 208, 211–19, 241, 245–46, 249, 252
accommodation, 226, 238–43, 245, 247, 252. *See also* reasonable accommodation; barriers; discriminatory barriers
acquired immune deficiency syndrome (AIDS), 40, 53, 243
action, strategy, 60, 111–18, 121–24, 132, 205, 207, 212, 233, 247
action/structure model, 98–109, 122
action theory, 17–19, 23, 25, 98–109, 132, 163, 256–58
activities of daily living (ADL), 32–34
adverse effect discrimination, 222–26, 230, 247, 250, 252–54. *See also* discriminatory barriers
advocacy, 172–73, 182, 209, 267, 278
Advocacy Resource Center for the Handicapped, 219, 222

affirmative action, 218–20, 222–23, 233, 241, 245, 249–50, 253, 271
agency, 15, 18, 258
Alberta Committee of Citizens With Disabilities, xix, 5, 23
   advocacy role, 86, 103, 135, 139–49
   history, 135–36
   organizational structure, 132, 137–39, 156
   service objectives, 88, 124–25, 145–48
Alberta Human Rights Commission v. Central Alberta Dairy Pool, 243
alienation, 22, 55, 112–14, 201, 265
awareness, 208, 212–14

Barrier Free Design Standard (BFDS), 212
barrier free environment, 212
barriers, 225–28, 246, 252. *See also* discriminatory barriers
   definition, 227

309

Bhinder v. Canadian National Railways, 229–30, 236, 238, 242, 247–49
body, the, 9
  and discipline, 37–39, 41–56
  as machine 67, 70
bona fide occupational qualification (BFOQ), 231–34, 237–38, 248, 250
bona fide occupational requirement (BFOR), 230–34, 237–38, 247
breakdown/crisis, theory of social movement, 99–100
brokerage, 173, 189–90, 195, 268
brokerage systems, xxi
  agency model, 191–92, 196
  history, 189–90
  operating principles, 192–93
  service model, 173–74, 189–91, 195–96
  structure and features, 174, 194–95

Calgary Association for Independent Living (CAIL), 172, 175, 177, 181–82, 184–85, 189–90
Canadian Assistance Plan (CAP), 212, 266–73, 278
Canada Clause [Charlottetown Constitutional Accord], 218–19, 222
Canada Elections Act, 210
Canada Employment Centers, 210
Canadian Association of Independent Living Centres (CAILC), 135, 174, 180, 186
Canadian Association for the Mentally Retarded, 215
Canadian Charter of Rights and Freedoms, xix, 88–89, 206, 208, 211, 213, 217–19, 221–24, 233, 244, 249, 253, 277–78
Canadian Disability Rights Council, 208, 211, 219, 222

Canadian Human Rights Act, 230–33, 237–38, 242–44, 249
Canadian Human Rights Commission, 208–10, 215–16, 228, 237–38, 242–43, 247, 250
Canadian Labour Congress, 209, 215
Canadian Paraplegic Association v. Elections Canada, 135, 211
Canadian Standards Association, 212
Canadian Transport Commission, 154–56
case services approach, 267–68
categorization of disabilities, 30–31, 125, 200. *See also* impairments
  mental/psychological, 30–31
  motor, 30
  muscular, skeletal, 30
  organic, 31
  sensory, 30
Census of Population, 213–14
Charlottetown Constitutional Accord, 218. *See also* Canada Clause
citizen participation, 255–73
Coalition of Provincial Organizations of the Handicapped (COPOH), xix, 4, 10, 12, 150–56, 183
  action principles, 79–80, 83–84, 105–7, 124, 127, 151–52, 160–61, 207–8, 240–43, 259–60
  annual forums, 153–56, 212, 216, 219
  history, 150, 215
  organizational structure, 133–36, 150–51, 156, 162, 173, 180
  service objectives, 65, 70, 83–84, 86, 88, 113, 152–56, 166–67, 181–82, 209–10, 246, 248–49, 267
coalitions, 96, 113–14, 128–32
colonization of the life world, 111–17

community, 20–25, 198–99
  definition, xxviii
  integration, 19, 23, 64, 123, 131, 156, 179–80, 212–13, 245
community building, 16, 20, 23, 62, 82, 122–26, 158, 161, 163–68, 174, 200, 206–7, 224–25, 252–53, 255–78
conservative individualism, xxvii
consumer coalitions, 11, 72, 91, 163–65, 179, 212–14, 262
consumer organizational model, 161
consumer organizations, structures and features of, 11, 92, 132–33, 156–57, 161
consumer rights, 91–92, 213–16, 252, 275
consumer sovereignty, 84–86
consumerism, xxvii, 10–11, 91–92, 123–24, 155, 267, 273, 277
consumption
  in context of industrial and advanced capitalism, 72–75, 103–5, 273–75
  in relation to production, 60, 72, 75, 101–2, 123, 274–76
  in relation to social identity, 10, 72–75, 92, 272–77
contention, minority protest, 94–95, 252
Court Challenges Program, 211
cross-disability focus, 129–34, 158, 172, 178–80
culture of participation, 253

decentralization, 107
decolonization, 112–13
decontextualization, 47–52, 93, 256, 262
dehumanization, 166
deinstitutionalization, 167
demedicalization, 166
depoliticization, 115–16

deviance, 39, 47, 54, 65, 93, 99–100, 125, 227, 262
dialectic of control, 19–21, 76, 123, 128, 160
dignity of risk, 154–55
disability, 3, 10, 50, 54, 56
  categories, 55, 175, 217–18, 269
  definition, 27–38
  etiology/pathology, 34
  history of, 37–39
  and the individual, 47, 50–51, 54, 62–68
  legal definition, 263, 270
  model, 35–36
  medical definition, 54, 263, 270
  as process, 48, 63, 269
  social consequences, 34, 262–64
  social role definition, 4–10, 34, 53–54, 126–27, 255–56, 264, 270
  statistics, 28–30, 34
Disability Information Brokerage System (DIBS), 173, 190
Disability Information Services of Canada (DISC), 178, 212
Disabled Consumer Movement, xvii, xxvii, 9–10, 61–118, 121, 205–9, 219–42, 252
Disabled Consumer Organizations, 128–59
  and advocacy, 216–18
  and information, research, 129–31, 212–13
  mandates, purpose, 129–32, 157, 166–67, 209
  structure, 130–32, 156–58
Disabled People for Employment Equity, 209–10
Disabled Peoples' International (DPI), 79, 133–35
Disabled Persons Participation Program, 209
Disabled Women's Network (DAWN), 129
disease, 43–44. *See also* illness

discriminatory barriers. *See also* adverse effect discrimination; barriers
  definition, 227–28
  discrimination of silence, definition of, 227
  failure to accommodate, definition of, 226
  insurmountable impairment, definition of, 226
  neglect of differences, 226–27
    definition, 227
  neutral standard, 225–26
    definition, 225
  purpose/effect, theories of, 220, 228
  social bias, 224–26
    definition, 225
  structural/systemic, 221, 239–40, 269
discrimination and the law, 215–19, 224–48, 255–57
discriminatory behavior
  intentional, 215, 222–23, 225, 227–31
  unintentional, 215, 225, 227, 231, 247
  definition, 229
domination, techno-bureaucratic, 101, 222
duality of social movement, 95–105
duality of structure, 260

ecological intervention, 183, 257
emancipatory politics, xxviii
Employment and Immigration Canada, 210, 238–39
employment equity, 209–12, 223–24, 238–41, 249–50, 253, 268–73
empowerment, xviii, xxv–xxvii, 121–35
  as minority goal, 93–118
  motivational, 92–118, 163–64
  relational or interactional, 15, 49, 76, 83, 92, 105–9, 123, 175–76, 207, 256
environment, social, 65
epilepsy, 38
equality, 205–30. *See also* rights
  concept/theory of, 219–20, 248–49
  and the disabled consumer movement, 219–78
  formal, 219, 221–22, 224, 250
    definition, 221
  political, individual, 220, 246, 250
  purposive, 220, 250–51
  substantive, 207–8, 219, 221–24, 250
    definition 223
ethnomethodology, 17
ethics
  the disabled consumer, 71
  medical, 67
  the professional ethic, 68–72, 179–80
  traditional rehabilitation, 66
  volunteer, charity, 66

Federal Contractors Program, 209
Federal Government initiatives
  access, 209–12, 238–45
  awareness, 212–21
  forums, 213–15
  legislation
    amendments, 217–18
    enacted, 209–21
    handicap amendment, 214–16
    human rights, 224–26, 229–31
    organizing principles, 208–11
    participation, 207–11
    statutory/constitutional, 224–27, 229–37, 242–46
fields, theoretical, 7sf., 96–98, 109
Five Star Community, 142–43
fixed point of responsibility, 169, 194
functional limitation approach, 32

funding, public and/or private, 182–83, 191, 207–12, 268–71

Gemeinschaft/Gezellschaft, 21
grassroots involvement, 199–200
Griggs v. Duke Power Company Ltd., 229

handicap(s), 25, 36
  definition, 36
  handicap amendment, 161, 214–15
handicapping, 93
Health and Activity Limitation Survey (HALS), 212–13
Health and Welfare Canada, 210, 212
Huck v. Canadian Odeon Theatres Ltd., 221, 234–35, 248
human immunodeficiency virus (HIV), 243

identical treatment/equal treatment, 221
identity
  defined by consumption model, 61, 272–77
  "as disabled," 61–66, 72, 255
  social and individual, xvii, 9, 41–56, 72–74, 115–18
illness, 44–46
image-building, 210
images of the disabled, 115–16
impairments
  mental and psychological, 30–31, 265
  muscular-skeletal and motor, 30–31
  organic, 31
  sensory, 30
  social, 52, 207, 226, 244, 263,
independent living, xvii, xxvii, 84, 88, 166

Independent Living Centres, xxi, history, 66–100
  organizational structure, 63–67, 80–81, 168–69, 177–79
  service objectives, 64–72, 80–85, 167–68, 176, 205
  as a social innovation, 65–118, 166–69, 176, 178–82, 201, 209
independent living model, 62, 78, 81–85, 155, 168–85, 272
Independent Living Movement, 25, 61–118, 121, 170, 198, 205–9
independent living principles, 78–81, 183–85
  accountability, 82–83, 90, 169
  equality, 82–83, 88, 170, 173–74, 223
  full participation, 82–83, 89, 170, 199
  individuality, 83, 90
  integration, 82–83, 89–90, 155, 167–71, 176, 198–99, 223, 225
independent living programs, 168–69, 176–78, 210
individual program planning, 185
information, as a consumer product, 76, 103–6
institutions/institutionalization, 41–47, 210, 253–54, 267
integration, 166–67, 223, 224–25, 252–53, 256, 263
intentionality, 17
interaction, 40–41
  social, 17, 43, 92–94, 106–8, 123, 165, 257
  symbolic, 16
International Year of the Disabled Person, 215

Joshua Committee, xxi, 10, 173, 184–202
  definition, 185

language use/discursive formations, 6, 110–12, 129–30, 144–45, 156, 177, 202, 245
life-world, colonization of, 111–12
life-world, as community and symbolic space, 109–13

mandatory drug testing in/for employment, 226–30, 244
marginalization, 93, 273
medical model, 60, 62, 65–71, 81, 124–26, 131, 166, 262, 272
medical/professional ethics, 62–64, 70–72
medicalization of illness, 8, 41–46, 50, 62–65
Meech Lake Accord, 218
MLA/Handicapped Joint Committee (Alberta), 136
minorities, 218, 220, 227, 251, 255, 257, 261
motivation, 87, 108–9

National Access Awareness Week (NAAW), 142, 213
National Policy for Transportation of Disabled Persons, 154–56, 210
National Strategy for the Economic Integration of Persons with Disabilities, 207
networking, 194–99
networks, 11–13, 186–202
Non-Government Organizations (NGO), 206
normalization, 167

occupational health and safety, 272–78
O'Malley v. Simpson-Sears, 229–30, 247–49

one person/one fare, 154–55
Ontario Human Rights Commission v. Borough of Etobicoke, 232, 248
oppression, 122–25, 225
organization theory, 96–105

Parlimentary Forum on the Status of Disabled Persons, 3, 8
participation, as benefit of identity, 78, 205–11, 263
participation, as a sense of belonging, xviii, 208–10, 253
peer counselling, 127–28, 172
personal support networks. *See* Joshua Committee
personhood, 257–60, 267, 273
poverty, 262, 265–66
post-industrial society, 206, 264
power, 17
    blocks, 159–61
    defined, strategies, structure, 6, 159, 225
    and institutions, 16, 61, 88–89, 99–102, 124–25, 276
    and knowledge, 71, 103–7, 123
powerlessness, 156–61
praxis, 124–25
privatization, 206
production
    definition of, 72
    in advanced capitalist, post-industrial society, 71–72, 111–15, 272–73, 276–78
    in context of industrial capitalism, 72, 101–2, 273, 275
    in relation to social identity, 60, 71–72, 101, 273
property
    development of, 274–78
    rooted in rights, 273–78
public/social utility service model, 267–68, 278
Public Works, Canada, 212

quasi-market society, 277–78

R. v. Big M Drug Mart, 220
radical voluntarism, xxv
rational actor model, approach to social movements, 97–98, 103, 112
reasonable accommodation, 207–78
   definition, 227, 234–38, 245
   guidelines, 230, 233, 246–55
   implementation, 235–46, 248–55, 258–78
   types, 227–31, 239–40
reciprocal relations, 113–17
reconciliation, 21
rehabilitation
   medical, 51, 63, 94, 101, 104
   occupational, 66
   paradigm, 77–81, 107–9, 266
   vocational, 66, 155
reproduction, 100–105, 109–15
resource mobilization, approach to social movements, 97–98, 101, 121–25
rights. *See also* equality
   development of, 14, 222–25
   before and under the law, 217–18, 223–24, 260
   employment, 252–53
   protection, benefit, 217–18, 222
   symbolic inequality, 218–19
   equality, 205–30
   human, 218, 227–33, 245–46, 253–56, 264–78
rights claims
   categorical, 14, 251–53
   collective, 250
   individual, 250–53
role(s)
   relationships, 6, 45–47
   and status, 42

scientific management, 264–65
segregation, 23, 68–70, 167, 200, 216, 225, 271
self-actualization, 87–92, 163–65, 258, 260, 263
self-determination, 85–87, 91–92, 107, 165–66, 184, 256–58, 263, 272–76, 278
self-efficacy, 107
self-representation, 89
service brokerage systems. *See* brokerage systems
social charter. *See* Canadian Charter of Rights and Freedoms
social identity. *See* identity, social and individual
social movement(s), 50, 96–97, 101–5, 109–18
social reform movements, 9, 96–107, 113–18
solidarity, mechanical/organic, 21, 115
Special Joint Committee of the Senate and the House of Commons on the Constitution of Canada (Hays-Joyal Committee), 214–15
Standing Committee on Human Rights and the Status of Disabled Persons, 66, 133, 143, 149, 207–8, 212
Statistics Canada, 28–30, 211
stereotypes, 250, 253, 264
stigma, 39, 41, 47, 50, 93–95, 225, 227, 253
stigmatization, 42, 47, 115–17, 165, 264, 266
strategic intervention, 127–28
structural-functionalist approach, 98–99
structuration theory, 17–22
   definition, 18
structures, 11
   external/internal, 256, 272

limiting/enabling, 18, 115, 121, 263
micro/macro, 18, 260, 262
normative/relational, 111–13, 262–63
organizational (self-help), 11–13, 122–23, 177, 252, 257
parallel/alternate, 11–12, 112, 128, 252, 262–63
permanent/temporary, 12, 262
preserving/transferring, 13–15, 255–56
as process, 27, 176–77
social, 123–25, 163–65, 248, 252, 256–58, 260–63, 272
subjectivism, 17, 47
support networks. *See* networks
supported independence model (SI), 189–90
definition, 182–83

temporary able-bodiedness, 69–70, 138
transformation, 47, 94, 101–2, 156–57, 256
Treasury Board of Canada, 211–12
Tymchyshyn v. Canadian Pacific Ltd., 232

undue hardship, 236, 243, 248, 250
unity in diversity, 207
United Nations Decade of Disabled Persons, 207
United Nations Declaration of the Rights of Disabled Persons, 216
U.S. Commission on Civil Rights, 235–36

Vocational Rehabilitation of Disabled Persons Act, 212, 266–73, 277
vocational rehabilitation. *See* rehabilitation
volunteer/charity ethic, 66

welfare/income security, 264–66, 268–73
welfarian economics, 85, 265–66, 268
welfarist interest theory, 85–86
World Health Organization, 34